FOUNDATIONS FOR SUCCESS

EIGHT WEEKS TO REAL ESTATE SUCCESS

Stephen L. Silver, BScPT, AEA, CNE

Broker

This publication is designed to provide information with regard to the subject matter covered. It is sold with the understanding that the author and publisher are not engaged in rendering legal, accounting or other professional advice. If legal advice or other expert assistance is required, the services of a competent professional person should be sought.

ISBN 13: 978-0-9939401-8-7

Contents

BUYERS, BUYERS, BUYERS - BUYERS AND BUYERS SYSTEMS

CHAPTER 1

CHAPTER 2

THE WORKBOOK - EXERCISES, TEMPLATES AND SCRIPTS

Foreword

Recently a new Salesperson revealed to me what most newly licensed individuals experience… *"Bruce, when I got my real estate license, it seemed like they gave me the keys to the car but then nobody taught me how to drive it."* There's a lot of wisdom in that analogy and…no doubt a lot of frustration for people starting out.

In his first book, ***List to Last***, Stephen Silver focused on prospecting for, closing on and managing listings. In his second book, ***Foundations for Success***, Steve takes you through a very detailed process of "how to drive a car." As a new REALTOR®, you need to take time to develop your business without wasting time and money. You'll learn how to:

- Develop a simple business plan that will take you on the trip from where you are now to where you want to be.
- Avoid the most common traps in which new REALTORS® get caught.
- Implement the systems that help you:
    - Become organized, in terms of managing time, finances and clients.
    - Connect with and cultivate the leads you'll need to develop in order to secure a consistent, reproducible business.
    - Manage listings and buyers from start to finish.

This book provides specific business building exercises for you to complete that will utilize the information provided and get you on track to success fast. You'll see how you can achieve the success you deserve and grow your business at a significantly greater rate than you ever thought.

I have known Steve Silver for a long time… he knows the business inside out and is an excellent "driving instructor." Follow these steps, take them on chapter by chapter and you too will be "a great driver". Good luck…turn the key and start your engine!

Bruce Keith

Bruce Keith is a leading Motivational Speaker and Trainer for sales organizations in North America, specializing in Real Estate Sales.

He has been in real estate in excess of 27 years, including 16 years as a top Coach for thousands of Sales Agents. Learn more at www.BruceKeithResults.com.

Acknowledgements

Bruce Keith, mentor, coach and long-time friend, for sharing his experience, his encouragement and recommendations, which made the publishing of this series possible.

Aileen Simcic, my best friend and business partner, for her support and encouragement through the many years of our shared real estate practice and beyond and her husband, Christopher Hairrell, for putting up with it all.

Bohdan Uszkalo, friend, business partner and general wild and crazy guy, who always had a joke (not always great) and an encouraging word.

Gerald Tostowaryk, whose personal and professional life defines the meaning of ethics and character and who kept me pointed in the right direction when I needed it.

Dan Gitzel, friend, Broker and mentor, who gave me the chance to find my way back to what I love, teaching and helping others and without whom none of this would have been possible.

David Yunker, ever present and ever available friend, mentor and sounding board, without whose guidance and advice this work would have oft gone astray.

Virginia Munden whose example of dedication to teaching and mentoring has been an inspiration and for taking the time from her ridiculously busy schedule to help me get this book into a readable condition.

George Zanette, friend and trusted advisor, whose advice has been instrumental in getting this book into a format that makes sense to more people than just me.

ACKNOWLEDGEMENT

Christina Davie, friend, major support and chief architect of my endurance, without whom I would have either called it quits or be sitting in prison for murder.

Josie Stern, friend, inspiration and SuperREALTOR®, for demonstrating, on a daily basis, that the main thesis of this book, having and consistently using systems as well as an unwavering commitment to client service, are the only ways to succeed in real estate.

Peggy Urieff, Associate Broker with Coldwell Banker in Roseville, CA, who graciously allowed me to include her outstanding website, www.popbyideas.com, in this series.

To my family; my father Gerald, and daughters Arielle and Andrea, who endured my neglect, ordered in food, and my mood swings and still gave me their unrelenting support, encouragement and love. Without you, this would never have been possible.

And finally, to my amazing partner, Harvey, best friend, kindred spirit, inspiration and dearest, most loving man I know. I can't imagine my life without you in it.

Introduction

Systems for Success

Real estate sales can be a siren song to many. To those outside the business it appears to be an easy way to make money. Watch any of the home improvement channels and you can see people flipping this house, flipping that house, real estate agents selling million dollar properties to the first people that walk in the door, turning junk homes into gorgeous properties and renting them out to the first group through. And all this happens during an hour-long show. So many get into the business with the dream of earning a huge income in their first few months, but it's a sad fact of life in the real estate world that almost 50% of new Sales Representatives fail and are out of the business within the first year of graduating from the training programs. And a further 50% of the remaining aspirants drop out within the second year.

This happens for a wide range of reasons, but the most common one is that the initial training programs don't adequately educate them on the realities of life in the real world as a REALTOR®. They're taught how to avoid getting into trouble with the provincial regulators. They're taught the basics of real estate law and they're taught such useful tools as the length of a "chain", metes and bounds or the Torrens system. There's little to no training on what is truly necessary to succeed in this most competitive business, systems.

That's why this series has been written. It's designed to provide new salespeople with the information, tools, skills and systems they'll require to help them get through those first couple of difficult years.

In this series can be found a step by step approach to implementing the systems that every successful real estate salesperson requires, beginning with business planning and time management and moving through organizational systems, prospecting, working with sellers and buyers and much more. Tools and business building exercises are included, both in the series, the workbook and online at www.foundationsforsuccess.ca which will assist the salesperson in developing those systems, their skills and confidence.

On the Right Foot will introduce you to the Business Plan, the real secret behind getting started without falling into the traps encountered by most new Sales Representatives. It will also introduce you to the key components of success, consistency and organization; doing what needs to be done, when it needs to be done, as often as it needs to be done, in every aspect of the business, including time, client and financial management.

Good Hunting will familiarize you with various types of prospecting techniques, and even more importantly than the types of techniques, you'll learn to develop the mindset required to be consistently successful at it. You'll be shown how to develop and maintain one of the most important long-term prospecting activities, a farm, an activity which will establish you as the best known and most knowledgeable REALTOR® in the area. We'll review the many different active forms that prospecting may take, including making prospecting calls, door-knocking, Open Houses, converting For Sale By Owners, networking, trade shows, and participating in client and community events.

Volume 2 will examine not just lead generation but will also help you develop a complete and organized lead follow up system, so that the leads you generate result in ongoing and future business. You'll read about how to follow up with leads rapidly, effectively and to set them up on a program that keeps you in touch with them until they're ready to act.

In **Listings, Listings, Listings** you'll read about, and prepare a listing system that differentiates you from other REALTORS® and helps influence people to want to work with you before they actually meet you. It discusses listing presentations that demonstrate to the potential client that you're able to provide them with the value they're seeking and what they feel is important, not what you believe your value is. You'll also learn to develop a highly organized listing system that ensures you follow a consistent process for every listing, thereby reducing or eliminating the possibility of missing any steps throughout the entire sales cycle.

Volume 3 will also review and discuss offer management, a key component of a well-constructed listing system. The management of offers, both single and multiple, can easily become disorganized and chaotic without a standardized method of handling the many aspects of what can be a complex procedure.

In **Buyers, Buyers, Buyers** you'll read about different buyer demographics, what the average buyer in each is looking for when purchasing a home and the questions that will help you determine what your client is looking for, what type of buyer they are and that will help you narrow down their needs and wants. By following the systems in this volume, you should be able to review the properties for which they're looking and help you find them the right property in the least amount of time.

As in Volume 3, this volume will help you develop a buyers' system, including an offer management system for your buyer which will enable you to protect your client's interests while obtaining the property with the least amount of difficulty.

And in **I'm Just Sayin'**, you'll be introduced to a critical skill you'll need to develop, objection handling. Using the BASIQ technique, introduced in this volume, you'll be able to quickly and easily determine what the true objection is and by asking the right questions and listening carefully to the answers you'll have the opportunity to understand what the client's concern is and, even more, how to handle it.

The next critical skill you'll need to cultivate is your communication abilities, in order to eliminate the major source of complaints against REALTORS®, a lack of communication or a miscommunication that was never resolved. This volume will discuss how your ongoing task will be to, through the use of open ended questions and active listening techniques, fully grasp what your client is trying to communicate to you as well as ensuring that the client is able to clearly hear and understand the information you're providing.

You'll also be introduced to negotiation, which, if not prepared for, can be a very disconcerting experience. You'll learn how to work towards a win-win resolution, how to prepare for the negotiation and how to develop and execute an effective game plan, complete with specific strategies to achieve the desired outcomes.

And last, this volume will provide you with direction on marketing and advertising. As with any other system, your marketing strategy must planned out for the year so that you don't miss any component or spend money where you needn't, a major point of failure for most new salespeople. You'll learn how to write ads that appeal to buyers.

And finally **The Workbook** will provide you with a weekly, step by step approach to building and managing your business. You'll have opportunities to develop, in a logical, proven, sequence by completing the exercises provided, the systems, skills, and tools you'll need to smooth out the learning curve, reduce the time required to implement the systems needed to ensure their success and begin earning a steady, reproducible and predictable income in a shorter period of time.

However, it is not the end of what you need to do and what you need to learn. As with any athlete, learning the rudiments of the sport is just the beginning. Stop learning and perfecting your skills and techniques and you end up being nothing more than average at best. Professional and high caliber amateur athletes all recognize that the key to ongoing success is to have someone who can teach them and hold them accountable for their performance, forcing them to take absolute advantage of their strengths as well as to face their weaknesses and overcome them; in other words, a coach. I strongly urge you to consider working with a real estate coach who can help you hone your skills and techniques as well as provide you with additional tools and skills designed to test your limits, push you to excel and ensure you reach the goals you'll set for yourself.

FOUNDATIONS FOR SUCCESS

Eight Weeks to Real Estate Success

ON THE RIGHT FOOT

Business Planning, Time Management, Financial Management, Client Management and Real Estate Etiquette

Get off on the Right Foot

A journey of a thousand miles begins with a single step
The Way of Lao-tzu

CHAPTER 1

Business Planning – How do I Get to Where I Want to Be?

Many new real estate salespeople aren't able to survive in this business. They fail as a result of a specific but common series of reasons, which include:

1. The lack of an overall vision about what it takes to succeed in the business.
2. Having poor or no systems in place to ensure their business is consistent and reproducible.
3. A lack of strategic planning which limits their ability to look down the road and define their direction as well as make decisions on allocating resources.
4. No understanding of the competition and what it will take to grow their market share.
5. No established performance measures, which means they have no way of knowing how well they're functioning, where they're making mistakes and no way of modifying their procedures to achieve optimum effectiveness.
6. A lack of knowledge and/or skills which limits their ability to perform at their optimal level.

These reasons can be overcome by developing and following a thorough business plan.

The Business Plan

If you can't see where you're going, it's not likely that you're going to get there. A business plan is the starting point in developing a consistent and focused pathway to getting where you want to be. Establishing a comprehensive business plan ensures that the Sales Representative avoids taking a "shotgun" approach to business. It provides detailed steps to be taken when undertaking different components of the business, such as marketing, prospecting, advertising and communicating with clients; it avoids duplication of effort and confusion about the next steps to be taken. A well thought out plan puts systems in place to proactively deal with market changes and challenges and allows for ongoing evaluation of efforts and modification of the plan as needed to adapt to the changes.

Elements of the Business Plan

Goals

A thorough business plan contains specific elements that shape the plan's development. The first component is the establishment of specific goals. These define what you want to achieve and must be specific, reasonable, attainable, measureable, and time sensitive. And they must be written down. Having a specific goal, achieving a specific task, within a specific timeframe will ensure that the goal doesn't languish or fall victim to procrastination. It's said that if a goal isn't written down, it's nothing more than a wish. Think about all the times you've decided to do something, but haven't set a specific time frame for completion. How many of them did you actually complete?

When defining your goals, there are three levels that will need to be examined. The first of these is your long term or lifetime goals, also known as your Life Purpose, which we'll examine in a different section of this chapter. The next level is your intermediate goals, your five year plan. Where do you want to be in five years in terms of your finances, personal life, health, career, education, family, pleasure and community? And finally, you need to set short term goals. How much do you want to earn this year, what do you want to accomplish personally, etc. It's important to make sure that these goals are ones over which you have as much control as possible and that you avoid creating a situation that can be dispiriting should you to fail to achieve a personal goal for reasons beyond your control! We'll define some very specific goals later in this chapter.

SWOT Analysis

The next step in building a comprehensive business plan is to figure out where you are at this moment. This is accomplished through taking a hard look at yourself and undertaking what's known as a personal SWOT Analysis, a review of your strengths, weaknesses, the opportunities you have to build your business and the threats you'll need to overcome. This will also be discussed in much more depth later in this chapter.

Strategic Plan

When planning a battle, generals have two components they need to include in any plan in order to win. The first is their strategic goal; an overall vision that says "We need to take this hill so we can control the surrounding ground." The second component is known as the tactical plan. This component sets the actual methods they'll use to achieve the strategic goal; the number of troops and transport they'll need, how the troops will be dispersed, how they'll attack and other aspects that will facilitate the taking of the hill.

Your strategic plan must be developed, with a defined path, indicating how you'll achieve the goals you've set. Then your tactical plan will establish critical success factors, in other words, a series of objectives you'll need to reach as well as a set of specific tactics you'll employ to reach those objectives and what resources will need to be allocated to pursue this strategy.

You'll also need to develop a method of monitoring the results of your efforts, so that you can develop new or revised strategies in the event that you're not achieving the results you planned. Far too often we see people who, despite clear indications that they're not moving forward, continue to repeat the same processes. Remember, Einstein said that the definition of insanity was *"Doing the same thing over and over again and expecting different results."*

The business plan must also incorporate the following elements:

- A **Mission Statement**, which defines a representative's focus, direction and sense of purpose. In other words, it's what you want your business to look like to the outside world.

  "To consistently provide professional, ethical and dependable real estate services to my clients and to ensure the integration of my core values of service, flexibility, dedication, enthusiasm, and integrity into that service."

- A **Purpose Statement**, which outlines what you believe in and works as the rationale behind your activities. This can be defined as a person's **"Life Purpose"**, their legacy. It's why you're here on earth.

- Estimated and actual business expenses that cover items such as:
    - Professional memberships, dues and fees
    - Marketing and advertising
    - Travel and auto expenses
    - Office supplies and expenses
    - Legal, accounting and banking costs
    - Contingency fees
    - Donations / Charity
    - Professional development
    - Entertainment
- Sales-related and business generating activities, including daily, weekly and monthly projected estimates of lead generating activities such as farming, prospecting and marketing.

Planning your Business is like taking a Trip

When you're planning a trip, you must know where you're going and why, where you are, how to get there and what you need to take to reach your destination. Before you start the journey, it helps to have a specific destination in mind and what you plan to do when you get there. Then you can determine which items you'll need to have with you to make the journey easier and more enjoyable. The next step is to set your car's GPS system to make sure you know exactly where you are and then plan the route you expect to take to reach your destination, including the amount of time it'll take to get there. The information gained from this will help you re-evaluate the things you're bringing on the trip and adjust your baggage. This is analogous to planning your business.

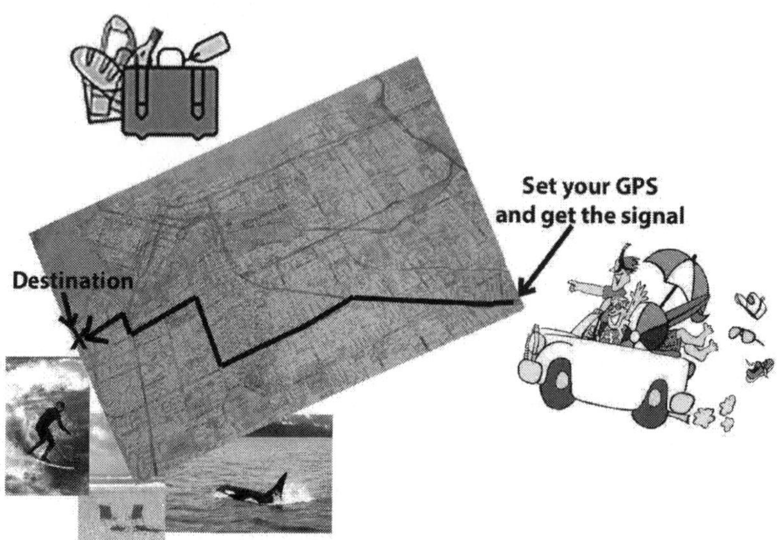

So, now that we understand the process, let's start you on your journey to becoming a successful REALTOR®.

Why are You Here?

The first step in your journey to success is to recognize and understand what success actually means to you.

When I ask the people I coach to explain why they're doing what they're doing, the most common answer I get is "to earn money". But when I ask them to look deeper and explain what that money will do for them, many find it difficult to really explain their deeper motivation.

This deeper reason can be called your Life Purpose. It defines why we do things and gives meaning to what we do. Richard Robbins describes it as, *"The difference we want to make in the world; a higher meaning in life."* He goes on to say that, *"It goes way beyond making money. The How brings solutions, but the Why brings meaning."* Robert F. Kennedy said, *"The purpose of life is to contribute in some way to making things better."*

When defining your Life Purpose, you'll need to define the impact you want to have on your family, your relationships, the community in which you live and work, and how your personal success will be achieved. Your Life Purpose statement gives direction to your life; chasing your Life Purpose can make you virtually unstoppable. One of the best descriptions of what a Life Purpose would look like comes from Richard Robbins, who describes it as follows:

> *"If someone was giving your eulogy, what would you want them to say about you? What do you want your legacy to be?"*

Makes sense if you think about it. What would you want people to say about you as a person? What would you want your friends and family to remember you for?

Here are two examples of Life Purpose statements.

> *"It is to build relationships with and contribute significant value to my clients while attracting success with my integrity and actions. To help people I have relationships with achieve wealth, be it financial, emotional or spiritual, while living a balanced life of my own. To give back to the world before it gives to me."*

> *"To develop a self-sustaining business that:*
> *Provides compassion, care and hope to the community, assisting others to achieve their potential,*
> *Enables me to ensure that my children are able to reach their educational goals, emotional potential and relationship hopes, and*
> *Allows me to maintain and grow my relationship with my children, family, friends and colleagues."*

Business Building Exercise

Your first business building exercise is to **create your own LIFE PURPOSE Statement.** Don't try to do this all at once. It can be a long and sometimes emotional experience and will require time to fully examine your values and motivation. But you need to get started on it now.

SWOT Yourself

Now that you've determined the reason for the trip, it's time to set your GPS and find out exactly where you are. This is where your SWOT Analysis comes in. It's your personal situational assessment and helps you understand not just where you are, but where you need to go and the type of training, support and tools you'll need to access in order to get you there.

It's composed of four parts, Strengths and Weaknesses, which are internal, personal elements and Opportunities and Threats, which are external community and environmental factors.

When analyzing your current situation, there are several questions you'll need to ask.

Strengths

- What are you good at, not just sales related strengths?
- What can you use to your benefit in this career?
- What advantages do you have?
- What do you do better than anyone else?
- What unique resources can you draw upon that others can't?
- What factors mean that you "get the sale“?

- What is your Unique Selling Proposition or Competitive Edge (the unique thing that you can offer that your competitors can't)?

Weaknesses

- What areas do you find yourself weak in?
- Where can you improve? Be honest!
- What should you avoid?
- What are people in your market likely to see as weaknesses?
- What factors cost you sales?

Opportunities

- What is happening in the outside world that you can take advantage of to find yourself a niche or create a business that people will want to use?
- What good opportunities can you spot?
- What interesting trends are you aware of?
- Useful opportunities can come from such things as:
    - Changes in government policy.
    - Changes in social patterns, population profiles, lifestyle changes, and so on.
    - Local events.
    - Relationships.

Threats

- What is happening in the outside world that can potentially create difficulties for you to develop your business?

- Market Variability
- Competition
- Technology
- Labor markets
- The economy

Once you've had a chance to analyze these factors, you should have a clear idea of where you stand in terms of the inherent strengths you can work with, the training and support you'll need to take advantage of to overcome your weaknesses, the opportunities you can utilize and the threats you'll need to work around to become a better REALTOR® and to grow your business.

Business Building Exercise (Workbook)

Create your SWOT Analysis. Remember, be critical, both about where your strengths lie as well as your weaknesses. The more in-depth your self-analysis, the better prepared you'll be.

Crunching the Numbers

Now that you know where you are and where you want to go, it's time to examine, in depth, your financial goals for the coming year. This process is used to determine many of the subsequent components of your business plan, including the number of contacts you'll need to make on a daily basis as well as from which sources you're going to get your business.

The forms needed to complete this section of the plan can be found in the Workbook as well as the book's website at www.foundationsforsuccess.ca. You may want to print out a copy and fill it in as you proceed through this section of the book.

And now for the fun stuff…

How many Transactions do you need?

The first step in determining what your business will look like is to determine how much money you would like to make in the coming year. I would suggest that you use a calendar year to make it easier to keep in line with your tax year. So, figure out what your **Desired Income** will be between now and December 31. Remember, since this is a goal, it must be Specific, Measurable, Attainable and Reasonable. If this is your first year in the business, you'll want to discuss this with your manager and get their input on what may be a reasonable and attainable income for you.

Step number two is to determine either what your **Average Commission per transaction** was from last year, or, if you're new to the business, the **Average Commission for the area** in which you live. Again, your manager is in the best position to be able to assist you with this.

You can then divide the **Average Commission** into the **Desired Income** and calculate the **Number of Transactions** you'll need to make to achieve your desired income. Remember to round up; it's always better to go for more. In the example below, I've determined that I want to earn $100,000 and that the average commission in my area is $7,500. This means that I need to have 14 transactions to earn my target income.

INCOME GOAL	AVERAGE COMMISSION	TRANSACTIONS NEEDED
$100,000	$ 7,500	13.33 = 14

Who do you Know?

The next element to determine is the size of your current database. This is your **Sphere of Influence (SOI)**, the people who you'll be really focussing on in order to grow your business. We'll discuss this in much more depth later in this chapter. But for now, you need to figure out how many people you know that may be able to help you develop your business, both through actually selling or buying, but also, and mainly, through referring other people to you. This number will assist you in predicting the number of transactions you'll be able to make through this source of business.

Sources of Business

Your next task will be to determine which potential sources of business you want to focus on and how many transactions you want to achieve from each. These may include, but aren't limited to:

- Referrals
- Prospecting
- For Sale By Owners
- Expireds (if allowed in your area)
- Just Listed and Just Sold properties
- Flyers
- Ad and Sign Calls
- Open Houses

- Website and Social Media
- Trade Shows
- Commercial Business

As a new Sales Representative, it's advisable to focus on a maximum of three to four sources. By only working on those specific sources, you'll find that you have the opportunity to achieve two major benefits. The first is that you won't be attempting to do too much, too quickly and thereby burning yourself out. The second benefit is that you'll be able to focus your energies on mastering the techniques involved in dealing with those sources and eventually become massively competent in those areas.

Following on from the example in the previous section, I determined that I need 14 transactions, and that I want 3 of them to come from referrals from my sphere of influence, 2 from running Open Houses and 9 from prospecting.

Buyer's Agent or Listing Agent?

In this step you'll decide whether you want to work predominantly with buyers or sellers. It's my belief that, while it's easier to develop and convert buyer leads, it's more effective from both a time and income perspective to focus on developing leads and working with listings. We'll examine this concept more fully later in this book.

Once you've determined which type of client will be your predominant target market, the next question you have to ask yourself is what percentage of business you want from each.

In the example below, I've chosen to have 30% of my business come from working with Sellers and 70% from working with Buyers.

Listings	Buyers
30%	**70%**

Next, calculate the number of listings and the number of buyers needed by multiplying the number of overall transactions by the percentage of listings and the percentage of buyers you set previously. Based on 14 transactions, with 30% of them from listings, I need to sell 4 listings. If 70% of my transactions come from buyer sales, I require 10 sales.

TRANSACTIONS NEEDED	% OF LISTINGS	NUMBER OF LISTINGS	% OF BUYER SALES	NUMBER OF BUYER SALES
14	30%	**4**	70%	**10**

What are the Numbers?

Once you've determined the number of closed transactions you require from each, there are a couple of twists which have to be added into the mix. The first twist is you rarely sell every listing you take. This results in what's known as a List to Sale Ratio. It means that in order to sell a certain number of listings, you'll actually need to list a certain quantity more. If you've been in real estate for a year or two, you'll know what your list to sales ratio is. If you're new, the easiest way to determine this is to use your Board's current list to sales ratio. Once you've determined this, multiply it by the number of listings you need to sell. For example, if I need to sell 4 listings and my list to sales ratio is 75%, I need to list an additional 25% more listings, or 1 more listing (4x25%=1), for a total of 5.

The next twist is that even more rarely do you get every listing when you go on a listing appointment. As a new Sales Representative, you should expect that you may have to go on 5 to 7 appointments for every listing you actually take. While this sounds frustrating, remember that every time you go on an appointment, whether you get the listing or not, you're gaining valuable experience and polishing your presentation skills. As a default for our new sales people, I use a 7:1 appointment to listing ratio, meaning that they'll need to go on 7 appointments to get 1 listing.

With these numbers in mind, complete the following:

- What's your List to Sales Ratio?
- What's your conversion rate on Listing Appointments / Listings Taken (How many Listing Appointments do you need to go on?)

In the example below, I've used a list to sales ratio of 75%, meaning that I need to take 5 listings. I've also set a Listing appointment to listing conversion rate of 15% (7:1).

This means that in order to take 5 listings, I need to go on 35 listing appointments (7 appointments x 5 listings).

To recap, I need to sell 4 listings. In order to sell them, and with a 75% list to sales ratio, I need to take 5 listings. And in order to take 5 listings, with a conversion rate of 15%, I need to go on 35 appointments.

Sold Listings Needed	4
List to Sales Ratio	75%
Listings Required	5
Listing Appointment Conversion Rate	15% (7:1)
Appointments Needed	35

Your next step is to figure out how many people you'll need to speak to in order to get an appointment. New Sales Representatives should expect to speak to a significant number of people (I've seen numbers ranging from 60 up to 125) as they develop their skills and learn to handle objections. The industry standard for more seasoned Sales Representatives usually ranges from 35 to around 50. If, for the example we're using, I calculate my numbers based on an average of 50 people for every appointment, I'll need to speak to at least 1,750 people over the year. Don't panic, it's not as bad as it sounds. We'll examine this more closely shortly.

All the previous calculations have been for determining how you're going to acquire the number of listings you decided you need. Let's now take a look at how many people you'll need to speak to in order to achieve the number of buyer sales you want.

Just as with listings, not every Purchase Contract you write will go through to close. Depending upon the market you find yourself in, a certain proportion of them will fail. You'll need to know how many Purchase Contracts you'll have to write in order to attain the number of sales you require for your goal. Again, your manager will be able to assist you with the average in your area.

In our example, I need 10 sales. If I have a 90% written to close percentage, that means I need to write 10% more contracts, or 1 additional contract. That would mean I need to write 11 contracts.

Using the same ratio of 50 contacts for each appointment, that would mean I need to speak to 550 people over the course of a year, giving me a combined total of 2,300 contacts for the year.

How Hard do you have to Work?

It's been shown that the average REALTOR® works approximately 275 days per year, what with at least 1 day off per week, a minimum of 2 weeks of holidays, 2 weeks of at Christmas and New Year's, and statutory holidays. How many days do you intend to work?

In our example, I need to make 2,300 contacts over 275 days, meaning I need to have a serious conversation about real estate with 8.4, or 9, people each day, or 48 per week.

How many contacts do you need to make on a daily basis? Mike Ferry has indicated that when using the telephone as a prospecting technique, the average REALTOR® can expect to make 8 – 10 contacts an hour. In my experience, when using doorknocking, you can reasonably expect to make 8 - 10 contacts in an hour and a half. So, based on these projections, how hard do you really have to work?

Below, I've summarized the example used in the calculations, using the form you'll find in the Workbook (Volume 6).

Define your Income Goals for the end of 1st year – Set Bar High but attainable

INCOME GOAL	AVERAGE COMMISSION	TRANSACTIONS NEEDED
$ 100,000	**$ 7,500**	**13.33 = 14**

Determine the Percentage of Listings to Sales desired

LISTINGS	BUYERS
30%	**70%**

Calculate the Number of Sold Listings Needed & Number of Buyers Needed

TRANSACTIONS NEEDED	% OF LISTINGS	NUMBER OF LISTINGS	% OF SALES	NUMBER OF SALES
14	**30**	**4**	**70**	**10**

Listings

Number of Listings Needed next 12 mo. __4___

Personal List to Sold Ratio __75__%

Total Listings Required	5
Listing Appointments / Listings Taken	**7:1**
Number of Listing Appointments needed (# of listings needed X # of appts/listing)	35
Number of Contacts per Appointment	50
Number of Listing Contacts per year	**1,750**

Purchases

Number of Purchase Contracts next 12 mo.	10
Written / Close Percentage	90 %
Number of Written Contracts needed	11
Number of Contacts needed / deal	50
Number of Contacts per year	**550**

TOTAL CONTACTS NEEDED	**2,300**
TOTAL DAILY CONTACTS NEEDED (WORKING 275 DAYS / YEAR)	**8.4 = 9**

Business Building Exercise (Workbook)

Using the workbook, **determine the sources of business** you plan to use and **calculate the number of contacts you need to make on a daily basis**.

Contact? What's a Contact?

Now that we've established how many contacts you'll need to make, it makes sense to define what's actually considered a contact. There are as many definitions of what constitutes a contact as there are trainers, but I would suggest that at the heart of it, a "contact" is someone with whom you have a conversation about real estate. If they ask you a question about real estate and you answer it, or vice versa, that's a contact. You don't necessarily need to get their contact information (although that would be even better) for them to be considered a contact.

I'm always asked about how many contacts a REALTOR® needs to make in order to get an appointment. As I said before, there are as many definitions of contacts as there are trainers. That extends to the number of contacts to set an appointment as well. The latest figures that I've seen that make sense take into account the years of experience of the REALTOR®. For those in their first year, the average appears to be approximately 120-130 contacts per appointment. As you gain experience in handling objections, polish your dialogue and become more familiar with speaking with people that number decreases to approximately 60 by the fifth year and 30-40 with more experience.

The 3 Point Stool

When deciding from where you intend to get your business, it may help to understand the concept of the 3-point stool.

It's an algebraic constant that a 3-point stool is stable, since for any three points chosen on an uneven floor, there is an even plane, with some slight tilt that passes through these points. In other words, having three points of contact will always provide stability, even when the floor itself is uneven.

In business, it's much the same. There's no such thing as an unfailingly constant source of business in real estate, so, consequently, we need to build our own 3-point stool of business sources. These will be the sources we need to become, not just competent with, but masters of. At this point you need to choose the three sources which you feel you can become an expert at and how many transactions you want to achieve using each. Then work consistently to become the master of each of these.

However, no matter which others you may choose to engage in, one of these MUST be through referrals from your database and sphere of influence. It's significantly easier to get people to work with and refer to you if they already know and like you. We'll examine how you can accomplish this later in this book.

The Task List

This part of the business plan provides direction in terms of anticipated completion of specific tasks. It is designed to allow Sales Representatives to set a quarterly schedule to achieve fixed mileposts in terms of the transaction goals set earlier in the business plan.

In the example below, you can see that in order to achieve three referral transactions, I've anticipated having one by the end of the second quarter of the year, one by the end of the third and one by the end of the fourth quarter. Similarly, to achieve two transactions through running Open Houses, I have planned on achieving one by the end of the first quarter and one by the end of the third. And finally, the prospecting transactions are planned to be completed with one transaction by the end of the first quarter, two by the end of the second and three each by the end of the third and fourth quarters.

The Task List

Source of Business	Number of Transactions	Quarterly Target	
Referrals from Past Clients / Sphere of Influence & Repeat Clients	3	Q1 - 0 Q3 - 1	Q2 - 1 Q4 - 1
Open Houses	2	Q1 - 1 Q3 - 1	Q2 - 0 Q4 - 0
Website / Social Media		Q1 - 0 Q3 - 0	Q2 - 0 Q4 - 0
Prospecting	9	Q1 - 1 Q3 - 3	Q2 - 2 Q4 - 3
Ad / Sign Calls		Q1 - 0 Q3 - 0	Q2 - 0 Q4 - 0
Other Networking		Q1 - 0 Q3 - 0	Q2 - 0 Q4 - 0
FSBO / Expireds		Q1 - 0 Q3 - 0	Q2 - 0 Q4 - 0
Just Listed / Just Sold Marketing		Q1 - 0 Q3 - 0	Q2 - 0 Q4 - 0
Commercial		Q1 - 0 Q3 - 0	Q2 - 0 Q4 - 0
Other (Specify)		Q1 - 0 Q3 - 0	Q2 - 0 Q4 - 0

Total Quarterly Targets

Q1 **Q2** **Q3** **Q4**

The Tactical Plan

So now you know where you're starting on this journey and exactly where you're headed. Before you load the family into the old station wagon and hit the road, there are just a few more things you'll need to figure out. The first is how you're going to get there; what route will you take, given that there are a whole bunch of different paths. And the second item on the agenda is that you just remembered you don't know how to drive, so you'll have to learn how to do that.

The Tactical Plan is a detailed overview of the tasks you need to achieve in order to reach your goals. It consists of the objectives for each source of business you plan on utilizing and the assignments you'll be required to achieve to complete each objective. Each assignment utilizes the SWOT Analysis and takes into account your strengths and opportunities and how you'll use them to achieve each task as well as your weaknesses and the education, skills, tools and people you'll need to help you overcome them.

The Tactical Plan

Task – 3 Referrals from SOI			
		Deadline	Achieved
Objective – Complete Database		Jan. 31	
1	Create Database of friends, family and past clients	Jan. 10	
2	Implement Contact Management System	Jan. 15	
3	Upload Database to CRM System	Jan. 18	
4	Contact SOI and Qualify / Eliminate	Jan. 25	
5	Set up Monthly Newsletter and Initiate Referral Management System	Jan. 31	

Task – 9 Prospecting Transactions			
		Deadline	Achieved
Objective – Warm Calls initiated		Feb. 28	
1	Refine and Rehearse Warm Call Script	Feb. 10	
2	Develop Objection Handlers	Feb. 18	
3	Implement Lead Follow Up System	Feb. 25	
4	Role Play and Initiate Warm Calls	Feb. 27	
5	Review Lead Follow Up System and modify if required	Mar 15	

Your Tactical Plan should be a step by step guide detailing exactly the procedures needed to move you forward in a controlled, consistent and logical sequence. As you build your Tactical Plan, you must take into consideration every step and how it will influence and provide a guidepost to the ultimate objective.

Business Building Exercise (Workbook)

Design your Task List and Tactical Plan using your SWOT Analysis and the sources of business you decided to work on.

Once you've completed this business building exercise your business plan will be ready to take you toward your goals, if you follow it and stick to the timeframes you've set for yourself.

A Silver Bullet

You'll find these Business Planning Forms in the Workbook and on the book's website at www.foundationsforsuccess.ca.

Build Your Business

In the 1970's, Faberge had a commercial in which a model stated that she loved her shampoo so much that she told two friends, who told two friends, who told two friends, and so on, and so on and so on. This is the concept around which successful REALTORS® have built their businesses. Real estate is a networking and interactive business. In order to succeed, a real estate Sales Representative MUST generate leads and the easiest method is to have your friends tell two friends and so on and so on.

In order to build your business, part of your plan must include a method of interacting with two groups of people; those people who already know you, like you and are willing or want to work with you (your Sphere of Influence) and the group of people who don't know you at all. It makes sense, therefore, that the easiest group, by far, to deal with is your Sphere. Understandably, then, the major focus of your prospecting should be directed to getting them to work for you and act as your Referral Team. The main thing to remember when working with your Sphere of Influence is that it's not about simply getting them to buy or sell, it's about who they know and having your sphere become your full-throated supporters.

They need to see you as their real estate resource person and, obviously, choose to work with you for all their real estate needs.

But they also need to be comfortable with referring you to anyone they know that needs real estate services.

Defining Your Sphere of Influence

The first step in building your database is to decide who to include. So, to quote Ghostbusters, "Who ya gonna call?" Who should be on your database?

Obviously, friends and family need to be included, but you'll also want to include any past clients with whom you've dealt in any previous careers, past co-workers, business contacts and any service people you've worked with, such as your doctor, dentist, vet, plumbers, car mechanics, etc. In short, you'll want to include anyone you know by their first name. In the Workbook section, I've added a list of people you may want to consider including when establishing your database.

When inputting people into your database, it's extremely important to have as much of their contact information as possible. Any additional information, such as the following, will also assist in your ability to both build rapport and influence your database:

- Names of their Spouse / Kids / Pets
- Birthdays
- Wedding anniversary date
- Profession and work address
- Interests and hobbies
- The date they moved into current home
- Details about current home and "dream home."

The second step is to decide on a Contact Management System to handle the automated aspects of managing your database. We'll discuss this aspect in the chapter on organization.

Have a Chat

Now that you've put your list of people together for your database, your next task is to find out if they're actually willing or able to be part of your Referral Team. To do this, you'll need to speak to each person and qualify them for their commitment and eliminate anyone who isn't a full-fledged supporter.

To do this, you'll need a script that lets them know or reminds them that:

- You're in the real estate business
- Your business is built on referrals
- You need them to refer to you

"I was thinking about you the other day and I just thought I'd give you a call and see how everything is going.

I wanted to let you know that I'm working in real estate, with XYZ Realty and my ultimate goal is to become the person that people think of when they have a real estate question or are thinking about making a move.

Can I ask you a quick question? If you were thinking about buying or selling a property, or knew anyone who was, would you be comfortable referring them to me?"

Of course, if they agree, you keep them on your database. However, if they have a cousin, brother, best friend, etc. in the business, you're going to eliminate them from your list. There's no point in spending time or money on marketing to people who aren't going to work with you. I had a friend who, when going through his list, had his mother, yes, his mother, tell him that she wasn't sure she'd refer her friends to him because he was too new and she wouldn't want to offend them. Ouch! As awful as it sounds, at that point, Mom's name comes off the list.

A Silver Bullet

You'll also find this list in the Workbook and on the book's website at www.foundationsforsuccess.ca.

Now that you've qualified them, you'll need to request permission to communicate with them regularly. One of the cornerstones of working with your Sphere of Influence is that you need to make sure you stay top of mind with them, so that, should they come across someone who's thinking of selling or buying a property, you're the name they give them.

Your task at this point is to schedule your next call with them in the next 90 days. As part of your management system for your sphere, you're going to make quarterly calls to every one of them. We'll discuss the specifics of the Referral Management System later, in the chapter on organization.

When making these quarterly calls you must have something of value to offer them, such as the latest statistics from your Board, current information from CMHC, any housing reports published by your office or franchise, or any local community information. Remember, you're there not just to ask them for referrals, your there to provide information so they see you as their real estate resource person.

Always end your calls by asking them for referrals; after all, it's not about them, it's about who they know.

"Just one last question. Do you know anyone who's thinking of selling or buying in the near future?"

It's about who they know, rather than "Are you thinking about…?"

Business Building Exercise (Workbook)

List as many people you know, using the "Who do you know" pages in the workbook and enter them onto the Database form.

Strategic Alliances

Later on in the book, we'll examine how to set up and manage a farm. As part of that process you're going to need to get to know not just the people in the community, but also the businesses. This is what's known as building strategic alliances.

At this point, though, as part of your SOI, you'll need to include the businesses or people with whom you already do business on an ongoing basis. These people, your doctor, dentist, mechanic, plumber, etc., have other clients, however, this source of referrals can very easily be overlooked.

Your nest task is to develop a working relationship with these people, one in which you have an opportunity to cross-promote each other; to offer a quid pro quo for clients of both parties. A successful strategic alliance needs to be mutually beneficial to the two parties involved. For example; when you refer your client to them for service, your client gets a discount. When they refer a client to you, their client gets priority service. In that way both businesses have the opportunity to grow their client list.

At one point, when I was selling, we had an arrangement with a company that repaired and installed central vacuums. If we had a client who had purchased a house with a central vacuum, we gave them the name and contact information of the central vac company so that they could have it serviced if they so choose. They'd get a discount for the service and on anything they purchased. We referred several clients to them and they, in turn, referred people who were considering selling to us.

You can also work with these alliances to co-market each other. One of the REALTORS® in one of my offices arranged to produce a large calendar. He solicited the businesses in a strip mall in his farm area to be part of the calendar. He'd have the ads for the businesses placed around the perimeter of the calendar (of course, his information would be prominent) and would produce and pay for it. In turn, the businesses would have to physically hand out a couple of hundred of the calendars to their patrons.

Once you've established these alliances, there are many ways to take advantage of the opportunities afforded, some of which we'll discuss in the chapter on farming.

Business Building Exercise (Workbook)

Speak to the businesses with whom you already work and find 5 that are interested in setting up an alliance.

CHAPTER 2

Let's Get Organized

One of the most common issues I hear about when coaching REALTORS® is their lack of ability to organize their business and, for a large part, their lives. All too often they're caught up providing service to their clients, completing paperwork, doing research, handling issues, and a myriad of other items inherent in this business. And because of this, they're unable to live the life they expected. They become stressed, frustrated and disillusioned.

In this business, it's far too easy to allow the business to run us rather than us running the business. This stems from the misguided belief that we need to focus on dealing with the "now" business rather than on developing future business. This type of thought process is what results in Sales Representatives living the "real estate roller coaster" lifestyle rather than a much more predictable, consistent and manageable one.

Many of the coaching clients I deal with spend a great deal of their time working with people who, if they had a choice, they would choose not to. This stems from the fact that they don't have anyone else to work with. They don't have anyone else in their pipeline because they've chosen to go after the now business instead of making the commitment to stick with the schedule that ensures that they prospect on a consistent basis to build the pipeline.

I've found that, in general, two major areas in their lives need to be modified in order to reduce their inability to live a more stable life. The first is to learn to better manage their time. Better time management leads to a more organized life leading to a less stressful one. The second, and one with which many REALTORS® struggle, is to learn to better manage their finances.

Time Management

"Half our life is spent trying to find something to do with the time we have rushed through life trying to save." – ***Will Rogers***

One of the basic concepts to understand about time management is that time is finite. There's only a specific amount of time in each day and it's essential that priorities be managed. When you fill your life with trivial things, you limit the amount of time you have for the important ones. However, when you fill your life with important things, you can still find time for the less important ones.

Here's a story that really exemplifies this concept.

A professor of philosophy stood in front of his class. From under the table that stood between him and the students, he pulled out a big glass jar and placed it in front of him. Next, he pulled out a bag of large stones and proceeded to fill the jar with the stones. He then asked the students if the jar was full.

They agreed that it was.

The professor then pulled out a bag full of pebbles and poured them into the jar. Shaking the jar gently, the pebbles slipped through the larger stones, until they settled into the open spaces between the stones. The professor then asked the students again if the jar was full.

They agreed that it was definitely full this time.

This time the professor picked up a bag of sand and poured it into the jar. The sand filled the remaining open areas of the jar. Once again, he asked the students if they thought the jar was full and they agreed it was.

He then explained that the jar signified their life. The rocks represent the truly important things, such as family, health and relationships. If all else was lost and only the rocks remained, your life would still be meaningful. The pebbles represented the other things that matter in your life, such as work or school and the sand symbolized the remaining "trivial stuff".

To demonstrate this further, the professor emptied the jar. He then poured the same amount of sand into the jar, which filled it about halfway. He then poured the pebbles back into the jar, which left only a little room at the top. When he tried to place the remaining large rocks into the jar, there was only room for a couple of them.

If you allow the smaller things (the pebbles and sand) in your life to take priority, your life will be filled with less important things, leaving little or no time for the things in your lives that are most important to you.

As Brian Tracy says, *"There's never enough time to do everything, but there's always enough time to do the important things"*

Your Life Purpose

Earlier in the book we discussed what I've called your "Life Purpose". This is the most important motivating factor that drives you to succeed. Achieving your Life Purpose must be the one element that keeps you focussed on consistently doing what you need to do, when you need to do it. By following the schedule we'll discuss later in this chapter you can ensure that your motivation remains strong and that you're consistently working towards reaching that goal.

The Time Vampires

There are several reasons for people to have difficulties with managing time. These are nicknamed "Time Vampires" because they suck the time from your life.

Multitasking

Count backwards from 26 to 1; easy, isn't it? Now recite the alphabet from A to Z; also easy? Now, recite the alphabet from A to Z and count backwards from 26 to 1 at the same time, i.e. A-26, B-25…, still easy?

Welcome to Multitasking. This Time Vampire creates the illusion of being able to manage more than one task at a time. However, many studies have shown that people are 25 – 40% less efficient when multitasking. It takes more time to complete tasks if you have to switch back and forth between them and you're more likely to make errors when you switch than if you manage one task at a time. If the tasks are complex, these time and error penalties increase.

The Garlic Bouquet

As any horror show devotee knows, the way you eliminate having a vampire hanging around is to hang a bouquet of garlic in the room. So what's the garlic bouquet for this Time Vampire?

Simple, focus on one task at a time. Avoid scheduling conflicts, which reduce your ability to concentrate on the task at hand while being distracted by the potential consequences of missing the conflicting appointment. Evaluate your priorities. Consider both the urgency and importance of meetings and events before agreeing to take them.

When working on a project, such as prospecting, dealing with clients, etc., eliminate the distractions. Turn your cell phone off and let callers go to voice mail. Turn your emails off. Get disconnected from the outside world and allow yourself to be unavailable. Don't allow interruptions to pull you off task; have your door closed and locked.

Clear your desk, clear your mind. It used to be said that a cluttered desk is a sign of a cluttered mind, but I'm not sure that's truly accurate. After all, Einstein's desk was a mess. But a cluttered desk does create an environment where distraction and multitasking can lurk. Eliminate the potential for multitasking and you'll find that it's easier to concentrate on one project at a time.

Procrastination ("I'll get to it later"-itis)

Do you suffer from "I'll get to it later-itis"? The symptoms of this crippling disease are:

- You can't see the benefits of completing certain tasks. So why start them?

- You have difficulties with time management, leaving no time to start things.
- You have difficulty with organization and scheduling, which means you're more likely to forget tasks and miss deadlines.
- You spend so much time running around doing non-priority things so you're too tired to get started.
- You fear the outcome of the project, which can be a:
- fear of failure in that you're afraid that you may not be able to complete the task to the standard expected, or
- fear of succeeding and what that success may bring
- You're easily distracted
- You feel overwhelmed by the project and don't know where or how to get started
- You read e-mails several times without starting to work on them or deciding what you're going to do with them
- You sit down to start a high-priority task, and almost immediately realize you need a cup of coffee
- You wait for the "right mood" or the "right time" to tackle the important task at hand.

Do any of these sound like you? If you suffer from two or more of these symptoms, you have "I'll get to it later-itis" in one form or another. But don't despair, as with multitasking, this time vampire can be beaten with a stake through the heart too.

The Garlic Bouquet

The first step is to recognize you have the disease, to recognize you're procrastinating. Since procrastination can be due to a wide variety of causes, you need to ask yourself WHY you're procrastinating.

One of the major factors is a lack of organization, which can create serious difficulties in managing a schedule and completing tasks within a specific time frame. This lack of organization can be overcome by following specific steps:

- Every night, set up a To Do List for the following day with the most urgent / important task at the top and follow it.
- Set up a daily schedule that will allow you to have sufficient time for each task on the To Do List.
- Use an Urgent / Important Matrix to decide which tasks are the most urgent and which can be put off until later.
- Is the task you're thinking about one that's Highly Important and Very Urgent? If so, do it now. If not, do it later and deal with the one that's of greater urgency and higher importance now.

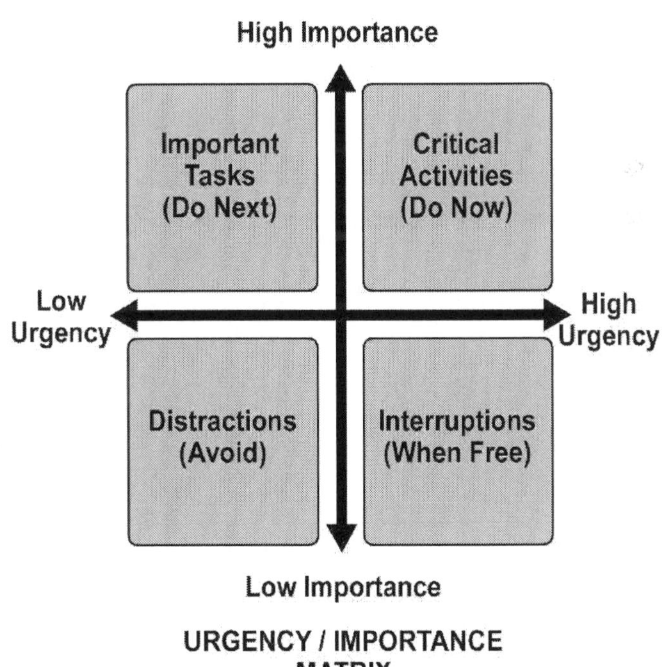

URGENCY / IMPORTANCE MATRIX

Do I really have to?

Another key factor at play in procrastination is the avoidance of having to do an unpleasant task. Do you hate having to change the kitty litter or take the dog out for a walk or clean the bathroom or make those prospecting calls? If so, remember that no matter when you get to it, it still needs to be done. And, as my father used to tell me, *"If you don't do it now, it just gets worse later."* That task you're putting off won't go away and gets larger in your mind as time goes on, adding more pressure and guilt. You need to get it done and over with NOW.

The Garlic Bouquet

Eat that frog!

Mark Twain has been quoted as saying, *"If the first thing you have to do each day is eat a live frog, you can go through the day knowing that this is probably the worst thing that is going to happen to you all day."*

The most effective tool in combatting avoidance behaviour is to learn to "Eat That Frog"; to face up to what needs to be done and do it no matter what. It's going to have to be done at some point and there's no purpose in hoping someone else will do it. Brian Tracy, in his book *"Eat That Frog"* said, *"If you have to eat two frogs, eat the ugliest one first"*. In other words, if you have two important tasks to complete, do the biggest and hardest one first.

By completing the biggest, most distasteful task first, the rest will appear to be much smaller and easier to complete. *"Hey, if I can get that one over with, I can easily do these."*

He also said, *"If you have to eat a live frog at all, it doesn't pay to sit and look at it for very long."* Just get it done! Don't spend time thinking about it.

There's just too much to do

Another significant player in procrastination is the feeling of being overwhelmed by the task. Often, people get caught up in the size of the task and spend so much time looking at the overall scope of the project that they sometimes feel beaten and are therefore unable to begin.

The Garlic Bouquet

Eat that elephant!

There's an old saying, "How do you eat an elephant? One bite at a time." Overwhelmingly large tasks can appear to be insurmountable, but when broken down into their constituent components can suddenly be seen to be manageable. Rather than dealing with the whole great scary task, it becomes easy to plan and manage when dealing with smaller, sequential segments. If you were asked you to go out and sell a house this week, I'm sure you'd feel overcome by the sheer amount of work needed. You'd have to find someone ready to sell, get it listed at the right price, handle all the paperwork, deal with the seller, manage the offer and the conditions, and so on. But, by breaking each process into its constituent parts and learning them thoroughly, it becomes a much less daunting task. Break the task into manageable bites, plan how long you'll spend on each segment and the task becomes achievable.

I Just Have a Quick Question

Interruptions can come from many sources: phone calls, information requests, questions from colleagues and unexpected events. No matter the cause, they all have the effect of causing a distraction and making you lose focus on important tasks. Once you've lost focus, time must be spent in refocusing on the original task, thereby taking time away from working on the task itself.

The Garlic Bouquet

Don't Bother Me

In order to use a garlic bouquet for this time vampire, you must first analyze interruptions to determine if they're a high urgency / high importance issue and if you have to deal with it now. The first barrier to interruptions is a closed door. Placing a "Do Not Disturb" sign on your door and making sure people understand you mean Do Not Disturb will add emphasis to the point, but only if you adhere to it yourself. Having a Do Not Disturb sign on the door and still allowing people to interrupt you is completely counterproductive! My friend Bruce Keith tells a story of a Broker he coaches who placed a Do Not Disturb sign on his door, but people kept opening it and asking him questions. That is until he bought a squirt gun and anyone who stuck their head in the door... well you guessed it. That stopped the interruptions cold.

Just Say No!

Learning to say "No" is an effective tool in reducing the number of times you are interrupted. Setting "Available" and "Unavailable" times and letting coworkers and family know when those times are will allow coworkers or family to adapt to when you're available. Another effective weapon in the war against interruptions is to schedule "Invitation Only" time. Schedule regular check-in times for the people you talk to most often, so that they know when you're expecting them to meet with you.

Off the Hook

Phone interruptions can be dealt with by the simple method of unplugging the land line and turning your cell phone off. Alternatively, you can have an assistant, or receptionist, screen your calls and take messages. However, we all know that unavoidable interruptions occur. After an interruption has occurred, take a few minutes to catch your breath, clear your head, and refocus on the main task.

It's NOT a Hobby

The successful real estate agent understands that real estate is not a hobby. Because we're self-employed independent contractors, it can be a challenge to treat it as a real job. We can set our own hours, earn as much as we want and take as many holidays as we choose, right? Think again.

It's important to understand that while we are able to set our own schedule, if we don't put in the work needed, it's going to be very difficult to earn the money we want. There's a direct correlation between the amount of time we work and the amount of money we can earn.

In any business where taking action results in earning income, it's vital that you treat your business as if it was a real job. Because it is. Certainly, it has some different flexibility options, but it's still a work in equals income out proposition.

The best way to understand this concept is to ask yourself the following questions:

- My salary is $_____________ / year.
- If I worked for a company, what would the company expect from me?

- Would their expectations of me be greater than those I have of myself?
- Would they hold me accountable for my activities?
- Would I have to follow a schedule?
- Would that schedule have to be filled with income-producing tasks?

It seems to me that the answer to the last four questions needs to be a resounding yes. If you're not working to the same level that you'd be expected to by an employer, if you're not holding yourself, or being held, accountable for doing what you need to do every day, if you're not religiously following a schedule that's filled with lead generating activities, how can you expect to earn an income that only comes from having and maintaining that level of commitment?

It's all a matter of priorities

Time management is nothing more than a matter of defining your priorities, setting them in a schedule and following that schedule. To get started, you have to first ask yourself, what's the most important activity that will help you reach your goals, what's the next most important, and so on. Using the Urgency / Importance Matrix previously discussed will help you make these determinations.

The whole point of this is to make sure that you work on what Brian Tracy calls the 'VITAL FEW' tasks rather than on the 'TRIVIAL MANY'. Once you've established the priorities, your Vital Few, the most difficult part of managing your time will be to ensure that the Time Vampires don't take hold of you. Avoid the pitfalls of trying to do too many things at once, putting off things just because they're unpleasant or large, allowing people or other things to get in the way of completing the priority task or forgetting why you're doing what you're doing. You must hold yourself accountable and be strict about it.

So much for theory

Now that we've discussed the theory of time management and how to deal with the time vampires, it's time to look at the practical side of managing what can become an incredibly hectic schedule if not organized properly.

Get a Calendar

The first decision in setting up a time management strategy is to choose whether you're going to use an electronic device, like a smartphone, tablet, laptop or computer or work with a paper version, such as a Day Planner. Whichever format you choose to work with, step one in the process is to have it with you at all times, so you can reference it whenever you need to add an appointment into your schedule and it's always handy to remind you of an upcoming appointment.

Now, go to your nearest office supply store and get a wall calendar for the year. A dry erase board may be the best option.

Put the calendar up on your wall at the office. There's nothing like seeing your entire schedule every day to keep you on track.

Yearly Holidays

Step two is to designate when you'll be taking your holidays. And yes, I know, it can be hard to envision taking holidays right at the start of your career, but planning when you'll be away is extremely important. So schedule the time into your calendar. If you don't go away at that time, you can rejig your schedule to correct the dates at a later time.

R&R Time

Next, set aside, at minimum, one day per week to rest and recuperate and spend time with your family, friends or significant other. Trying to handle business for seven days straight, over a period of weeks, will, in all likelihood, end up with you feeling exhausted and unable to operate at a reasonably efficient level, not to mention the toll it can take on a relationship. You need to take time off on a regular basis.

As well, set aside some time to exercise, meditate, or whatever you need to do on a daily basis to look after your own health needs. Remember, if you don't take care of yourself, you can't take care of everyone else.

Heigh Ho, Heigh Ho, It's off to Work I Go

Next, decide what time you're going to start work and when your last appointment will finish and plan on designing the schedule around those times.

Munchy Time

Next, schedule time for lunch and dinner. You need to eat and you don't want to end up eating a rushed lunch at some fast food restaurant on a regular basis, or having dinner late at night and then falling into bed. Not healthy prospects! Look after yourself first.

Lead Generation

Remembering that your first priority in real estate is lead generation, it only makes sense that the first appointments to be scheduled will be slots for prospecting. I would suggest these be 90 minute slots each day, 5 days per week.

Follow-Up Time

Traditionally, lead generation is done in the mornings, when your energy levels are at their greatest and lead follow up is handled in the early afternoon, at which time your energy is usually somewhat reduced. Schedule slots after lunch for your lead follow up.

Preview New Listings

One of the most important things you can do when working on a farm area is to make sure you're as knowledgeable as possible on all the events and changes in the community. The best way to be able to speak intelligently to sellers about any new listings which occur in the community is to preview them. In order to be able to do that you need to schedule at least one appointment slot, on a weekly basis, to preview those new listings.

Open Houses

Later in this series, we'll discuss methods of prospecting for new sellers and buyers. One of those methods is holding Open Houses. In order to run effective Open Houses, you'll need to schedule four to five hours for the Open House at least one day per weekend.

R&D Time

Part of your responsibility to your clients will be to furnish them with information that will help them make informed choices. To this end, you'll need to spend some time performing research and therefore will need to schedule slots for research twice weekly.

Training & Courses

Schedule at least one 90 minute slot every week for training, courses and/or webinars.

All the Rest

After scheduling all the other times, you can then schedule appointment slots within the remaining time, giving yourself at least half an hour to get from one appointment to the next.

Post a copy of your schedule in your office, in different places at home and set it up on your mobile device and computer with reminders for each of the time blocks.

Now, follow the schedule consistently. If you don't have appointments booked, use the time constructively to work on building your business, such as prospecting, training or role playing. Do **NOT** use it to sit around and socialize with the other salespeople in your office. Remember, if they're sitting around and socializing, they're probably not busy and they're not the people from whom you'll learn good habits.

Take a top producer out for lunch and ask them how they got where they did. And then listen. It's amazing what you'll learn.

Business Building Exercise (Workbook)

1) **List as many of your Time Vampires as you can.**
2) **Decide how you can avoid or eliminate them.**
3) **Following the instructions in the workbook, complete your Yearly and Weekly Schedule, blocking in the times in which you'll be away and in which you'll be working on your business.**

A Silver Bullet

You can find a blank Weekly Schedule in the Workbook and on the book's website at www.foundationsforsuccess.ca

	MONDAY	TUESDAY	WEDNESDAY	THURSDAY	FRIDAY	SATURDAY	SUNDAY
8:00 - 8:30 am	Role Play	Role Play	Role Play	Role Play	Role Play	Role Play	OFF (Sorry I'm competely Booked)
8:30 - 9:00 am	Prospecting Calls & SOI	Prospecting Calls & SOI	Prospecting Calls & SOI	Prospecting Calls & SOI	Prospecting Calls & SOI	Prospecting Calls & SOI	
9:00 - 9:30 am							
9:30 - 10:00 am							
10:00 - 10:30 am							
10:30 - 11:00 am							
11:00 - 11:30 am	Appointment Available	Appointment Available	Appointment Available	Appointment Available	Appointment Available		
11:30 - 12:00 pm							
12:00 - 12:30 pm						Open House	
12:30 - 1:00 pm							
1:00 - 1:30 pm	Lead Follow Up	Lead Follow Up	Lead Follow Up	Lead Follow Up	Lead Follow Up		
1:30 - 2:00 pm							
2:00 - 2:30 pm							
2:30 - 3:00 pm	Appointment Available	Appointment Available	Appointment Available	Appointment Available	Preview New Listings		
3:00 - 3:30 pm							
3:30 - 4:00 pm							
4:00 - 4:30 pm							
4:30 - 5:00 pm	Doorknocking (Farm)	Appointment Available	Doorknocking (Farm)	Appointment Available	Doorknocking (Farm)		
5:00 - 5:30 pm							
5:30 - 6:00 pm							
6:00 - 6:30 pm							
6:30 - 7:00 pm							
7:00 - 7:30 pm	Appointment Available	Appointment Available	Appointment Available	Appointment Available	Appointment Available		
7:30 - 8:00 pm							
8:00 - 8:30 pm							
8:30 - 9:00 pm							

Activity vs. Results

One of the "secrets" to being successful in prospecting is to relentlessly continue doing the activities that are necessary to reach the goals you've set for yourself. All too often, we see salespeople try a technique for a short while, then give it up if they don't see immediate results. They refuse to try the technique again because "it doesn't work."

Rather than focusing on the results, it's important to recognize that the issue preventing the desired result may only be one facet of the technique that may not work and it may require revision. Focus on the activity, not the results; long-term vision vs. short term vision. Keep prospecting and the results will come. Bruce Keith maintains that "The main thing is not to focus on how long it takes... just make sure you are moving forward every single day."

So, in summary, time management is all about making sure you've set a schedule, that you follow it consistently and that you don't allow the time vampires to pull you off that schedule. By following your schedule, doing what you need to do every day, when you need to do it and focussing on your Life Purpose, you can avoid the biggest reason new REALTORS® fail, losing sight of what needs to be done. Remember, people don't fail because of what they don't know. People fail because they don't put into practice the things they know they need to do on a consistent basis.

Financial Management

If you've worked as an employee, you've gotten used to the employer taking the taxes and other deductions off your cheque before you get it. As an independent contractor, you have sole charge of your finances and unless you've set it up with your brokerage to withhold taxes and HST/GST, it can be very easy to overlook these deductions when you receive a commission cheque. It becomes very seductive to just use this extra money rather than make the hard choice of deducting it before calculating your income. This is a trap that many REALTORS® have fallen into, and one from which it can become extremely difficult to extricate yourself.

This, however, can be avoided by following some simple rules. First, remember, the HST/GST is not yours. It doesn't belong to you; it belongs to the government. All you're doing is collecting it, holding it and then remitting it every quarter or every year. It's the same with taxes. You can reduce your tax burden with write-offs, but you still owe it, so don't get caught thinking that you can use the money and then pay it back when you get a chance. The government isn't that forgiving. In other words, you need to stash that money away, hold it and then pay what you owe when it comes time to do so.

So, here are those simple rules. Before progressing further, it's important to understand that this is NOT a course on accounting and that this advice is simply a basic set of principles that will help keep you out of trouble. It's strongly advised that you seek professional advice about setting up and managing your finances. So, on with the rules.

First, set up three bank accounts.

The first account will be your Business Account, into which you'll deposit your entire commission whenever you're paid. Your Business Account should be used to pay business expenses, fees, dues and other real estate related costs.

The next account will be your Tax Account. As soon as you deposit your commission into your Business Account, you'll need to transfer the entire HST/GST amount as well as around 30 - 35% of your commission into your Tax Account (your accountant can give you a more accurate idea of how much you should deduct for taxes).

And the third account will be your Personal Account. This is the account that you can transfer either a set salary or the amount of money you need for the month and from which you can pay your personal expenses, such as your mortgage, food, etc. If you choose, you can also set up a fourth, or Savings Account, into which you can deposit an automatic 10% of your commission to save for the future.

The next step is to set up and use an accounting package, or any other program which will help you with your accounting. It's much less expensive to take the printouts from an accounting package to your accountant at tax preparation time than it is to have them sort through a shoebox of papers, bills and receipts and do all the calculations and input. Take it from painful and expensive personal experience.

Step number three is to have two credit cards, one for personal expenses and one for business expenses. It's extremely important to keep your personal and business expenses separate; don't let them play with each other, personal card for personal expenses and business card for business expenses. Keeping them separate will ensure you're able to accurately track your expenses and will help avoid confusion at tax time. Of course, it goes without saying (but I'm going to say it anyway) that it's really important to pay off the cards when they come due, to avoid the biggest reason for people getting into debt trouble, the interest.

When you purchase anything on your card, write the reason for the expense on the receipt. You can then enter it into your accounting software and file it immediately in the appropriate expense file.

One more bit of advice. Keep a log book for your business mileage in your car. Whenever you're working with a client, jot down the client's name and the odometer reading when you first set out. By keeping track of your personal and business mileage, you'll be able to keep the taxman off your back. There are some great free ones available online.

I really hate accounting and bookkeeping, so I use a very simple filing system for my expenses. I have 12 manila envelopes labelled for each month. Once I've added the expense into my accounting program, I put the receipt into the appropriate envelope and at the end of the month, place the envelope in order by month in a banker's box. My version of the KISS (Keep It Simple and Straightforward) principle.

Client Management

A recent study by the National Association of REALTORS® in the US revealed that 84% of clients would use the same REALTOR® or provide a referral for the REALTOR® they used (NAR 2010 Profile of Home Buyers and Sellers). However, this number dropped significantly when the REALTOR® didn't stay in touch. A comprehensive client retention management (CRM) system is the foundation of a consistent, predictable business model. Your client management system must be based upon a model of communication in which you stay in touch with your sphere of influence on a regular schedule and thereby stay top of mind with them.

A fully integrated CRM program includes the ability to organize and automate client management tasks, such as lead follow up, drip email campaigns, monthly newsletters, flyers, letters to clients and special event cards, such as birthday, anniversary and holiday cards. It allows you to spend the time needed to generate leads and deal with clients rather than working on less important or urgent tasks.

Be Touchy-Feely

As discussed earlier in this chapter, it's not just important to stay in touch with your sphere of influence, it's the most important action you can take to develop and maintain a consistent and predictable business. This is where your CRM system will come into its own and earn the money you pay for it.

Having your SOI act as your referral team is a factor of what's known as Top of Mind Marketing. You must be the person they think of whenever they, or someone they meet, is thinking of buying or selling real estate or has a real estate related question. This can only be accomplished if they remember that you're a REALTOR®. And the only way that can happen is to stay in touch consistently with them by means of an effective system of interactions, or touches.

The Referral Management System

Let me begin by explaining that this system is based on the minimum number of touches you need in order to stay top of mind with your SOI, and that more is better. However, it's not really about the number of touches, it's about what you provide to your SOI with each touch.

If you provide people with valuable information that gives them the opportunity to make informed decisions, you have a much better chance of them wanting to work with you and refer you to the people they know, than if you provide generic, stock information. People have access to loads of information through the internet. What they don't have is the background knowledge to be able to accurately interpret it. Instead of being simply another information source, your goal must be to become viewed as the trusted advisor; the person they know they can turn to if they have questions. Your Referral Management System must ensure that what you're providing them fosters that perception. It must also ensure that you maintain personal contact with your SOI.

The basic Referral Management System comprises the following items:

- 12 Monthly Newsletters, which can be emailed or snail mailed depending on the client's preference.
- Four Quarterly Phone Calls
- One Birthday Card (hand signed) for each person in the contact's family
- A Home Purchase Anniversary Card
- Holiday Cards for each major Holiday
- Mother's Day and Father's Day Cards
- Two to three Invitations to Client events (movie morning, bowling day, family photo event, charity BBQ, educational seminar, giveaways, etc.)
- An annual Calendar
- Various small items which can be dropped off as a quick keeping in touch gesture. Brian Buffini calls these "Pop-bys" and I would encourage you to take a look at his systems for more information on these great little ideas.

As well as the touches mentioned above, you can send a Market Snapshot, essentially an update on the properties that have listed and sold in the clients' areas in the last 6 months, which will give them an idea of the prices in their area. This can be sent twice a year, along with making a follow up call to them to ask if they have any questions.

The number of touches can be increased, but the essence of the system is that each time you contact each person, you must provide them with useful, valuable information or you risk becoming more of a nuisance than someone they value.

A full service CRM system will enable you to maintain this type of contact with your sphere and allow you to modify any message they produce. For more information on the different CRM systems available, I would highly recommend reviewing Gary David Hall's website at www.garydavidhall.com/GarysTopPicks as well as speaking with your more experienced colleagues.

Business Building Exercise (Workbook)

Set up your CRM and your Referral Management System. Transfer your database onto the CRM and set up your Monthly Newsletter for distribution to your database.

CHAPTER 3

Real Estate Etiquette

It's more than just Ethics

As REALTORS®, we subscribe to a Code of Ethics. However, our day to day interactions with the public and our colleagues are ruled by something even higher. The "Golden Rule" says "Do unto others as you would have them do unto you." In real estate, that concept becomes of the ultimate importance as you'll be dealing with colleagues, clients, and service people and want to make sure that you develop a reputation that you can be proud of. There's nothing that destroys a REALTOR®'s reputation faster than taking a less than ethical or flagrantly nonchalant approach to your dealings with others.

Think of your fellow man...

"Politeness and consideration for others is like investing pennies and getting dollars back." - Thomas Sowell

In no particular order of precedence or importance, here are some key "Golden Rules" to help you grow your reputation (parts of this list have been reproduced with the kind permission of Einas Makki, OREA Young Professionals Network Committee Member and OREA Guest Blogger).

1. Present a professional appearance at all times; first impressions matter. Your appearance sets the stage for all other interactions and creates an impression in the mind of the client that often determines your future professional success.
2. Be aware of and respect cultural differences.
3. All materials and supplies should be organized and readily accessible. You may want to consider carrying a few spare copies of all necessary paperwork in a container in your trunk.
4. Always have lots of business cards on hand and hand them out as much as you can.
5. Due to the increasing number of people with chemical sensitivities, limit the amount of perfume or cologne worn.
6. Keep all the areas which a client would visit (office and car) clean, organized and smoke-free.
7. Avoid smoking before any appointments. Many people are significantly affected or offended by the smell of smoke.
8. Underpromise and overdeliver. Promise only what you can deliver and keep your promises.
9. Build mutual respect through honest and courteous communication.

10. Read all viewing instructions and agent's remarks before going to the property.
11. When posting a new listing, drive the most direct route to a listing first. Correct driving directions are critical.
12. Make sure the keys work before leaving them in the lockbox. It's really annoying to Buyer's agents to find out that the key doesn't work when they're standing on the doorstep of your listing with a client, especially in the rain or snow.
13. When inquiring about a property or when talking with another REALTOR® or seller, identify yourself and your company and when leaving messages, be sure to include your contact information. A handy rule of thumb is to clearly state your name, repeat your phone number twice, and briefly state the nature of your business.
14. Schedule appointments and showings as far in advance as possible and always be aware that 24 hours' notice means 24 hours.
15. Be on time for all appointments and meetings.
16. If you are running late for a showing call or text the listing agent (or your client) and let them know your estimated arrival time.
17. Communicate with all parties in a timely fashion. There are very few things more frustrating than trying to discuss a question or issue with someone who takes a day to respond, or doesn't respond at all.
18. Respond promptly to inquiries and requests for information and provide feedback on showings when asked for it. Even if it's just a generic response. Imagine how you'd feel trying to get feedback to provide to your clients and not getting it.

19. If a prospective buyer decides not to view an occupied home, let the listing agent know immediately, so they can notify the seller or occupant.
20. Leave your business card when showing a property.
21. Always use the sidewalks. People can get cranky if you walk on the lawn.
22. Remove your shoes inside the property, unless doing so would pose a danger to you and/or your client.
23. Never allow buyers to enter a property unaccompanied or hand out the lockbox code to a buyer.
24. Advise your sellers to leave the property during a showing or simply become scarce and not to speak to the buyers or their REALTOR®.
25. When showing an occupied home, always ring the doorbell or knock and announce yourself loudly before entering. Knock and announce yourself loudly before opening any closed interior door.
26. If occupants are home during showings, ask permission before using the restroom and remember to flush. No one wants to get that phone call from their client.
27. Honour the listing agent's relationship with the seller and encourage the seller to direct all questions to his or her agent.
28. Lockboxes are a single use item. Once you've completed a showing, always lock the key back in the lockbox. Don't hand the key to anyone else.
29. Don't send your cousin's uncle's ex-wife to look at houses with an unsuspecting REALTOR®, then email over an offer from 500km away. You are licensed throughout the whole province. Earn it, or refer it.

30. If there will be a pet at home during showings, prominently post a note with the pet's name and the location within the room on an interior door, i.e., "in kennel."
31. Always leave the property as you found it and ensure all doors and windows are closed and locked.
32. Do not allow anyone to eat, drink, smoke, dispose of trash, or bring pets into the property.
33. Refrain from making sarcastic or negative comments about the property or neighborhood, you never know who may be listening or how it might get back to the Seller.
34. If you notice any irregularities in a property when showing, report them to the listing agent; also report any error or incorrect information you notice on the MLS posting.
35. If you encounter a doorman/building manager during your showing, be polite, even if they aren't. Remember you are leaving a lasting impression that will impact us all.

SUMMARY

So that's the dry part. But it's the part that most new Sales Representatives don't learn and don't apply. And it's the part that, if they had, would have ensured they got off on the right foot and saved them so much trouble in the first place.

It comes down to the old adage, "Plan your work, Work your plan". A solid, well thought out and realistic business plan is the starting point to long term success, much like the GPS System in your car. You need to determine your starting point, plan your destination, the route you wish to take and what you wish to take with you on the journey. In other words, you need to set realistic, achievable goals, complete a SWOT analysis to determine your starting point, set out clearly defined tasks you need to achieve to reach the goals you've set and then break each task into specific objectives with specific timeframes, the Task List.

Once you have the framework of the business plan completed, the next key component of success is consistency and organization. Doing what needs to be done, when it needs to be done, as often as it needs to be done is far and away the most difficult aspect of making a go of it in this highly competitive and challenging industry, with all its opportunity for distraction and diversion.

Organization, in every aspect of the business, including time, client and financial management, if not developed and followed routinely will inevitably lead to sloppy and inefficient management of your business. Setting up systems that ensure consistent and reproducible processes will help produce the kind of successful results that lead to long term success.

One of the greatest challenges you'll face as a new Sales Representative will be that of managing your time. There are four major components involved in building your business, which, if you concentrate on, will ensure you're successful. These are, in order of importance:

- Lead Generation
- Lead Follow Up
- Going on Appointments
- Writing and Negotiating Contracts

Every activity you undertake must be directed at fulfilling these. Your daily and weekly schedule, therefore, must be planned with accomplishing these tasks first and foremost.

As with everything, a good financial management system will help avoid most of the pitfalls which new Sales Representatives encounter. Your system must include a method of tracking your expenses, putting the money away which you'll need to pay taxes and saving money for your future. It must be one which you find easy to use and allows you to easily calculate your expenses and taxes.

And last, but certainly not least, client management will be one of the most important issues you'll deal with throughout your career. Unquestionably, maintaining a consistent, personal, value-driven and client-centred management system is the single most critical item that will ensure a much smoother and more predictable path right from the beginning.

Our ability to provide outstanding service to both our clients, customers and our colleagues is ruled by the Code of Ethics to which we all must adhere. However, it should be viewed as a starting point. I've always gone by the belief that if you have to ask, "Should I do this," the answer is a resounding "No!"

Your reputation will be built on how you conduct yourself in situations in which opportunities to do things the easy way instead of the right way abound. There's an old Zen saying that goes, "How you do one thing is how you do everything."

On the Right Foot

And now, your task will be to complete the Business Building Exercises in the **Workbook**; getting your Business Plan built, your schedule set and everything else you need to have in place to get your career started off on the right foot. Good luck!

FOUNDATIONS FOR SUCCESS

GOOD HUNTING

Lead Generation and Lead Follow Up

Good Hunting

"Every morning in Africa, a gazelle wakes up. It knows it must outrun the fastest lion or it will be killed. Every morning in Africa, a lion wakes up. It knows it must run faster than the slowest gazelle, or it will starve. It doesn't matter whether you're the lion or a gazelle, when the sun comes up, you'd better be running."

Christopher McDougall, Born to Run

GOOD HUNTING!

CHAPTER 1

Panning for Gold

In the late 1890's, a small, barely known mountain pass underwent a massive transformation. The Chilkoot Trail became one of the most travelled stretches of the Rockies, all because someone had discovered gold in the Yukon. Thousands of prospectors and would-be prospectors traversed that pass in order to seek their fortune looking for gold.

The traditional method of prospecting they used involved combing the countryside, along ridges, through riverbeds and creeks, scooping up mounds of dirt and washing them through a sieve or pan, hoping to find any traces of gold that may have been present. If they located a trace, or show, they had to then begin working the area with a pick and shovel and other tools to find the larger seam.

Sounds like a lot of work, doesn't it? Well, prospecting hasn't really changed much in the last 120 years. In real estate, you have to comb the countryside, which in this case is your farm area, scooping up (talking to) lots of people in the hope of finding a small nugget, in other words a motivated, qualified lead. In this volume we'll look at many, but not all, of the ways of doing just that.

Mindset

Old time prospectors had a tough go of it. They had to negotiate the trip from many different ports to Skagway, Alaska and then up and across the steep and arduous Chilkoot Pass, carrying enough supplies, about one ton, to last them a full year. This kind of journey required a certain type of mindset. Only those willing to undergo the punishing cold, the steep climb and the exhausting hours, days and weeks it took to finally get the chance to make their fortune, survived.

While prospecting in real estate doesn't require that kind of extreme mindset, it does require a complete commitment to doing what needs to be done, when it needs to be done as much as it needs to be done.

The first thing to realize is that you're not just in real estate sales. Your main job is Lead Generation; looking for and finding qualified, motivated leads. You can't sell homes you don't have listed and you can't work with buyers if you don't have any.

Riding the Roller Coaster

The diagram below represents what's known as the Real Estate Roller Coaster. It demonstrates what a typical REALTOR®'s income over a year can look like when prospecting is not a priority.

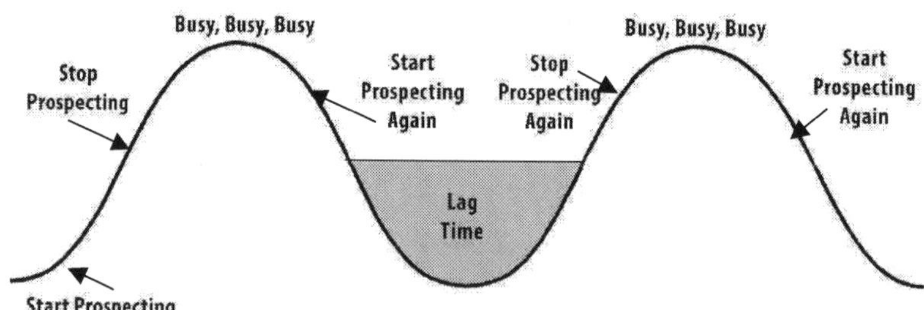

The Real Estate Roller Coaster

At the beginning of the cycle, Sales Representatives begin with no, or few leads, so they begin prospecting consistently and conscientiously. Then as they begin to get busier and deals begin to close, prospecting begins to become less important and occurs less frequently. Once all the deals have closed, there's a sudden recognition that the Sales Representative has no more leads and no deals coming in, so they frantically begin to prospect again. However, there's usually a lag time between the start of prospecting and the next deal. And once again, as the deals begin to flow in, the same cycle is repeated, over and over.

There's only one way to avoid riding the roller coaster, and that's to maintain a consistent, active prospecting program and develop lots of new leads.

So how do you refill the bottle? How do you find those leads?

Well, there are 3 ways of finding business in real estate.

You can sit around and wait for people to call you, which is an extremely passive and very ineffective method of prospecting.

You can spend loads of money on advertising and flyers and then sit and wait for people to call you or spend loads of money on lead generation programs that promise you "x" number of "qualified" leads every month; people who are just looking for a real estate agent to work with, and again, sit and wait for people to get in touch with you.

Or you can go out and find those new leads every day, which is much more effective, less costly and offers the greatest return on investment.

Here are examples of the different prospecting methods and the type of prospecting they represent.

Passive

These techniques result in slow, if any, results and can be costly in terms of money and time.

- Direct mail campaigns
- Duty time
- Internet referral sites
- Marketing
- Referrals from lawyers, etc.

- Web-based email marketing

Active – Future Business

These techniques will not result in immediate business, but will build for the future.

- Doorknocking (cold call)
- Phone cold calls
- Community involvement
- Volunteering
- Social networking
- Seminars
- Passive SOI marketing – monthly newsletters, email campaign

Active – Immediate Business

These techniques are most effective in developing immediate business.

- Doorknocking (with Just Listed / Just Sold information)
- Warm calls
- Open Houses
- Contacting expired listings (if allowed in your jurisdiction)
- Personal contact with your Sphere of Influence and past clients for referrals
- Working present clients for referrals
- FSBOs
- Trade shows
- Client appreciation events

Jim Rohn said, *"Success is neither magical nor mysterious. Success is the natural consequence of consistently applying basic fundamentals."*

What we're now going to do is examine the fundamentals of what it takes mentally to set yourself up for success.

What's in Your Attic?

To become successful at this, you must have clarity of purpose. You need to understand and consistently focus on the reason you're here. What's the single most important motivating factor driving you to succeed? This is your Life Purpose and it defines your purpose for working. Everything you do must be focused on helping you achieve your Life Purpose. Lose sight of this and you'll lose focus on what it is you need to do to reach your dreams.

This part of the chapter is based on a course I teach, called *Getting Beyond Good, Overcoming Your Limits*, and is all about how to knock out the bugaboos and cobwebs and scary stuff that live in our attics; in our minds.

The first step in massively succeeding is to understand that it's OK to be average. Average allows you to work as hard as you feel and if you just don't feel like it, that's OK too. Average allows you to be satisfied with average work instead of exceptional work. Average says, "Don't worry about getting that pre-listing package put together. Most people don't have one and they still make money." Average lets you be part of the 90 percent who are making a few deals a year, instead of the 10 percent who are doing massive numbers of deals. Average is acceptable; if that's what you want to be. If so, stop reading here!

But if it's not, then ask yourself if you truly believe that you can:

- Succeed beyond your wildest dreams?
- Do way more business than you are now?
- Move from having a good life to having a great life?
- Be more than average?

Understand that, no matter what the market is doing, success in real estate depends on doing what you need to do every single day. It's very easy to blame the market for our failure. "It's a seller's market. I can't find any listings because people are worried about where they'll go when they sell," or "It's the winter market. No one wants to sell in the winter. They all want to wait until spring." It may be more difficult to find buyers or sellers during certain times of the year, however, from December 2013 to February 2014, the Toronto Real Estate Board recorded a total of 23,821 new listings and 13,944 sales. There are still people out there who want or need to sell or buy, so REALTORS® are still able to find properties to list and sell, even in the heart of winter. Your job, if you truly want to succeed, is to get out there and find them.

Jim Collins, in his book, "*Good to Great*", says that *"good is the mortal enemy of great, and...that's why we have so few things that become truly great."* He gave a lecture in which he explained that, *"most people will wake up at the end of their lives and need to look back and accept the horrifying truth that they did not have a great life, because it is oh so easy to settle for a good life."*

So, why do some people have a great life while others have a good one? People who have a great life live in a constant state of dissatisfaction with the status quo; they're never satisfied with doing the same thing the same way if there's an opportunity to do something in a better way, such as improve how they deliver their services, constantly grow their knowledge and skills and improve the client experience.

Confront what Jim Collins calls the Brutal Facts. He explains that you are where you are because you've done business the way you've done it – for good or bad. This is your Status Quo. In order to move toward achieving your goals, you have to be prepared, if needed, to abandon your Status Quo and do things differently. You need to ask yourself, "Is what I'm doing moving me forward at the pace I want, or holding me back?" If the answer is that it's not moving you in the direction or at the pace you want, you're going to need to change the way you're doing things. Ask yourself if you need to abandon your Status Quo.

Next, recognize that you will have to do things that make you uncomfortable. You're going to have to do things you may never have done before and that can lead to a certain level of discomfort. However, it's important to remember that discomfort is not a bad thing. It means you're gaining experience and learning what works and how to fix what doesn't.

When I first started skiing, I was very cautious about falling. I wanted to make sure I did everything carefully and correctly. I remember my instructor coming over one day and telling me to stop being so careful. He explained that I would never really get any better if I didn't take chances, and that meant taking the risk of falling, a lot. Well, I started to take those chances and I fell, a lot. And I fell some more and some more, but I learned what did and didn't work, eventually having the opportunity to do some minor racing in college.

You have to take chances, put yourself out there and accept that you're going to have to do some things that will make you uncomfortable, but that it's OK in order to grow and learn.

You must have absolute faith in your ability to achieve the results you want. Faith is described as the confidence that what we hope for will actually happen. You must believe that you can achieve whatever you put your mind to achieving. This will allow you to be fearless and powerful, not fearful and powerless.

Anthony Robbins says, *"The only thing keeping you from getting what you want are the stories you're telling yourself about why you can't have it."*

You must act without fear and with complete confidence in what you do. We'll examine this a little later in this chapter.

Being successful in this business takes a lot of discipline. You have to be disciplined enough to prospect consistently, to follow up with leads when you need to and to ensure that everything you do for your clients is done correctly. People fail in this business because they don't do what they know they need to do on a daily basis. Develop the discipline you need, to do the things you must.

In order to develop that discipline, the first step is to dump the excuses. An excuse is not a reason for not doing something you need to do, it's a way to justify or obtain forgiveness for not having done it. If it's important, you'll find a way to get it done. If it's not, you'll find an excuse.

One of the best methods of developing the necessary discipline is to harness the power of routine. A consistent, effective routine creates a pattern for life that ensure success. Your routine could look like this:

- Make a To Do List, every night, for the following day.
- Be in the office at the same time every morning
- Role play your script for half an hour every morning
- Make the number of calls you need to make in order to reach the number of contacts you need to make every day.
- Do what you need to do every day, when you need to do it and not make any excuses.

- Give up the habits that are preventing you from doing what you need to do when you need to do them.

And finally, set goals that challenge yourself. Don't settle for what you can reach easily. Set your goals so that you shoot for the moon every day. If you reach for the moon and fail, you'll still fall among the stars.

"Most people fail in life not because they aim too high and miss, but because they aim too low and hit." - **Les Brown**

Here are some random thoughts about how to start your day to make sure it allows you to be the best you can be and do the best job you're able.

- What's Your Ultimate Goal, Your Life Purpose? Focus on achieving that and your priorities will become clear.
- Begin each day with an Attitude of Gratitude.
- Take care of your needs first. You can't take care of them, if you don't take care of you.
- Set realistic intentions for your day. "How much money do I want to make today? How many people do I need to see?"
- Dress for success. It helps you psych yourself up for the day.
- Make a TO DO List and JUST DO IT.
- Have personal reinforcement tools available. These help you deal with rejection and reinforce your self-confidence. (i.e. mantra, music, poetry)
- Never mind the Results; FOCUS ON THE ACTIVITY. The results will take care of themselves.
- Deliver Value first. People don't care what you know until they know that you care. Provide people with value and they'll recognize that you're the person they want to work with.

- HAVE FUN!

Be a Hunter-Gatherer

Prior to 10,000 BC, hunter gatherer societies consisted of small groups of 10 to 12 adults and children. They were nomadic people, regularly on the move, who searched for nuts, berries and other plants and followed the wild animals to hunt for meat. Theirs was a society in which feast or famine was an all too common experience and their lives depended on the ready supply of nutritional plants and the migration patterns of their preferred meat source.

Between 10,000 and 7,000 BC, humans began to acquire capabilities that would eventually lead them to re-fashion much of the planet's surface to meet their own particular needs and the agrarian, or farming, culture began to develop. The domestication of selected grasses (wheat and barley) began occurring. As well, something similar was occurring with some animals. Sheep-keeping starting around 9000 BC, followed soon after by the domestication of goats, pigs and cattle. These animals, bred to improve their usefulness to humans, were soon yielding meat for food and skin for clothing. These major evolutionary changes led to a society which no longer had to suffer from famine as their hunter gatherer forefathers did.

Courtesy – Dan Piraro, Bizzaro Comics

It became a society in which a ready supply of food, clothing and trade goods could be expected.

In real estate, both of these societies still exist as separate entities. The hunter gatherers still go out and hunt and collect to find their next transaction, living from deal to deal, while the farmers concentrate on planting the seeds in their farms, maintaining them and reaping the harvest on a consistent basis. Independently, neither of these mind-sets can be truly successful. If you're a hunter gatherer, and satisfied to be one, stop reading and return the book. If you're a farmer, and satisfied to be one, also stop reading and return the book. However, if you're a hunter gatherer who wants to have the consistency of a successful farmer or a farmer who wants to be able to generate even more new leads in a shorter period, read on.

No matter what your main source of leads is, there appear to be three distinct reasons that prevent REALTORS® from becoming successful. In no particular order, these are fear, inertia, and projection.

Fear

Fear is an instinctive emotion that can paralyze people and prevent them from taking the steps necessary to achieve success. Fear leads to self-immobilization, self-defeating and self-destructive behaviour. One of the greatest of these fears affecting real estate salespeople, is one we learn in childhood - the fear of rejection. If not resisted, this fear stops people dead in their tracks and prevents any chance of success.

However, this fear is manageable; the secret to managing it is to realize that some rejection is inevitable and learn how to look at it differently.

The first principle in managing the fear of rejection is to focus on the benefits of prospecting and what it is going to help you achieve. It is the lifeblood of sales, without which the sales cycle becomes stagnant and withers. Prospecting ensures you have a steady supply of leads which, in turn, creates a steady, predictable source of transactions and income.

The second principle is to avoid beating yourself up after a rejection. Most people avoid taking an uncomfortable action. You've gone for what you want, taken positive action toward achieving your goals and even though the result wasn't favourable, you did it! Be proud of yourself for having acted!

Next, remember that you can't lose what you don't have. When you start out, you have nothing. When you prospect, only a few possible results can occur and the worst of these is that you don't get what you wanted. You end up where you started, but at least you've acted.

Knowing a classy way to get out of rejection can help reduce the sting of the rejection and reinforce your resilience. Have a face-saving expression;

"OK, I understand. Thank you for the chance to speak with you. Have a great day."

Don't take it personally. Realize it's not you who is being rejected. People don't want to be "sold" and as a result, their natural reaction is to say no. After all, they don't know you!

By accepting that some rejection is inevitable and deciding to go for it anyway, you become more powerful.

Carl Jung said, *"What you resist persists. What you accept, you gain power over."* To overcome the rejection, all you need do is accept that it will happen and it no longer matters.

Change what rejection means to you. Rejection can make people feel weak and powerless. Changing the meaning in your mind to something more positive means you're more likely to take action.

"I didn't get the outcome that I wanted. Fine. This is not a comment on my worth as a person, but rather about my approach to getting what I wanted."

And as you'll hear over and over, focus on the activity, not the results. Do what you need to do, every day.

"Do that which you fear, and the death of fear is certain" - **Ralph Waldo Emerson**

Inertia

Isaac Newton's First Law of Motion is "An object at rest will remain at rest until an unequal and opposing force acts on it." There's a natural tendency of objects (and, unfortunately, people) to keep doing what they're doing unless something makes them change direction. We don't do the things we need to do because we're already busy doing other things. We all occasionally get into a rut. The issue becomes serious when that rut becomes a habit and we continue doing things that are counterproductive or non-productive.

Oddly enough, one of the best motivators for overcoming inertia is our old friend, fear. Fear of not having enough money at the end of the month has a huge motivating effect on getting people to change their daily habits and take action. To overcome inertia, you need to create a clear vision of what you're trying to achieve. Keep your Life Purpose in sight. You may also want to shock yourself into taking the action. Ask yourself the following questions:

"What are the consequences if I don't get started?"

"How much money am I losing by not getting started on this?"

"How much interest would I be earning if I were investing all the money that I'm currently losing and what would that money mean for my retirement?"

Dangle a carrot in front of yourself but use a stick to get yourself moving. You already have a big, giant carrot; your Life Purpose. But you can also use smaller, short term carrots, like going out for dinner with a spouse or friend when you complete your prospecting for the week. You need to reward yourself for your accomplishments.

The stick comes in when you don't complete your task. Be accountable to another person, an accountability partner. Accountability ensures consistency in effort and activity. It creates an environment where you can overcome uncertainty by being able to call on someone who can provide positive reinforcement, review and support. You can overcome fear through practice and encouragement. You can learn to ignore distractions by having guidelines and directives in place to ensure concentration on critical items. And you can learn to manage time more effectively by establishing structures and outcomes designed to meet specific targets.

Projection

Projection is a defense mechanism we subconsciously employ in order to cope with difficult feelings or emotions. It occurs when we unconsciously protect ourselves against unpleasant emotions or thoughts by subconsciously denying the existence of the impulse or feeling in ourselves, while attributing them to others. This condition can inadvertently limit a person's ability to take a specific action.

Complementary projection is a type of projection where one assumes that other people share the same opinions that you do. As a result of this type of projection, a REALTOR®, who consciously recognizes that they dislike getting cold calls, may avoid making prospecting calls.

Since they feel that way, they make the assumption that everyone feels the same way.

Overcoming projection can be a difficult problem and is well beyond the scope of this book. However, simply recognizing that this is at the heart of your avoidance behaviour and taking the action anyway, can go a long way to overcoming your unwillingness to take the necessary action.

Now that we've had a chance to take a look at what factors create issues for REALTORS® in moving from a hunter gatherer mind-set to a farming mentality, let's look at what it takes to become consistently successful by incorporating both strategies.

Think like a Farmer

Farming in real estate can be viewed as being analogous to agricultural farming. It is a process in which a Sales Representative consistently plants seeds by making their presence known in the community in various ways, maintains the farm by providing valuable information and services and, if done correctly and consistently, reaps a harvest of listings and buyers. The key to success in this is consistency, both in effort, the message and time commitment. Forget one of the first two components in farming and you can forget the last.

Robert Louis Stevenson said, *"Don't judge each day by the harvest you reap but by the seeds that you plant."*

Choosing the right area to farm is critical to your success. When choosing a farm several factors need to be considered, including:

- the size of the farm,
- the turnover rate,
- the absorption rate,
- the inventory,
- the competition, including their market share and the services they provide,
- the growth potential in the area,
- the demographics,
- desirability of the homes in the area,
- the sales trends (whether prices are rising or falling).

You should not choose an area just because it's where you live and you know the area, or an area where you'd like to live, or if the area has a higher price tag attached and you feel you can make more money per transaction. Selecting a farm area takes research, consideration and time.

Once you've selected your farm area, your task is simple. **Get yourself known!** That's it.

How you choose to accomplish that is up to you. However you communicate with your farm, it must be consistent and designed to ensure that the residents within your farm keep you "top of mind" whenever they think of real estate. If they have a real estate question, are you their go-to resource person? If they have a friend or family member who has a question or a real estate need, do they refer you to them?

We'll look at some of the methods and tools that can be utilized to develop and maintain this "top of mind" awareness, such as a Farm Area Update, later in this book.

My friend Josie Stern, for whom I have tremendous respect, has been the premier Sales Representative in her area for the past twenty-five years and has this to say about her experience in developing her farm.

"Twenty-five years ago, before privacy laws, an agent could pursue an expired listing contract. So after the first two months of entering the business I pursued the seller of a house on Wychwood Ave (currently in Hillcrest Village). I got the listing in July of 1989 when the market started its rapid downward seven year spiral. The seller had to sell so I marketed the heck out of that place. Cold called, held daily evening open houses in the month of July and door knocked. There was no internet, so face to face and phones were the only way. During that period I met the people in the community and fell in love with the area. I began to see that this lovely community (now known as Hillcrest Village) was being overlooked because the area had not been promoted and so I decided to become its ambassador, flaunting its merits to everyone. More affordable than the Annex, north Toronto and Yonge/Eglinton, yet just as centrally located, beautiful architecture, many green spaces, family programs, a growing retail area etc. The first ten years were hard because the area wasn't as trendy as other areas so bringing in buyers was like pulling on a rope but I knew it was just a question of time before everyone saw what I saw in the neighbourhood. The Toronto Star noticed my efforts and they printed a half page article in November 2002 about "people with a mission that affect neighbourhoods" and that's when the area began to be noticed. Thirteen years after I started farming it. Farming an area requires patience, passion for and

commitment to the betterment of the community daily and a reputation that will honor the trust people place in you. This is how you plant the seeds of your career which will last a lifetime. You have to become engaged and interested in bettering people's lives by placing them first above all else... and do it for a long time. When you do that you become entrenched in people's lives and they learn to trust you because they know you care and you become their confidante. That's a hard feat for your competitor's to beat. So farming is not just sending out flyers and waiting for the calls. If it doesn't come with a heart it won't be lasting."

One simple, but immensely important aspect of farming is the concept that is best described by Jim Rohn; "Giving is better than receiving, because giving starts the receiving process". It's critical to "give back" or build "goodwill" within your farming area, so that you become known as the trusted "go-to" advisor and that people in your farm area understand that you have THEIR best interests at heart and not your own.

Josie related a couple of incidents that occurred in her community that clearly define how vital that concept is in building relationships in a farm.

"I received a phone call from a woman in my farm area this year who told me she had received a private offer. She asked if I would do an appraisal on her house so she could make sure she was getting market value and she would pay me. I told her it was not necessary to pay me because I was happy to do it for free. When I went to appraise her house she told me she had asked the agent who sold her the house to do the same and because it wasn't going to pay off for him he did not want to waste his time, so he gave her a ball park value on the phone. She told me the price of the private offer and I told her to accept

it. Two weeks later she called to tell me the private offer did not go through and she gave us the listing. She said she never considered using the agent who sold her the house because he didn't care enough to go over to give her an appraisal."

The second occurrence illustrates that it's far more important to keep the best interests of the people in your farm at the forefront than it is to just get the sale.

"We get called in all the time to help people with their renovations, to give them ideas or to advise them on whether they should renovate or sell. Many times we tell people to renovate and stay where they are because it makes the most sense for them. Last year we did just that. We told a person to renovate and after she renovated she asked if we would go see her reno because she wanted to show it off to us. Of course we went. A year later, another client of ours told us she had had a street party at her house for thirty people. She said that the lady whom we had advised to renovate and not sell had come to the party and was bragging about how honest we are to everybody. Thirty people now think we are great. The time we spent with her was not about commission, it was about building goodwill."

This will happen only with time and by you consistently acting in the best interest of the people who live in your farm area.

Size

When selecting a farm area, it's important to choose an area that will allow you to contact each home once a month.

Depending upon your preferred means of communication with your farm, this could be anywhere between five hundred and eight hundred homes. I used doorknocking to farm and could knock on about forty doors in an hour and a half. That meant that I was able to reach about two hundred doors a week, or eight hundred a month. Too many homes and you risk not being able to stay in touch on a consistent basis, not to mention that the expense of sending out marketing pieces can become prohibitive. Once you've become the neighbourhood "go-to-person," you can then begin to expand your farm.

The simplest method to determine the size of your farm is to take a look at the Letter Carrier Walk maps for the postal code in which you want to work on the Canada Post website. You can then choose the walk and find out how many homes are in that particular walk.

Turnover and Absorption

Let's begin by defining each of these terms.

Turnover is the percentage of homes in your farm area that sell over a given period, traditionally one year. An acceptable turnover rate can vary depending on the area. For example, at the time of writing, the minimum acceptable turnover rate to look for in the Greater Toronto Area (GTA) is 4%.

Absorption Rate is defined as the total number of available homes divided by the average number of sales per month. This calculation shows how many months it will take to exhaust the supply of homes on the market. A high absorption rate indicates that the area is in high demand and may be an area to be considered when looking for an area to farm.

Competition

When selecting a farm, you need to take into account who your competition will be, their market share and the services they provide. Trying to become established in an area in which another REALTOR© has a 50% market share is nothing short of hopeless. Most sources tend to suggest that a market share of 30% is the threshold for determining whether or not to consider an area as a potential farm. Having some knowledge of the potential competition's services will allow you to determine what services you want to provide. And is there opportunity to integrate additional services which aren't being provided by your competition, into your sales systems?

Knowledge

Once you've reviewed all the factors involved and you have selected a farm, it's time to become the most knowledgeable person in the area. It's said that knowledge is power, and in negotiations, it truly is. In farming and prospecting, being knowledgeable about the area is more about your ability to deliver valuable information to the people in your farm area when it's required.

The secret to successful farming is to hyper-specialize; become the neighbourhood expert; know the demographics, the real estate market in the area, including all of the new listings as well as sales, both recent and historic, the average prices, the types, sizes and ages of the homes as well as any zoning changes or construction which may be coming. It's also important to be able to provide information on the local schools, transit, amenities, doctors, dentists and other services. Having this knowledge will enable you to become the resource person to whom the residents of your farm area will turn to when they have any real estate questions or concerns.

In Canada, an easy way to get a handle on how the schools rank is to use the report cards published by the Fraser Institute (www.fraserinstitute.org). This provides a numerical ranking of both elementary and secondary schools based on the students' performance on standardized tests. There is, however, some controversy about the validity of these tests (which I will not get into here), so I strongly recommend that you speak with the vice-principals at the schools in your area to find out about the services and programs available at each facility. In my experience, school principals tend to be predominantly administrative, while the vice-principals tend to have their finger on the pulse of the school and can offer a more student-based view.

Utilizing social media in your campaign is also an increasingly important method of building knowledge and credibility. Join any resident's groups, chat groups and share local events and issues, restaurant reviews, promote businesses, schools and other community interests.

Establish a community based website, in which you have current information specific to your farm area updated on a regular basis. This type of website will greatly increase the perception of you as the REALTOR® with whom people will want to deal as well as become a great lead generation source.

By maintaining consistent and informed communication with the residents, you will come across as the expert and as someone who cares.

Producing community-centred videos is another excellent method of keeping the residents and any potential residents informed of what's going on. We'll discuss this later in the book.

Now that you've established where your farm will be and armed with the knowledge you've gained about it, it's time to slip into hunter mentality; it's time to begin to prospect consistently, using a lead generation system that is structured to ensure that your focus is, and remains, on lead generation and lead follow-up in order to build a sustainable and predictable supply of qualified leads.

Business Building Exercise

Complete the following:

1) **Determine where you want your farm area to be.**

2) **Find out about the schools in the area. How do they rank on the Fraser Institute Report Cards? Speak to the vice-principals about the resources they have.**

3) **Develop a monthly Farm Area Update (go to www.foundationsforsuccess.ca for a template) and use it for doorknocking.**

4) **Begin doorknocking in your farm area AT LEAST 3 times per week.**

Hunting Season Starts TODAY

We've discussed the necessity of having a farm and what's involved in setting one up. Now let's take some time looking at what's involved in being a hunter; prospecting for "right now" leads.

Prospecting can take many forms; however, the ultimate goal is generating both immediate and future leads. The only way to successfully achieve these results is to regularly and consistently speak to as many people as possible about their real estate needs.

This can be achieved by using many methods including:

- Prospecting Calls
- Door knocking
- Just Listed/Just Sold Flyers
- Open Houses
- For Sale by Owners
- Networking
- Trade Shows, and
- Client and Community Events

There are many ways of using these pathways to achieve success. Some believe that it's all about numbers, and that works for them. Some believe that it's all about delivering value, and that works for them. No matter to which school of thought you belong, the bottom line is that it has to be done consistently and daily.

Giving Starts the Process of Receiving

"For it is in giving that we receive." – **St. Francis of Assisi**

At some point, we've all been taught that you have to memorize a script to deal with every prospecting opportunity or objection. However, memorization leads only to duplication and, in my opinion, depersonalization. Scripts or dialogues are necessary only insofar as they ensure that, when speaking to people, the Sales Representative uses the same format every time. An effective script or dialogue is personalized and internalized by the person delivering it. It must sound natural and conversational. Having a specific framework for a prospecting conversation reduces the opportunity of getting drawn off track or "stepping on your tongue". The conversation must not sound rehearsed or "canned" and must be delivered easily. The only way to make sure it's perfect is to rehearse.

Now that you have your conversation down pat, change what used to be a cold call to a warm call by providing some valuable information to the person on the other end of the phone and you will see a difference in their response.

It sounds funny to have to say this, but many new salespeople forget this basic premise; even though it should sound like the person speaking, a script must have the same format every time, so that nothing is missed during the conversation. It must start with an introduction:

"Hi, my name's __________ and I'm with _____________."

Next, you need to provide useful hyper-localized information:

"A home just listed (or sold) in your neighbourhood yesterday. It's listed at (or It sold for) _________."

This leads to providing the homeowner with an opportunity to ask questions:

"Do you have any questions about the real estate market in this area?"

Once they've had the chance to get some information, you now have an opportunity to begin to ask questions which will qualify them and probe for the possibility of setting an appointment:

"Do you have any idea of what your home may be worth in this market?"

This then leads to closing for the appointment:

"Would it be of value to you if we were to get together and I could give you some information about what it might be worth?"

Rapport

Now that you have a script and have fine-tuned it, there are some key points to remember when standing in front of, or being on the phone with, a prospective contact.

The first and foremost responsibility is to build rapport. This is accomplished through the following techniques:

1. **Mirroring**. You match the other person's speech patterns and body language. If they're speaking softly, then speak softly. If they're speaking loud and quickly, then speak loud and quickly. This allows you to meet them at their comfort level and establish a connection at that same level. People are more likely to engage in a conversation with someone who speaks in the same manner as them, rather than overpowering, or being overpowered by, the caller.
2. **Active listening**. This is the skill of being able to listen to what the other person means, rather than what they're saying. At the heart of

this technique is learning how to ask a question and then really listen to the answer. Avoid trying to come up with a response before the other person is finished speaking. Then repeat the answer back to them confirming that what you heard is what they actually meant.

"So, what I'm hearing you say is... is that right?"

3. Once you've confirmed what you've heard, **express your understanding** thereby confirming that you understand their point of view.

4. **Find common ground**. Find something that allows you to establish a connection to the other person, such as children, a pet, a similar hobby, etc.

   A friend of mine was out prospecting one day. He knocked on one door and a gentleman answered who wasn't interested in talking. However, my friend noticed that he had a picture of a NASCAR race hanging on the wall behind him. Now, my friend is somewhat of a NASCAR nut. He knows everything about it and regularly goes to many of the races. So he mentioned the picture to the homeowner and they began discussing NASCAR. Later that year, the man decided to sell his home and my friend got the listing. It pays to spend some time building rapport.

5. **Be honest and authentic**. Don't try to be someone you're not. People can sense when you're faking, which will make it more difficult for you to build rapport.

6. **Provide value**. Providing the other person with something of value to them shows that you will focus on their interests, rather than yours. This begins the process of building trust and respect.

The Phone is Your Friend

Say the phrase "cold calling" and sales people begin to shudder. We've all heard colleagues say, "Cold calling doesn't work anymore," or "Everybody's on the Do Not Call list now, so why bother." Well, I'm not going to get into a discussion, in this book, as to whether it does or doesn't work. In my opinion, making prospecting calls is just another tool to be included in our prospecting toolbox.

I would propose, however, that the days of the "cold" call are indeed gone and that, instead, you make "warm" calls. And that the way you accomplish that is by providing the person on the other end of the call with something of value before you ask them to give something back.

Here's the difference.

Cold Call - Asking for something without giving anything

> *"Hi, it's ________________ with XYZ Realty. I was wondering if you were thinking about selling your home in the near future?"*

Warm Call - Giving some info and asking if they would like more, before even asking for something.

> *"Hi, it's ________________ with XYZ Realty. I'm calling to let you know that a home just down the street, number 123, was just listed. It's a beautiful 2 storey home with 3 bedrooms and 2 baths and it's listed at $___________. I was wondering if you had any questions about what's happening in the market in your area?"*

I believe there are four important components involved in making a successful prospecting call.

1. The time the calls are being made.
2. The dialogue (script) involved and how well it's being delivered.
3. The demographic and mindset of the community being called and,
4. The reason for the call.

When and Who

When deciding on the best time to make calls within a particular area, the best results will be obtained by doing a little research. It's important to know the predominant demographic in the area. Is it comprised mostly of young couples with children, seniors, "millennials", or older couples with teenage children? Each of these demographics will be at home at different times of the day and your best opportunity to maximize your time will vary depending on the community. No matter what time you choose to call, it has to be done consistently and daily. Warm calls can be an effective prospecting technique, not just in a farm area, but can also be used to prospect in areas outside your farm. After all, does it really matter where you find a listing or a buyer, as long as you find one?

Speak up boy, I can't hear you!

Scripts. There is a lot of discussion around what to say, how to say it, whether you should use a specific script, modify it for yourself or even use one at all.

For what it's worth, this is my take on scripts. It's my belief that scripts or, if you prefer, dialogues, are a very important skill that need to be mastered by new Sales Representatives. This is for no other reason than that it gives you a starting point upon which you can build your own personalized conversation with people. I don't believe that you should take someone else's script, memorize it and regurgitate it like a trained seal. By doing that you become nothing more than someone playing a role, rather than growing yourself into a wholly independent, fully capable and competent agent, who's capable of building the rapport that is so important to the establishment of a long term relationship.

The scripts you'll find in the Workbook are meant as nothing more than a skeleton upon which you need to flesh out your own dialogues, a guideline of how to say things, not what to say. When you speak to someone, it needs to be you coming out of your mouth, not someone else. But remember, the skeleton is a solid framework that has been created and modified through years of experience, trial and error. The words can be changed, but the framework, or the overall structure, should remain constant. There's no need to reinvent the wheel.

A significant part of having powerful scripts are the questions you ask during them. It's said that the person in charge of a conversation is the one asking the questions. However, that only works if the questions are ones which evoke a response that provide information back and allow for discussion to occur.

Closed questions result in yes or no answers and therefore, eliminate the opportunity for discussion.

"Have you thought about selling or buying in the near future?"
Yes or No, end of discussion.

Open ended questions, on the other hand, encourage answers which lead to further conversation.

"When (How soon) are you thinking of moving?"

"Why are you thinking of moving?"

"Where would you move to?"

"How long have you lived here?"

"What do you like or not like about the neighbourhood?"

"What kind of services would you want from your agent?"

"What's your ideal agent's service look like?"

Give people something to talk about, especially themselves, and then actively listen. Listen, clarify what you believe you heard and then ask more questions. We'll deal with more about communication and the skills involved in Volume 5 – I'm Just Sayin'.

Why are You Calling Me?

"A single question can be more influential than a thousand statements." - Bo Bennett

When you provide someone with information that they find valuable and can use to increase their knowledge and improve their decision making, you have a significantly better chance of establishing a relationship and building rapport with them. It gives you a reason to call them and is the essence of what changes it from a cold call to a warm call.

One of the techniques I've begun having my coaching clients use is to put together a market area snapshot and send them to ten homes in the area into which they intend to call. The snapshots provide information about the latest sales in the area, the average prices and a loose price range for the homes. They then make follow up calls to those ten homes to ask if the owners have any questions about the snapshot. It's been found to greatly increase the potential to have a serious discussion about real estate and has resulted in an increased opportunity to close for an appointment.

Business Building Exercise

Develop your Just Listed or Just Sold script, rehearse it five times with someone at your office and then begin making a minimum of one hundred warm calls every day from Monday to Friday. And remember, as discussed earlier in the book, it's the activity that's important, not the result. Focus on just doing the activity, not the results, because if you consistently do the activity, the results will take care of themselves.

Knock, knock, knocking on...

Door knocking is much like making warm calls in terms of the basic principles; there must be a set time to do the prospecting and you must have a script or dialogue that allows you to provide valuable information to the person being called upon. The difference is that, rather than being a disembodied voice on the end of the line, you're able to meet people face-to-face, giving them the opportunity to form an impression of you and build rapport.

The whole point of this type of prospecting is to engage people in a conversation and begin to build a relationship. That relationship is built around your ability to provide them with local information that they'll find valuable; a newsletter, flyer or some other tangible handout with statistics, market information, the latest interest rate news or news about upcoming developments in their area.

"Here's some information about what's been happening in the area."

You can then ask if they have any questions, thereby offering to provide them with even more information.

"Do you have any questions about what's happening in the market?"

Once you've answered any questions they may have, you can then ask more questions that will enable you to find common ground and build rapport with them.

"How long have you lived in the area?"

"What do you like / dislike in the neighbourhood?"

"What made you choose this community?"

And finally, you can then try to close for an appointment or their contact information.

"Would it be of any value to you for me to come over and give you an idea of what your home could be worth?"

"One last question. If you were thinking of buying or selling a property or knew anyone who might, do you have a REALTOR® that you'd refer them to?"

This technique can drastically improve name and face recognition within your farm area, but has the disadvantage of being less efficient in terms of time spent prospecting. It's very easy, when talking face to face, to get caught up in conversations. Avoid being pulled off task; your job is to speak to as many people as you can in the time you have available.

With an average of approximately two minutes per door knocked, you can expect that you would be able to knock on forty-five doors over a period of ninety minutes. Prospecting five days a week, you could reasonably be expected to knock on approximately two hundred doors during that week or approximately eight hundred homes over the period of a month.

You can find the doorknocking scripts in the Appendix, but again, remember to modify them so that they sound like you.

Right now, in your neighbourhood

One very effective tool, if done well, when door knocking is making use of "just listed" or "just sold" properties as a prospecting tool. (See the "Just Listed" and "Just Sold" scripts in the Appendix.)

It's well-known that, within a few days of one listing occurring in an area, several more tend to pop up. This is called the Domino Effect. Since people are generally interested in what's happening in the neighbourhood, incorporating the houses that have just been listed or sold into both warm calling and door knocking gives you a reason for making your prospecting calls.

You may also elect to either personally distribute the "just listed" or "just sold" flyers in an area or have them delivered and then follow-up with a warm call.

> *"Hi, it's _______________ with ________. I'm just calling to see if you received my flyers and to see if you have any questions about what's happening in your area."*

This technique can easily lead to a conversation about real estate and then further, to determine if the contact may become a lead. However, the drawback to this is that, due to the cost of producing the flyer and having it delivered, it can become an expensive method of prospecting.

Come One, Come All – The Open House

The first listing I got in my career was the result of having conducted an Open House for one of my colleagues. My second listing was the result of conducting an Open House for my first listing. Over the years, I've heard many colleagues opine that Open Houses just don't work. I would argue that, if run properly, Open Houses can be an excellent opportunity to prospect.

The first thing to realize is that if you do things the same way as everyone else, you'll get the same results as everyone else. Running an Open House that is significantly different from the others gives you the chance to stand out from the herd, to be something unique and create a memorable experience for both visitors and prospective clients.

Create the Demand

The first step in holding an effective Open House is to create the demand to see the home. This is accomplished by getting the neighbours and their friends involved. On the Monday, or Wednesday at the latest, prior to the Open House, hand deliver seventy-five to one hundred invitations to the neighbours and personally invite them to the Open House. Also, invite them to bring their friends. Let them know that this is a special VIP invitation and that this event is being held specifically for them one hour before the full Open House and that it will be catered. On the Wednesday or Thursday prior to the event, follow up with warm calls to the neighbours to remind them of the event and to inquire if they plan on attending. This gives you the opportunity to demonstrate the type of service that you provide to your clients and to deliver the unexpected and make it a memorable event. Some simple options for the event include food trays from your local grocery store and water bottles with your name and contact information wrapped over the labels (go to www.Etsy.com).

Create the Traffic

Advertise, advertise and advertise! Take every advantage you have to advertise the event:

- MLS, REALTOR.ca / .com
- Social Media, including Facebook, Twitter, LinkedIn, Pinterest, Instagram
- the internet, including your personal website and blog (if you have one), your company website, if possible
- Kijiji, Craigslist, Backpage, OpenHouse.ca
- Email invitations to your Sphere of Influence, other REALTORS® and brokerages in the area.

Get it Noticed

Making sure that people know that you're having an Open House is extremely important in increasing the number of people who may visit the event. Make sure you have enough signs out to direct people to the house. Simply having a couple of signs at the nearest intersections is not sufficient. You'll want to have several directional signs out, pointing in the right direction. Having one sign on each side of the intersection isn't going to be enough to direct people into the area. However, have 5 to 10 yard bag signs out on each side of the intersection leading up to your Open House sign and this will ensure that people are aware of the Open House as they approach the intersection rather than when they actually get to it allowing them to make the turn.

An additional method of prospecting is to knock on the door of every house where you want to place a directional sign and ask permission to place the sign on their lawn. Once the Open House is over, this gives you the opportunity to stop by, say thank you to the home owner and give them a small token of appreciation, such as a $5.00 gift card to a coffee shop. It's an additional prospecting opportunity and it gives you an opportunity to stand out from everyone else!

Be Prepared

One of the many lessons I learned quickly about holding an Open House is to be prepared for the type of questions that people visiting the home may ask. Preparation for the Open House includes:

- knowing the neighbourhood
- where the schools are and what they offer
- what type of amenities are available
- what is the competition
- how the currently available properties look and how they're priced.

It's always a good idea to visit the other properties in the area during the week leading up to the Open House so you've actually seen them and can speak intelligently about them should questions arise.

Make them Welcome

First impressions are very important. Making people feel welcome at your Open House is a very important aspect that, unfortunately, is frequently overlooked by many REALTORS®. This begins by greeting them at the door, shaking hands and welcoming them to the home. Once you've invited them in, hand them one of your highlight brochures and let them know you're available to answer any of their questions. You must engage them and make them feel comfortable.

Get them Interested

Give them a short description of the home and, if the Open House isn't busy, follow them through the home. This will allow them to discover the home for themselves and will allow you to answer any questions they have.

Keep them interested

Prior to the Open House, set up several stations with information that potential buyers may find helpful, such as how to get financing, what to expect from an inspection, what type of services they'll require from a lawyer and any other information you feel may be of benefit.

Another station may be where you've set up some food and water. This tends to be where many people will congregate and gives you the opportunity to engage them in conversation, begin to build rapport and ask them open- ended questions designed to qualify them.

"So where do you folks live?"

"How long have you been looking?"

"When are you planning on making a move?"

"Have you seen any homes you like so far?"

"What price range are you considering?"

"Have you been preapproved and for how much?"

Show and Tell

One of the most important stations in your open house system will be your laptop, set up with your applicable MLS system, opened to the map search facility and connected to a large monitor. This will give you the opportunity to engage people after they've had a chance to view the home and assist them in finding homes that may interest them.

"So folks, it sounds like this isn't the home you're looking for, am I right?

Are you looking online for homes?

Let me show you what I have access to and see if we can find some homes that may work better for you?"

You can then input their search criteria into the map search and see which homes meet their needs. Once you've narrowed the search to three or four properties that they may be interested in viewing, you can then close for an appointment to show them the homes.

Close, Close, Close

Forget about getting their contact information, you're not going to simply email them the new listings; they've probably already got other REALTORS® doing that. You're going for the appointment!

This is where your closing skills will come to the front. Closing at this point is about showing them you have the value, skills and knowledge that they want to work with to help them find a new home or sell their current one.

When moving toward the close you'll want to confirm that you've answered their questions and that they see the value in working with you.

"Folks, let me ask you this. You've seen how I do things differently from other agents, right? And you've seen that I make sure that the properties I show you will match as closely as possible to the kind of home you're looking for? Doesn't it

make sense then to spend a few minutes with me to make sure that we can find your new home with the least amount of headaches, in the time frame that best suits you?

When they say "Yes", you can now close for the appointment with a simple close.

"OK, then. We could meet today at 6 or I have Monday at 5 pm or Tuesday at 7 pm. Do either of those times work for you?"

Help Me, I Want to Sell my House!

As REALTORS®, we must always be looking for a ready source of people wanting to sell their homes. For Sale by Owners are one source that stands separate from the crowd, jumping up and down and waving their arms, yelling, "Help me, I want to sell my house!" Statistics have shown that eighty five percent (85%) of successful FSBO sales occur through the involvement of an agent. Despite the statistics, this still remains one of the least tackled sources of business. While this book is not designed to be a comprehensive treatise on the conversion of FSBOs, we will take a look at a few methods designed to increase the chances of having FSBOs sell through you.

To be truly successful, you must be convinced they need you, even if they don't know it and that you can get them more money through MLS than they can on their own. It's crucial that you earn their trust by proving that you care and are truly there to help.

To be consistently successful, you must find out why the FSBO is selling on their own. A 2006 NAR study evaluated the reasons that For Sale by Owners sold on their own. 51% said they wanted to save the commission, 22% sold it to a relative, friend or neighbour, only 8% said they did not want to deal with an agent, and only 3% said that their previous agent had been unable to sell the home.

Converting a FSBO becomes much like objection handling, in that, by asking loads of open-ended questions designed to get the FSBO talking about themselves, you can discover the underlying cause for their decision to sell on their own, their motivation and what it might take to have them sell with a REALTOR®. Certainly the most common reason is to save the commission, but they may have also had a bad experience with a REALTOR®. It may also be due to ego; "I can do this better than anyone else," "If you can do it, so can I," or "I know my home better than anyone else, why would I want to use a REALTOR®?" And last but not least, they may just be underestimating the amount of work required in selling a property.

One of the first things to realize is that, while most REALTORs® contact FSBOs by telephone, it's far easier for the FSBO to reject making an appointment with a disembodied voice than if the REALTOR® were standing directly in front of them. Therefore, the first meeting must be face-to-face.

Once you've introduced yourself and asked permission to view their home, the entire focus of your meeting must be to create and build rapport, find common ground and get to know them as you walk through their home. Discover what motivates them; what's their main issue? You may want to ask some of the following questions:

"Why did you decide to sell on your own?"

If it's due to wanting to save the commission:

"Is saving the commission the only reason?"

"Why is saving the commission so important for you?"

If it's because they don't want to work with a REALTOR®:

"Have you had any previous experience working with a REALTOR®?"

"Can you tell me about your previous experience?"

If they've had no previous experience with a REALTOR®:

"What is it that makes you not want to work with a REALTOR®?"

Is it about the challenge of selling on your own?

"What is it about selling on your own that attracted you?"

"Are there any other reasons that made you choose to sell on your own?"

Once you've had the chance to inquire and determine their main concern, it's important to acknowledge their issue(s), provide reassurance, defuse the issue and show you care. While you're at it, DON'T discuss the price they've set for their home or make comments on the appearance of the house.

Now that you've had a chance to determine the source of their concern, you can use a closing question to arrange for a follow-up appointment. For a commission objection, you may use either a Sharp Angle Closing Question or a softer approach, such as Feel, Felt, Found.

Sharp Angle Closing Question

"If I can show you how I can make you more money, even after paying the commission, would you be willing to set up a time to meet when you and your significant other are home together?"

Feel, Felt, Found

"I understand how you feel. I know many people have felt that way, but what I've found is that if I can show you how I can make you more money, even after paying the commission, many people are interested in finding out more. Can we set up

a time to meet when you and your significant other are home together?"

If you find yourself dealing with a FSBO who doesn't want to work with a REALTOR®, due either to a bad experience or simply having a negative opinion of the profession, you can use one of the following closing questions:

"If I can show you how the services that I provide are different than other REALTORS®, would we be able to set up a time to meet when you and your significant other are home together?"

"I understand how you feel. I know many people have felt that way, but what I've found is that, if I can show you how I'm different than other REALTORS®, many people are interested in finding out more. Can we set up a time to meet when you and your significant other are home together?"

In most cases, converting a FSBO is a five-week process. You must always go in with a game plan. There are several different approaches that can be taken when dealing with FSBOs, however, one of the most successful methods of handling FSBOs is to provide them with information and an offer to help, such as, Open House tips, safety pointers, market statistics, or current comparables.

The Helping Hand Approach

Using this approach, you must find a reason to visit the seller every five to seven days. This will ensure you are ready to catch the seller when they're ready to hire a real estate agent. The key to this approach is that you are providing the seller with valuable information without putting any pressure on them.

"Hello my name's ______________ with ______________. I noticed your sign. First I want to tell you that I am not here to ask for your listing and I respect your decision to sell on your

own. But I do have a quick question. I've put together a For Sale by Owner kit for people thinking about selling their home on their own. It's a free service that I offer. It includes information on many different aspects of selling your home. Would you like one?"

The benefit to this system is that you're building rapport and demonstrating a willingness to help. I've found that in many cases they will eventually seek advice from you and ultimately give you the listing if they can't sell their home on their own.

Cooperating Agent Approach

This approach has the advantage of being the simplest and fastest way to contact a large number of private sellers in a short period of time. However, since you're attempting to build a relationship, it's important to remember to use this approach only if you have a client looking for a home in this specific area.

"Hello my name's ______________ and I'm with ______________. I noticed your ad/sign. First of all I want to tell you I am not here to ask for your listing today, and I respect your decision to sell on your own. But I do have a quick question. If I had a buyer that would fit your home, would there be a possibility that I could show your property? Great, may I take a look through your home to see if it would work for my client?"

Relocation Approach

Utilizing this approach gives you an opportunity to get in the door by offering a service that has nothing to do with listing the seller's home. Instead, you offer the seller relocation services to help them find their next home.

"Hello my name is ________________ with ____________. I noticed your sign/ad. First I want to tell you that I'm not here to ask for a listing and I respect your decision to sell on your own. But I do have a quick question: When you sell your home will you be staying local or moving out of the area? I have access to hundreds of homes through our MLS system that may fit your needs. Would that be of interest to you? Great, can we sit down together so I can go through it with you? Would Wednesday or Thursday be more convenient?"

FSBO's are more receptive to this approach as it has nothing to do with the home they are attempting to sell. It provides you a way to lead with the sellers' need and offer them something of value before you ask for anything in return.

As stated earlier in this chapter, converting a FSBO is most often a five week process. After having visited them on the first week, built rapport and used a gentle close, the closes on the following weeks become stronger.

Week 2 - Gentle close

"Have you found the information I provided helpful? Is there anything else I can do to help you?"

Week 3 – Mild Close

"If I can show you how we can put virtually the same amount of money in your pocket on closing, would you be willing for me to come over so we can discuss it?"

A Silver Bullet

You can find a free FSBO Kit and Script on the book's website, www.foundationsforsuccess.ca.

Week 4 – Stronger Close

"In this market, homes on the MLS System are selling in an average of ___ days. You've had yours for sale for ___ days. Would you like me to come over and discuss how I can help you actually get your home sold?"

Week 5 – Strongest Close

"Mr. / Mrs. Seller, you must be getting tired of all the tire-kickers and sight-seers going through your home. Why don't we get together so I can get your home in front of qualified buyers? When would be a good time for us to meet?"

I Get Around...

One of the most effective long-term prospecting strategies is networking, which has a distinct advantage in being low-cost and high-return combined with a great deal of flexibility. It's a well-known fact that people prefer to do business with someone they know, and networking, when done properly, can ensure you have the opportunity to meet and develop relationships with a wide range of potential clients. However, networking is not a selling opportunity. It must be viewed as a long-term strategy in which you take the time to get to know and work with others, focusing on their needs. Giving starts the receiving process.

Certainly one of the most difficult aspects of networking is walking up to a complete stranger and starting a conversation. Given the fact that the other person is also there to develop a relationship, whether it be business or social, this difficulty is easily overcome. Since most people are always willing to talk about themselves, the easiest starting point is to ask about the other person's business, kids, hobbies or interests. This demonstrates that you're interested in the other person and gives you an opportunity to learn potentially valuable information. All you need to do then is sit back and listen.

One of the most critical factors in being successful at networking is to remember to follow up. This requires time and repeated contact and by placing these people on your contact management system, you'll give them the opportunity to get to know you and build trust. Since you never know who might become a referral source, an information provider or a lead to another valuable contact, it's important to remember that, even though prospecting is all about finding good prospects, someone you may not consider a prospect shouldn't be ignored. Everyone you meet must be treated with respect, warmth and thoughtfulness.

Show me what you've got

A successful technique used in prospecting by many industries is hosting a booth at a trade show. However, I've had the experience of seeing many booths which were poorly organized, poorly laid out and whose purpose was poorly defined. There are several factors involved in planning which will help ensure the maximum effect and the best prospecting opportunity.

The first is to define your goal. What are you trying to achieve by being part of the trade show? In most instances it will be to obtain leads or clients and to develop relationships with existing clients. It may also be used to increase brand recognition, educate people about your company and services and as a networking opportunity. It's important to decide, well in advance, on which one or two key goals to focus in order to avoid muddling your message.

The second factor is to pick the right event. The goals which have been decided upon will be specific and you want to ensure the biggest bang for the buck. It's important to analyze the predicted traffic through the show and to determine if this provides the best opportunity to reach your target goals. For example, does the Home and Garden Show provide a better opportunity to reach your goals than the Renovation Show or is the spring or fall Women's Show or the Bridal Show more appropriate?

Once the show has been selected, the next step is to develop a strategy and timeline. The strategy selected will depend upon the goals and will also determine the size, layout, graphic design requirements, staffing, banners, handouts and promotional material required for the booth. Preliminary plans will need to be drafted, discussed and analyzed with all participants involved in the booth. A timeline outlining the work required is necessary in order to ensure that everything is completed on time and is in place when needed and that nothing is left to fall through the cracks.

Next, you will need to consider a budget for the project. The cost of the booth itself may be the most significant portion of the outlay, but signage, promotional material, raffle items, staffing, marketing, and food will need to be included in any budget. The inclusion of suppliers and the percentage of the budget they may be able to defray should also be considered.

Since you're going to be confined to a fairly small area over a period of least a couple of days, it's important to pick the right people to man the booth. Staffing the booth with like-minded people who have the same goals and the same drive will help set a positive tone and atmosphere for the booth and will go a long way to help to draw potential leads to the booth as well as minimizing friction between the participants.

Getting people to visit your booth will be the next major hurdle to be managed. One of the major failures in drawing people in to a booth is the lack of engagement between visitors and the people staffing the booth. It's important not to hide inside the booth, but to step outside it, be friendly, make eye contact, smile and engage people. Drawing people in to the booth is more than just having material to give them; it's about meeting them, initiating a conversation and providing valuable information. Of course, having candy and chocolates doesn't hurt.

Free giveaways, balloons for the kids, answers to questions and an easy-to-carry, memorable and useful piece of branded swag will also help encourage people to visit.

Most shows will have internet availability for the participants; however, assume the internet will occasionally be down. It's advisable to have an alternate source of internet access readily available in the event this occurs.

One of the greatest lead generation tools at a trade show is to have a raffle; especially for whatever happens to be the most recently sold-out product in the world. If there is a lineup for something to buy at Best Buy you can be assured there will be an even longer line to get it for free at your booth.

Once you have the leads collected and the prize awarded, follow up with everyone who entered the draw and thank them for joining the raffle. You can then let them know that, while they didn't win the draw, you are inviting them to a free "investing in real estate" or other type of seminar, thereby offering them something else of value.

Eye-catching signage is another extremely important method of drawing people to the booth. Signage should be clearly visible above crowd height as well as being simple and straightforward. Having a graphic artist design the signage may be an initial cost, but will pay dividends in the numbers of people it draws.

Take the opportunity to circulate through the show giving away free merchandise, candy or other promotional material. Remember to network with the other show participants as well as the crowd, since they too may develop into a lead or a source for leads.

Hold a post-show recap with your team to evaluate the results, divide the leads and review any suggestions for future events.

And finally, avoid making the greatest mistake in running a trade show - the lack of follow-up once the show is over. After having spent the time and money involved, it is absolutely vital to follow up with every lead and contact made during the show.

The Bottom Line

Prospecting can be a truly daunting proposition. There are a wide range of options to find and generate new leads. You can spend time, money and lots of energy on using many different methods. As they say, if you throw enough spaghetti against the wall, some of it's gotta stick.

The bottom line when it comes to prospecting is to choose one or two methods and become a rock star at it. Ask yourself, "What do I need to do to become incredibly successful at using this method?" Once you've explored the answer to this question, it becomes a matter of using trial and error to determine what works and what doesn't and then putting it into practice on a consistent basis.

Business Building Exercise

1. **Choose two or three methods of prospecting, research ways of being super-successful at them and then implement them as quickly as possible.**
2. **Begin making warm calls for 90 minutes a day using the script of your choice. This way you get the chance to make your own decision as to whether it works for you or not.**
3. **Begin doorknocking in your farm area using the script.**

CHAPTER 2

Use It or Lose It

According to the National Association of REALTORS® (NAR), 48% of real estate agents fail to follow-up on leads. Nearly half! And when they did, the average time it took them to respond was 15 hours. Eighty-eight percent of leads are abandoned within thirty days and the average number of call back attempts after the initial contact was 1.5 times, with the average number of email contact attempts being 2.07 times. This, despite the fact that most conversions occur between the 2nd and 12th contact, or between 2 weeks to 1 year after the initial contact.

Does these sound familiar?

"I never have time to follow up because I am too busy."

"I have deals that are blowing up and it takes me all day to save them."

"I prospect throughout the day and do lead follow up when I have the time."

If you find yourself saying any of these, it may be that you need to review your time management or prioritization skills. If lead follow-up isn't your second highest priority, after lead generation, or you find yourself being distracted from it by other lesser important tasks, you'll have wasted all your lead generation efforts. If you're not following up with your current leads why generate more?

What about this?

"I have business calling me. I don't need to follow up or prospect."

This can be attributed to a case of short-sightedness. It's ideal to have that supply of referrals and repeat clients. But at some point, that source will slow down or cease. At that point, it becomes critical to get back to lead generation and follow-up, but it also means that your business will have to go through the lag time that is the hallmark of the real estate roller coaster.

I like to use an analogy to explain this. Imagine that you have a bottle of water and you take sips from it over a period of time. As you drink the water, the level in the bottle gets lower and lower until you finally reach the bottom. If you haven't been refilling the bottle, you have no more water to drink. It's the same with your business. Lead generation is the tap that lets you refill the bottle, but lead follow-up is what ensures that you have a steady supply of good, clean water to drink on an ongoing basis.

Here's another very common reason for not following up.

"Most of the leads I get are garbage, so I just don't bother with any of them."

This is what's known as Bad Lead Fatigue.

NAR's 2014 White Paper on Agent Responsiveness concluded, *"Agents get too many bad leads and develop bad lead fatigue. Bad lead fatigue happens over time when agents realize that most leads are bad, so they begin to ignore them. Unfortunately they are ignoring good and bad leads at the same time."*

It's important to remember that while many of the leads you may get will be of limited, if no, value, that this is a process of sifting the gold nuggets from the silt. If you don't look for the nuggets, there's really no point in prospecting.

"If they're serious they'll contact me."

I know, you threw out a couple of ads and now you're waiting for the world to beat a path to your door. How likely is that to really happen? If someone responds to your ad or calls on a flyer, that would suggest they at least have an interest in finding out some more information. They may not be a true lead, but why wouldn't you take the time to find out? Why would you assume that waiting for them to contact you is a good method for prequalifying a lead's motivation? A good follow-up system with a qualifying script is the only way to really find out who you're dealing with.

"I don't know what to say."

There's an easy fix for this. Develop quick, simple and direct responses and then practice each of these responses through role playing so that they become second nature.

"The last person I called was rude to me so I'm not calling anymore leads."

Brian Buffini so correctly says that the business is easy, but dealing with people is hard. Not everyone will be patient or courteous. You have to develop the skin of a rhino. Remember, "Some will, some won't, so what...NEXT." In other words, suck it up and move on.

"I need to figure out a way to automatically follow up."

Business is built on personal and professional relationships. Use technology when appropriate, but don't forget the power of your voice and personality.

"I always follow up within 3 days but I'm not getting good results."

Studies on the importance of timely follow up show that the chance of qualifying a lead is 20 times greater if the follow up is done within 5 minutes versus just 30 minutes later! If you are taking over 24 hours to follow up with your leads, your effectiveness is greatly diminished and your chances of success almost non-existent.

Why is follow up so important? A lead is nothing more than someone raising their hand and saying they have a question, or are interested in something you may have to offer. The point of lead follow up is to cultivate the lead and establish a relationship. Successful lead follow up moves people through three stages.

The first stage is what I call the "Stranger Danger" phase. In this stage a prospect is only interested in the particular piece of information they can get from you at that moment. Their attitude is that of, *"Who are you and why do I care? I just want some information."*

By engaging them and providing them with the information they're looking for, as well as asking them if there's any other type of information they may want which you can provide, you move them to the "Awareness" phase. In this phase they begin to recognize that you have some value and that there may be some benefit in working with you. *"OK, now I know something about you. Maybe you can help me."*

And finally, the third, or "Comfort", stage is the one in which you've developed sufficient rapport and trust and they're ready to begin working with you.

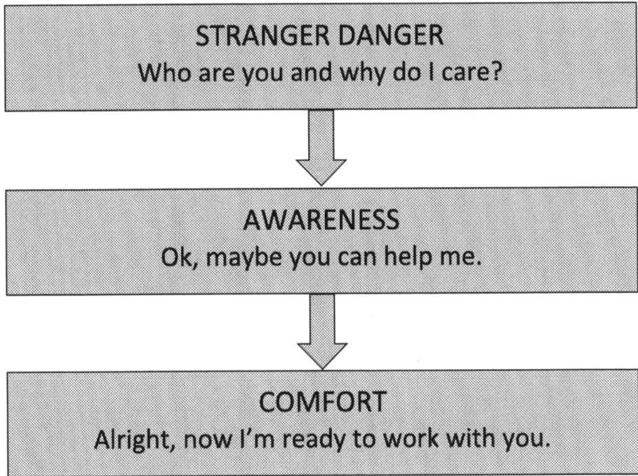

Lead follow up MUSTS

First and foremost, respond quickly; it's been shown that minutes matter! Prospects generally use responsiveness as a proxy for quality. If they don't know you, the faster your response to their inquiry the more value they place in you. Responsiveness equals quality.

Prospects don't look for reasons to work with you, they look for reasons to eliminate you. If your response time isn't within the parameters the prospect has set as a reasonable time frame, there's little chance that they'll consider you as someone with whom they want to work. The 2014 Lead Response Report, conducted by Insidesales.com, revealed that responding to a lead inquiry within 5 minutes meant that the odds of the lead actually having been contacted were 100 times greater than if they were contacted 30 minutes after the lead was generated. It also means that your chance of converting them doubles.

Lead follow-up is also a disqualification process. It's just as important to find the "no's" as it is to find the "yes's". If we can confirm the prospect isn't interested, we can invest our time, resources, and energy in a better prospect or in finding more and better prospects.

A significant part of following up with prospects is to qualify them for motivation. This can best be achieved through the use of open ended questions.

"When (How soon) are you thinking of moving?"

"Why are you thinking of moving?"

"Where would you move to?"

"How long have you lived here?"

"How long have you been looking"

"If we were to agree on a price / find you the right home, would you be ready to sell / buy right now?"

The type of prospect with which you're working can be gauged based on a matrix in which a prospect's motivation and ability to act determines the follow up required.

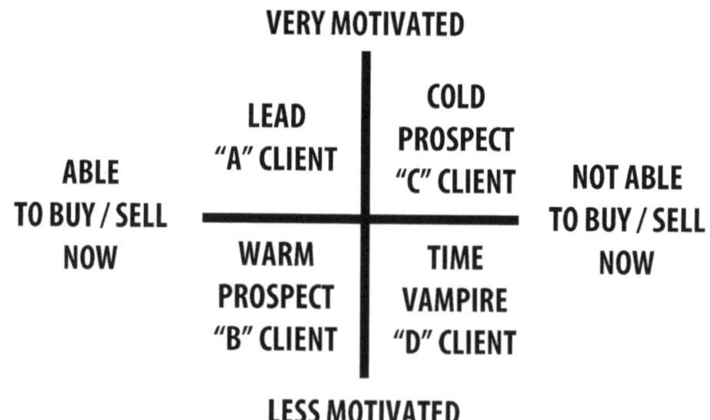

A person with a high level of motivation, who is prepared to act within the next 30 days, and the ability to buy or sell would be considered a hot lead or an "A" client and would demand your immediate attention. Someone with a lower level of motivation, who is prepared to act in the next 30 to 90 days, would be considered a warm prospect or a "B" client, since the only thing needed to convert them to a hot lead would be to alter their level of motivation, such as finding them exactly the right home, thereby removing the barrier to acting. Another warm prospect, the "C" client would be someone who has a high level of motivation, but due to a restriction in their ability to act, is prepared to take action only once the restriction has been lifted. Finally, a person who has a low level of motivation and is not able to act now would be considered a time vampire, or a "D" client and should be avoided.

When you do follow up, make your follow-up about the prospect. You need to find out what they're looking for and customize your response to their need. You also need to make your response personal. It needs to say "Hi, I'm human and I understand your concerns and values." People respond much better when they get a sense that they're dealing with another human and not just a "salesperson." People don't want to be sold and trying to sell them too soon, without getting them from the "Stranger Danger" phase to the "Comfort" stage, is more likely to scare them away than it is to secure an appointment. Think about how you feel when you walk into a big box store and start looking at electronics and a "salesperson" asks you if you want some help. Your first reaction is probably, "No, just looking," isn't it? That's because you're not at a stage where you want them to sell you on anything yet. But when you actually would like some help, you'll find someone to provide you with information and, perhaps, advice.

Demonstrate that you have value. If they just have general questions, answer them. If they want area information, send them the statistical data. You can also include links to additional area resources on your or other websites. But make sure you're able to provide them with the information for which they're looking. That will help establish your value to them.

As stated before, the average number of call back attempts was 1.5 times, with the average number of email contact attempts occurring a meager 2.07 times. To be successful in converting leads, it's vital to follow-up more than once. Since most conversions occur between the 2nd and 12th contact, you need to follow up, up to eight times with personalized messages.

The Lead Follow-Up System

All this can become overwhelming if you try to accomplish it alone. You, therefore, need a solid lead follow-up system that ensures that you stay in touch with leads. A complete automated lead follow-up system comprises the following components:

- It must be easy to use
- The ability to qualify leads as Hot, Warm, Lukewarm
- The ability to access information about the leads
- The ability to track the source of the leads
- A rapid response system that allows you to respond to inquiries NOW!
- An ongoing drip marketing campaign
- The ability to easily provide valuable information to the client
- The ability to be easily modified to fit your particular method of communication

Successful lead follow up results in good lead conversion. This depends on having a comprehensive system, an all-inclusive plan and scripts which qualify and encourage the lead to work with you.

A comprehensive lead follow-up system starts with the ability to easily track each lead. As we move into even more technology based systems, I'm going to suggest that you use an old-fashioned technique to track leads. This begins with setting up a, dare I say it, paper based binder for lead tracking. Into this binder you'll want to insert pages with a Lead Tracking form copied onto different coloured paper. You can categorize the leads as a Hot Lead and Warm and Lukewarm Prospects based on the colour of the form. I would suggest using a bright coloured paper for the Hot Leads and different, paler colour pages for each of the other leads, allowing the more important leads to stand out.

A simple Lead Tracking Form allows you to enter the following vital information:

- The lead's name and contact information
- The date the lead was received
- The date of the first contact
- The next scheduled contact date
- The type of lead, i.e. buyer or seller, and the basic requirements of the lead
- The source of the lead
- If the lead was referred, whether the referring party received a thank you note and gift.
- Any additional information which may assist you in following up and building rapport.

A Silver Bullet

You can find the Lead Tracking Form and other Lead Follow Up forms at www.foundationsforsuccess.ca.

Lead Tracking Form

LEAD NAME		DATE OF LEAD		
RES. PHONE	CELL PHONE	DATE OF FIRST CONTACT		
BUS. PHONE		FOLLOW-UP DATE	DAYTIMER	F/U DONE
BUYER		SELLER		
WANTS:		NOW:		
SINGLE FAMILY ☐	CONDO ☐	SINGLE FAMILY ☐	CONDO ☐	
PRICE RANGE:	ZONE:	STYLE:	BASEMENT:	
STYLE:	BEDROOMS:	SQ. FT.:	BEDROOMS:	
GARAGE:	OTHER:	BATHS:	GARAGE:	
		ZONE:	COMMUNITY:	
LEAD SOURCE	LEAD DATE	THANK YOU NOTE SENT	GIFT SENT	
PHONE:	ADDITIONAL INFO:			
ENTERED ON DATABASE:				

Once you've completed the Lead Tracking Form, your next step is to enter the information into your Client Management System (CMS) and set a date for the next follow-up activity.

In order to ensure that this follow-up occurs, you must have a reminder set up. Next, you'll need to set up a drip marketing campaign with valuable, client-centric information, such as your Informed Buyer or Seller Guide, a mini-CMA or community information and then follow up with the lead once the information has been sent to determine if they have any questions.

I believe that the simpler the system the more likely it is that it will be used. Therefore, I advocate the use of the following basic three point system.

1. Respond to the inquiry NOW. As said before, responding within five minutes massively increases the likelihood that you'll make contact with the lead.

2. Use all three communication methods; call, text and email. This ensures that you have the best chance of responding in the manner most preferred by the prospect and that you'll get through to them.

3. Follow up weekly using all three communication methods until you make contact with the prospect and determine their preferred method of communication. Your communication program should be spread across the week and may entail calling them on Monday, emailing them on Wednesday and text messaging them on Friday or any other combination you choose. Take them off the scheduled texts, calls and emails once they engage with you by their preferred method of communication and ensure that that method is the form of contact you use for future messages.

   Some do's and don'ts when following up with leads.

Don't use wishy-washy statements such as, "We should…", "Perhaps we could…", "Maybe...", "If you could…", "If you want...", "It would be great if…", "I'd appreciate it if…"

Use statements that have a definitive call to action, such as "We will need to get together in the next day or two..."

Don't use exclamation points, all capitals, bold letters or emoticons. These are all messaging mistakes and demonstrate your lack of technological etiquette.

Don't provide too much or too little information in your message. Use the KISS (Keep It Simple and Straightforward) principle. Provide no more than two to three points only.

Don't try to sell them at this stage, they're not ready yet. Your job is to provide client-centric information and to qualify them and determine their motivation.

Never assume a no. Keep following up until they actually say Yes or No. Remember, most prospects, unless they're a hot lead, take 2 weeks to one year to convert to a solid lead. Giving up too early means that you'll lose the ones who just aren't ready to do anything yet.

The Message and the Medium

Systems are based on creating a reproducible, consistent structure that allows a REALTOR® to manage their business. When dealing with leads, it's important that part of the lead follow-up system includes a script for phone messages and templates for text messages and emails. These templates should include the following:

- An introduction
- Why you're calling / writing and why it's good news for them
- Define and then confirm the prospect's objectives
- What you can do to help them achieve their goal (buying or selling)
- A plan of action, including time frame, objective & potential date to meet
- A call to action

Here are some sample templates.

Sample Email Template

Dear Mr. and Mrs. Smith,

Thanks for speaking with me yesterday at our Open House at 123 Anywhere St.

You expressed an interest in selling your home and I wanted to make sure I followed up and answered any questions you had about that process.

Selling your home can sometimes be a daunting procedure, but it's my job to eliminate the stress and worry from the process. The most important difference in the way I do things is to tailor the services I offer to the specific ways you want them provided, rather than providing the same services to everyone.

Sound intriguing? Then let's connect by Tuesday, so I can demonstrate more about how I can help you get your home sold, in the time frame that best suits you, for more money, with truly personalized, worry-free service. Call me at 123-456-7890 and we can schedule a time.

Sample Text Message Template

Hi Mr. and Mrs. Smith,

Thanks for speaking with me yesterday at our Open House at 123 Anywhere St.

You expressed an interest in selling your home and I wanted to make sure I followed up and answered any questions you had about that process.

Selling your home can be daunting, but it's my job to eliminate the stress and worry from the process by tailoring the services I offer to the specific ways you want them provided, rather than providing the same services to everyone.

Sound interesting? Then let's connect by Tuesday, so I can demonstrate more about how I can help you get your home sold, in the time frame that best suits you, for more money, with truly personalized, worry-free service. Call me at 123-456-7890 and we can schedule a time.

Sample Phone Call Script

"Hi Mr. / Mrs. Smith,

It's ____________ with ______________ calling. We met yesterday at our Open House at 123 Anywhere St.

You expressed an interest in selling your home and I wanted to make sure I followed up and answered any questions you had about that process.

I know that selling your home can sometimes be a daunting procedure, but it's my job to eliminate the stress and worry from the process. The most important difference in the way I do things is to tailor the services I offer to the specific ways you want them provided, rather than providing the same services to everyone.

Does that sound intriguing?

Then let's schedule a time when I can demonstrate how I can help you get your home sold, in the time frame that best suits you, for more money, with truly personalized, worry-free service."

4 Week Prospect Follow-Up System

The following system has been developed to ensure, once you've made contact with the prospect, that you maintain ongoing contact with them until they're ready to take some action.

Day 1

- Follow up by email, text and phone (2 times if they don't answer on the first call) on the same day, using prepared templates
- Send your Media Kit, a business card and a Market Report concerning the area about which the prospect is inquiring.

Week 1

- Follow up by email, text and phone (2 times per day, every day) unless they've indicated what their preference is.

  "Hi, this is ________________ from ______________. Did I catch you at a good time? I just wanted to make sure you received the information I sent you. Did you happen to get a

chance to take a look at it? Do you have any questions about it or about the real estate market?"

Week 2

- Continue calling 2 times per day until they speak to you. Set the prospect up on a drip campaign via email and mail with information specific to their needs, i.e. 6 month Buyer Campaign, 3 month Renter Conversion Campaign and then follow up using their preferred method of communication

Week 3

- Continue the drip campaign
- Follow up by phone

Week 4

- Continue the drip campaign and add a Pop-by.
- Send a client-centric tip such as a real estate investment or home maintenance tip

If the prospect is still not ready to take action, move them over to your database and include them in your drip marketing system.

Every week you must offer an item of value. Prospects are looking for something that makes you valuable to them. What are you offering that will make them stick with you? What makes you stand out from others? It's important to make the prospect feel important, remember, they're thinking WIIFM (What's In It For Me?) and your job is to find out what's in it for them and then deliver it.

WIIFM??

Some concepts on follow up for you to consider.

- The best value is unexpected value – Give them something different
- Shift your focus from prospecting to educating

- Clients have loads of tools to buy and/or learn just about anything online, but they don't have your experience, wisdom or insight.
- Stop burying people in information and start offering them insight, start becoming a trusted advisor
- Value needs to be communicated.
- Your value comes in educating consumers on what they didn't know they didn't know.
- You must believe in your value.

The Bottom Line

Lead follow-up is every bit as important as lead generation, for without follow-up, generation becomes a waste of time and effort. Successful lead follow-up depends on several factors, including:

- Following up within minutes of getting the lead. Remember, if they don't know you, your responsiveness will be how they judge your competence.
- Following up using a comprehensive lead follow-up system that ensures every lead is treated the same and followed up with on a consistent basis.
- Following up using the medium of communication favoured by the prospect.
- Qualifying the prospect and setting them up in the appropriate follow-up system.
- Following up until they take action or tell you to get lost.
- Providing the prospect with the value or information for which they're looking.
- Avoiding trying to sell them right off the bat. Most prospects won't act until some time has passed and they're ready. Rushing them will drive them away.

- Becoming their trusted advisor, not just by providing information, but by being able to interpret it for them.

Business Building Exercise

Start setting up your lead follow-up system.

1. **Set up your Lead Tracking Forms in 3 different colours and place them in a lead follow up binder.**
2. **Set up your drip mail campaigns in your CRM System.**
3. **Set up your 4 week prospect follow-up system.**
4. **Set up your phone, text and email templates. Remember, they need to sound like you.**
5. **Set up your list of qualifying questions to determine a lead's motivation.**

SUMMARY

There are four key daily tasks involved in being a successful REALTOR®. In this volume, we've dealt with the first two, Lead Generation and Lead Follow Up.

Lead Generation is, without doubt, the single most important component of your tasks in order to build a successful career. In this volume, we've discussed the reasons that prevent Sales Representatives from carrying out their lead generation and ways to overcome them. We reviewed the many different types of lead generation;

- Mobilizing your sphere of influence
- Farming
- Making prospecting calls
- Doorknocking
- Running Open Houses
- For Sale by Owners
- Trade Shows

When prospecting, it's extremely important to remember that asking someone to do something without building rapport and providing them with something of value to them is a sure-fire way to fail. When you provide someone with information that they find valuable and that they can use to increase their knowledge and improve their decision making, you have a significantly better chance of establishing a relationship and building rapport with them.

The next most important component is that of Lead Follow Up. It makes no sense to generate new leads if you don't follow up on the ones you generate. Lead follow up consists of ensuring that you communicate with any lead as quickly as possible, in the form with which they prefer to be communicated. It also means providing them with information that they'll find valuable and useful on an ongoing basis until they're either ready to act or they decide not to move forward.

On the Right Foot

And now, your task will be to complete the Business Building Exercises in the Workbook; developing your Lead Generation and Follow Up systems and everything else you need to have in place to get your career started off on the right foot. Good luck!

FOUNDATIONS FOR SUCCESS

LISTINGS, LISTINGS, LISTINGS

Finding, Closing and Managing Listings

LISTINGS, LISTINGS, LISTINGS

**"Selling is not something you do to someone,
it's something you do for someone."
Zig Ziglar**

CHAPTER 1

Listings, Listings, Listings

We've all heard the old adage, "List to Last" and "List to Live", but what's really the big deal about being a Listing REALTOR® as opposed to working with buyers? After all, it would seem easier to find buyers than it is to secure listings, right?

In this chapter, we're going to review why listings are so important, how to manage them and how to use your current listings to find more listings and buyers.

The agent who has properly priced listings will always collect a commission at one point or another. Buyers will always come to you, the listing agent, eliminating the need for you to have to chase them. The listing agent can leave town, go on vacation, be lying on a beach or skiing in the mountains and STILL be making money when someone makes an offer on one of your properties. A buyer's agent has to be available for their clients, spend time showing houses, write offers, deal with third parties and buyer loyalty issues and a myriad of other things that enter into finding and securing the right home for a client. As well, you might be faced with the possibility of having to deal with multiple offers on a house.

Let's take a look at this concept from both the amount of time required and the potential income generated by each type of sale.

Let's assume that you're working with a buyer who is looking for a $600,000 house. You've spent a couple of hours meeting with him, finding out exactly what he's looking for and then searching for the right homes. You've taken him out several times, shown him four or five homes each time, and have finally found the house he wants. After writing the offer and filling out all the needed forms and documents, presenting and negotiating the offer, you finally have an accepted conditional offer.

Now you have the responsibilities of ensuring the buyer gets his financing, arranging for and spending three to four hours attending the home inspection and completing all the necessary paperwork. All in all, you've likely spent a total of twenty-five to thirty hours working with this one client. That's assuming that you haven't had the misfortune of having to deal with multiple offers a couple of times and losing.

Once the purchase closes, you receive your commission of around $15,000. Your satisfied client may refer you to another client from whom you'll earn another commission of $15,000, meaning that you have the potential to earn a total of $30,000 from managing this one transaction.

Now, let's assume you're working with a client to help them sell their home. You've spent about four hours putting together a complete Comparative Market Analysis and your Listing Presentation. You've spent an hour or two meeting with the seller securing the listing and perhaps another hour arranging for the staging specialist and photographer to deal with the property. Add another two hours for managing the listing, writing ads, distributing the Just Listed flyers in the neighbourhood and another hour for your email, social media and website campaign and a couple of hours to make sure that all the conditions are removed at the appropriate time and all the paperwork has been received. All in all, your time for a well-managed listing would amount to somewhere around fifteen to twenty hours from listing presentation to sold.

The total commission from the sale could be approximately $15,000. Other potential income could include one purchase ($15,000), the possibility of one deal from an Open House ($10,000), one from your Just Listed and Just Sold flyers and prospecting ($15,000), one from mobilizing your Sphere of Influence ($15,000), one from an ad and/or sign call ($10,000) and one from the internet and social media marketing ($10,000). That would amount to potential earnings of $90,000 from this one listing. One of the main differences between being a listing agent and a buyer's representative is that some of the activities involved in a listing will generate new clients, while none of the activities involved with acting for buyer clients will result in immediate leads.

It is obvious that by concentrating on securing your business through listings, you have a greater potential to earn a steady, and greater, income with less time commitment than a Sales Representative whose business comes mostly from working with buyers.

But, I hear you say, trying to find listings is much more difficult than finding buyers. I respectfully disagree. It's my belief, that, as long as you have systems in place to find, secure, manage and use your listings to prospect for new ones, it's no more difficult to become a listing agent than it is to find buyers.

So, what are the systems that you need to put into place to ensure you have a ready supply of seller leads, to have them want to work with you, to thoroughly, efficiently and effectively manage the listing and to get more listing leads from each one? We're going to review each of these systems which, when followed consistently, can lead to an outstanding and successful career.

The Kick-Butt Listing Presentation

It's All About Them!

It's my belief that, for far too long, REALTORS® have been using the listing presentation to try to impress a potential client, to try to convince the potential client to work with them by demonstrating just how wonderful they are, how much money they spend on advertising and just how marvellous their service is, to outdo other REALTORS® and justify their commissions. The argument has always been that they want to provide outstanding service and value to the client. However, value has always been interpreted as what services and marketing the REALTOR® believes they can provide the client. But, this is where the biggest challenge is. It's like a juggler trying to show just how many balls they can juggle at once to impress the audience. Sure, it's exciting and impressive, but, many times, it misses the whole point of the presentation.

I would suggest that we take an altogether different view of the definition of value. Value must be viewed as the services and marketing which the client believes is of utmost importance to them.

In order to secure more listings and ultimately more referrals, it is incumbent upon the REALTOR®, during the listing presentation, to elicit which activities and services the sellers consider to be of the most value to them and then to explain how the REALTOR® will be able to best provide them.

To accomplish this, a complete listing presentation must satisfy four requirements.

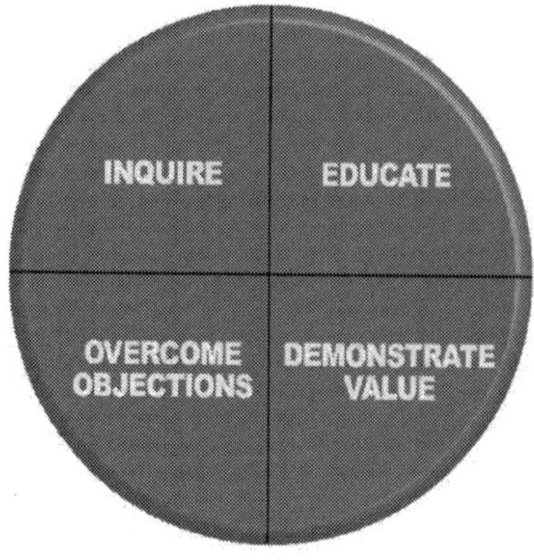

Inquire

The first segment of the listing presentation must allow the Sales Representative to find out as much information about the seller as possible and, at the same time build rapport. During this phase, the Sales Representative must discover what the sellers are looking for in their ideal REALTOR® and the services they expect him or her to provide. A conversation with a seller might include questions like these:

"Mr. and Mrs. Seller, Let me ask you; what are you looking for in a REALTOR®?"

"What are the three most important things your real estate agent can do for you?"

"Of the services I provide, which do you consider the most important?"

"You shared that communication is important. Can you tell me more about that? How often would you like to have communication and what type do you prefer? Do you prefer phone calls, emails, written reports or....? To give you a feeling of security and that you're in-the-know, what form would you like our communication to take and how often would you like it?"

"You shared that internet marketing was important. Can you be more specific? What methods, sites and types of internet marketing do you feel are most effective and which have the biggest impact? Which ones do you feel are a waste of time?"

Along with determining what the sellers conceived value to be, the Sales Representative needs to discover what information the sellers have, whether the information they have is accurate and what information they need. By asking open-ended questions, the REALTOR® can determine the concerns they have, their time frame for moving, and their motivation. This will help provide information on potential objections and how to deal with them.

Educate

Market demographics are changing, and Sales Representatives must understand that the traditional sources of information are being replaced with online providers. As a result of the variety and sheer number of articles available on the Internet, the public has access to unprecedented amounts of information, which can lead them to believe they know more than people in the industry. However, a great number of those articles can be misleading. REALTORS® need to spend time educating both potential clients and the public on the realities of the real estate market by providing relevant statistics and filling in gaps in their knowledge. Information must be provided on how homes are priced, the sales process, including what's involved, who's involved and at what point, the contracts required, and the costs involved in selling. REALTORS® must be ready and able to answer questions with accurate and up-to-date information.

Demonstrate your Value

Why you? And are you worth the commission you're charging? The Listing Presentation must answer those questions and prove to the seller that you're the REALTOR® they want to work with. The entire Listing Presentation must be tailored to define the REALTOR®'s Unique Selling Proposition and what it is that makes them different from other REALTORS®. Rather than explaining why you think you and your services are valuable to them, the Listing Presentation must reflect your initial conversation with the sellers and demonstrate that your services and marketing plans are determined by what the sellers believe is valuable to them. This can only be accomplished by asking open-ended questions and actively listening to the answers provided during the initial stage of the Listing Presentation and then adapting the presentation to those answers.

Overcome Objections

Throughout the Listing Presentation, based on the earlier conversation and issues raised by the sellers, the Sales Representative must predict the type of questions and concerns that may be raised and provide the answers before they are asked. The more frequently the answers are provided, the less likely it will be that the objection will rear its ugly head. Asking for feedback, understanding and buy-in (also known as trial closes or tie-downs) throughout the presentation will ensure the sellers have heard and understood the information and this will also assist in reducing the likelihood of an objection occurring. Some examples of these trial closes are:

"How do you feel about that?"

"Does that make sense?"

"Does that help?"

"How does that sound?"

The Complete Package

Any discussion of a Listing Presentation must also encompass the components that go into preparing the client for the presentation. A complete Listing Presentation kit includes three modules; the Media Kit, the Pre-Listing Package and the Presentation itself, each with a distinct use and time of implementation.

The Media Kit

This module is an information package designed for delivery to potential leads who have expressed some interest in selling but are not quite ready to do so. Its function is to provide them with information they can use while considering the move and, at the same time, demonstrate the Sales Representative's value and commitment to providing people with helpful and useful information and to keep their name foremost in the lead's mind. It also has the advantage of enabling the Sales Representative to have the opportunity of staying in touch with the lead until they indicate their readiness to sell.

The Media Kit consists of four sections:

1) Information about the Sales Representative, such as their biography, their Mission Statement, their statistics (or the company's stats for those new Sales Representatives) and any testimonials they may have gathered.

2) Information about the Brokerage or franchise, such as the market share it holds, its internet presence, international status and any other relevant information.

3) Information for the seller to consider before deciding to sell. This could include how the price for their home will be determined, positioning their home for the best price and sale time, how buyers search for homes, an overview of the Sales Representative's marketing system and ideas on how to prepare their home for showings, including the use of pre-

listing inspections, ideas on maximizing curb appeal and decluttering as well as information on potential closing costs.

4) A Sellers' Questionnaire which they can complete to assist the Sales Representative in gaining a better understanding of what the sellers deem important in marketing their home.

The Pre-Listing Package

The Pre-Listing Package, much like the Media Kit, provides information for the seller and answers some of the most common seller questions. It also includes samples of plain language versions of the Listing Contract and the Agreement of Purchase and Sale, allowing the seller to review and familiarize themselves with the contracts prior to meeting with the REALTOR®. It includes a Sellers' Questionnaire which allows the REALTOR® to gather information which can later be used in the marketing plan.

Delivered at least 48 hours prior to the listing appointment, the Pre-Listing Package allows the Sales Representative to contact the sellers at least 24 hours before the presentation to follow up and ensure that the sellers have read the package and to see if they have any questions. At this point, the Sales Representative may also take the opportunity to confirm the appointment and the attendance of everyone involved in the decision-making process for the listing.

"Mr. and Mrs. Seller, it's ________________ with ______________. I'm just calling to confirm that you received the Informed Seller's Guide I sent you yesterday and that you've had a chance to check it out. I wondered if you had any questions about any of the information in it?....OK, that's great. I also wanted to confirm that we're meeting tomorrow at 7 pm and that you're both going to be there. Also, if there's anyone else that you may want to

consult about the sale, I'd love to have them join us so they can get the information first hand...See you tomorrow night."

The Listing Presentation

This is where you get to shine and to prove to the sellers that you understand what services they consider to be valuable and that you can adapt to provide your services and marketing to meet, and possibly exceed, the seller's expectations.

A presentation can take many forms depending upon the relationship with the client, the situation for the presentation, whether you're in competition with others and a myriad of other factors. The following discussion will focus only on making a formal presentation.

The Secrets to making a Kick-Butt Listing Presentation

Be Prepared

Your listing presentation shouldn't sound like a canned speech that you trot out whenever you meet with people to discuss the sale of their home. It has to be natural, with a flow, tonality and speech quality that is your natural way of carrying on a conversation. This shouldn't be a sales pitch to get them to buy "you", but rather a listing conversation that will focus on what's important to them. The only way to get to this point is to rehearse your presentation, on video, until you have it down cold.

Chris Bradford, in *"The Way of the Warrior"*, said "Tomorrow's victory is today's practice." However, practice in itself isn't enough. To paraphrase Vince Lombardi, only perfect practice makes for perfect performance. By rehearsing over and over and over again, we develop the syntax and flow and confidence needed to make an effective and coherent presentation. By taking advantage of videoing our rehearsal, we're allowed to see ourselves as others see and hear us, thus allowing us to modify what we say and how we say it each time until we get it right. And once we have it right we can continue to rehearse it so that it becomes natural.

Know the neighbourhood

When I first began my career in real estate, I went to a listing presentation where the seller challenged me on a couple of the comparables I had chosen in the neighbourhood. They wanted to know if I had seen the other homes that I was comparing against theirs, and I had to admit that I hadn't actually seen them. Their next question, as they ushered me out the door, was how I could possibly make a fair comparison between their home and homes of which I had no knowledge. That's both a fair and reasonable question and it taught me a vital lesson. If you haven't seen the comparables, how can you truly know how to make any adjustments to the home? You must have physically seen the comparables before going in to the presentation; yet another reason for setting an appointment forty-eight hours after the original meeting or discussion. As well as having the time to deliver and have the sellers review your pre-listing package, it gives you the time to study the currently available comparable properties.

Understand the Sellers

When you first met the sellers and spoke with them, part of your discussion would have been to qualify them. You'd have asked them what was important to them in selling the home, why they were moving, where they were moving and many other questions that would have allowed you to determine their motivation. Now that you're making a formal presentation, it's important to remember and discuss their answers to those questions. It will help you define more clearly what's important to them and will also help you dig deeper during the initial stage of the presentation to determine how you can provide additional services that the sellers will feel are of significant value.

Bring Visual Aids

People are generally visual and tactile. They appreciate the opportunity to see and handle actual samples of the flyers, highlight sheets, ads, photos, and any other marketing tools you've used in the past. Sellers appreciate the ability to touch and feel the type of stock you use when you print things, the quality of the photos and the write-ups you've created. It helps them to quantify and evaluate your professionalism. Bring as many different samples of the marketing material you use with you. If you haven't listed anything previously, or don't have any samples, bring samples of the material your brokerage uses.

Visualize your Presentation

High caliber and professional athletes have been using visualization for many, many years in helping them achieve the greatest results possible in their sport. We've all seen Olympic downhill skiers stand at the top of the hill with their eyes closed while they sway back and forth while their hand traces the best line down the course. Or Usain Bolt rehearsing the first second of his start, as he blasts out of the blocks. It works for them and it works for us. It allows us to mentally run through the presentation, so we have it firmly implanted before speaking to the sellers.

Visualizing yourself actually presenting the information and seeing the sellers finally signing the listing contract produces positive reinforcement that allows you to go into the presentation in a more relaxed and positive frame of mind.

Use Positive Reinforcement Tools

Listen to your favourite music, a mantra, your own personal affirmation program on the way to the presentation - anything that will allow you to project a positive, self-confident attitude that will carry the sellers with you.

Review Objection Handlers

Take some time to review your objection handling system, the most common objections and how you're planning to handle them. Try to put yourself in the sellers' place and imagine how you'd want the information delivered. This will reduce any apprehension you may have regarding potential objections and allow you to exude a confident, positive attitude.

Arrive Early

Nothing interferes with trying to make an effective presentation as having to rush in and get your mind wrapped around what it is you want to say or do because you arrived just in the nick of time, or worse, a few minutes late. You've just set yourself up for failure. Having to rush into a presentation or any meeting for that matter, creates chaos and a loss of focus on the task at hand. It reduces mental clarity while trying to perform the tasks necessary to successfully negotiate the presentation, to handle objections and to do the paperwork involved. It also creates doubt in the sellers' minds about your ability to prioritize and provide the quality of service they expect from a professional REALTOR®. When you arrive early and have the time to relax and become mentally prepared, your performance improves, your ability to handle the twists and turns that regularly occur in a listing presentation increases and you will have more mental clarity. All of which will translate into a better, more coherent and more client focussed presentation.

Remember, It's All about Them

WIIFM?? What's In It For Me?

As stated at the beginning of this chapter, the purpose of the listing presentation is not to prove you're the best sales person on the planet and have better quality pictures than anyone else. It's designed to find out what the sellers are looking for and to demonstrate how your services and marketing plan can provide what they're expecting. To accomplish this, you have to listen to what the sellers are telling you and ask questions to clarify or dig deeper and then listen again. It becomes much more than just a listing presentation; it becomes a listing conversation.

One of the easiest methods of achieving this is to review the answers they gave in the Seller Questionnaire they received as part of the pre-listing package. This questionnaire allows you to ask more probing questions, reiterate their concerns and clarify any misimpressions you, or they, may have. The more you inquire about their needs and wants, the more you're likely to understand what they believe your value needs to be. The listing presentation must be a commitment to them and their best interests, not yours.

Positives Attract

We've all heard of "The Law of Attraction", which simply says that "like attracts like", In other words, positive people attract other positive people. Now, whether you believe that or not, your dominant thoughts do find a way to manifest themselves and can have an influence on those around you. I'm quite sure you've been around people who you can sense are fun and vibrant, as well as those who, like Joe Btfsplk from Li'l Abner, seem to have a black cloud hovering over them. Who would you prefer to spend time with? Be energized, positive and engaged and clients will sense it and will feel more inclined to want to work with you.

Laughter is the best Medicine

Use stories, especially humorous ones to illustrate a point. People love to laugh. They appreciate a bit of humour at a time when things may be somewhat tense. Relating a funny story, especially one where you or a client has had an interesting experience, can help clients relax and better understand the issue. However, there are a few points to remember when using stories.

- Avoid a story that is too long in making a minor point.
- The story must be easy to understand and doesn't require specific knowledge and information.
- The story must not contain language or humour that is inappropriate for, or offensive to, the audience.
- The story must not have a point that conflicts with the key beliefs of the audience.
- The story must not be confusing, hard to follow or doesn't illustrate the point well.

It's not a Fire Alarm!

Turn off your phone. Not onto vibrate…off! Pick up a phone call, or even check your phone during a listing presentation and you've just said to the seller, *"This call may be more important than you."* Definitely not the impression you want to give someone to whom you're trying to demonstrate your commitment.

A Sales Representatives at one of our offices told me she actually makes it a point of taking the phone out, right in front of the sellers and says, *"Let me just make sure I turn this off, so it doesn't disturb us."* and she, quite visibly, turns it off.

The Listing Presentation

During the initial segment of the presentation, your main tasks are:

- to build rapport with the sellers,
- to find out more about them,
- to find out what they're expecting from you,
- to ascertain what information they have,
- to determine how accurate that information is,
- to identify what information they still need to assist them in selling their property.

One of the most common questions you're likely to encounter when you walk in the door at a presentation is if you'd like to look around the home. There's a lot of discussion about this, with different trainers and coaches saying different things. In my opinion, at this point, your main job is to build rapport and discover what the sellers want and how you can provide it. So you'll need to defer that activity until you've had time to sit down and get them talking about themselves.

I recommend that you sit in the family room (since that's where the family gathers) if possible and spend some time reviewing the Seller Questionnaire and asking open-ended questions to encourage them to talk and allow you to find out more about them and for them to become more comfortable with you.

> *"Mr. and Mrs. Seller, I would love to look around your home. But right now, I'd like to take a few minutes to find*

out more about you and what you'd like to do about selling your home. Would we be able to sit in the family room (or living room) and chat for a bit?"

"Mr. and Mrs. Seller, let me begin by asking you this. What does your ideal REALTOR® look like? In other words, if you could define exactly what services you believe ***your*** *perfect REALTOR® would deliver, what would they be?"*

"Are there any fears or concerns that you have about the sale of your home?"

Once you receive answers from the sellers, it's extremely important to follow up with further questions that delve deeper into what's important to them.

"So what I heard you tell me is that communication is very important to you, is that right? Let me ask you, how would you like to be communicated with and how often. Do you prefer phone calls, emails, written reports or....? To make sure that you feel secure and that you're in-the-know, what form would you like our communication to take and how often would you like it?"

"It sounds to me that internet marketing is important to you, am I right? Can you elaborate for me? What methods, sites and types of internet marketing do you feel are most effective and have the biggest impact? Which ones do you feel are a waste of time?"

Now that you've had an opportunity to determine the sellers' perception of value, you can begin to define the issues they may have regarding the sale of the property, their subsequent move and their motivation.

"When do you want to make this move?"

"Why have you chosen to move at this time?"

"Have you definitely decided to move?"

"Are there any issues that need to be resolved before you move?"

"Will you want to purchase another home?"

"Are you ready to list your home on the market?"

"Do you have an idea of what you're expecting to get for your home?"

Once the initial phase is complete, you can then explain the process of the listing presentation.

"OK, Mr. and Mrs. Seller, now that we've had a chance to get to know each other better, here's what I'd like to do. Let's take a look at your home. Then when we're done, let's go back to the kitchen table and we can talk about how I can help you get your home sold, look at the contracts and get the paperwork done. How does that sound?"

Take the Tour

Now, it's time to take a look at the home. I've always found it advantageous to ask the sellers to show you the home as if you were a prospective purchaser. I want them to show me everything they believe is important for a buyer to know as I may want to use some of these in my marketing plan. One very important point to remember during this exercise is to not make any comments regarding the appearance of the home as anything you say may be misinterpreted by the seller and may have an impact during the pricing discussion. Occasionally, you may find they ask if they should go ahead and make some minor alteration, such as painting, or if they should leave a particular appliance in the home. The simplest answer is, "I would". There's no point in getting into a discussion of the pros and cons at this point.

And now it's back to the kitchen table to continue with the rest of the listing presentation. Should the seller, at this point offer you something to eat or drink, I believe you should "Drink the Kool-Aid".

With the exception of orange and apple juice, I hate fruit juice. I have lost track of the amount of mango-peach-banana type glop I've been offered over the years. In order to not offend sellers, I've had to hold my nose, put my taste buds on hold and drink this stuff. I've had sellers offer me food made with garam masala, a pretty hot spice, which had me sweating and needing several glasses of water, and which I ate so as not to offend them (I actually really enjoyed it). So, my advice is to, with the exception of alcohol, or if you're allergic to it, at least accept what they offer, even if you don't drink or eat it.

The Presentation

Let's now take a look at the physical aspects of the listing presentation. Listing presentations have changed drastically both in content and appearance. If you're still doing listing presentations as they were done in the 1990s, it's time to make some serious modifications and bring them into the current century. This must involve the use of technology such as laptops, tablets, projectors or whatever the latest form of technology happens to be, as opposed to traditional paper-based presentations. Whatever format you choose to make the presentation, it must look professional, must be organized and must be simple and straightforward. Make it visual, with lots of images instead of text. Too much text has been shown to actually decrease the amount of information people can take in and retain. Graphs can be used to help clarify information and data, as long as they're simple and easy to understand. Dare to be different; use colours and graphics that attract the eye. Branding, especially corporate branding, can be very useful but don't allow your presentation to become overburdened with corporate logos and colours.

It's important that your presentation is tailored to the audience. With changing demographics come changes in methods of communication. The style of communication of the presentation will be determined by the age, preferred communication style and comfort and knowledge of technology of the target audience.

At the time of writing this book, the Silent Generation, people aged seventy and older, comprise almost five million people in Canada. People of this generation predominantly use referrals to find a REALTOR® and tend to prefer communication by phone or in person. The reliance on and use of too much technology in a presentation can be a deterrent factor in the selection of a REALTOR®.

The Baby Boomer Generation, aged fifty to sixty-five years comprise nine and a half million people, also predominantly utilize referrals to select their REALTOR®. These people are familiar with computers and will conduct research before choosing a REALTOR®.

The next generations, Gen X and Gen Y, are much more familiar with technology. Generation Y, also known as Millennials, aged twenty to thirty-five, make up some nine million people. This demographic is sceptical of referrals and therefore exhaustively research properties and the REALTOR® online before working with them. They prefer communication by text message, want rapid responses and demand as much information as possible. Presentations to this demographic must be technology based as much as possible with emphasis on providing both information and value.

The listing presentation itself needs to be remembered and is a recitation of the following components:

- who you are,
- your vision of your service,
- the marketing and services you traditionally provide (which will be modified to meet the needs and requirements of the seller as discussed during the initial stage of your meeting with them)
- the Comparative Market Analysis.

Remember that the style, colours, graphics and "impressiveness" of the presentation are much less important in securing the listing than the time you take to find out what the sellers are actually looking for and what is of value to them. By spending that initial time digging deeply and asking the questions to understand what the sellers consider valuable, you will greatly improve your "appointment to listing conversion rate" and stand a much greater chance of obtaining a listing when in competition with other Sales Representatives who rely on "glitz".

An important component to demonstrate the quality of your services is to have your presentation visual and tactile. Sellers will have a better understanding of the type of marketing that you do when you're able to demonstrate it by providing samples of every type of marketing used, including:

- photos of previous listings,
- examples of virtual tours,
- before and after staging photos,

- samples of flyers, feature sheets,
- copies of ads,
- screenshots of websites.
- samples of previous reports.

It's also during this phase of the presentation that you're going to take the opportunity to reduce or eliminate a significant number of potential objections. This can be accomplished by reviewing how you're going to provide the value that the sellers have already revealed. Throughout the presentation, it's important to check with the sellers to ensure they understand and have no questions about the information you're providing. By eliminating any questions or concerns they may have, you can drastically reduce the likelihood of having to deal with objections. Once you've completed reviewing the marketing section, a simple way to ensure the sellers have understood and are on board with you is to use what's known as a trial or "small" close.

"So, based on the marketing that I'm going to do and the services that I'm going to provide, how do you feel about me handling the sale of your home?"

If the sellers agree that they're comfortable with your marketing and services, you are now ready to move forward, review how you've priced their home and present the CMA.

It's important to separate the pricing from the marketing, to determine if they have any concerns or objections relating to your marketing or services. Should they avoid agreeing until they hear how you've priced their home, you'll need to create that separation.

"I understand your concern. Of course you want to sell it for the best amount possible and that makes perfect sense. Let's assume we agree on a price. Based only on the

marketing I'm going to do and the services I'm going to provide, how would you feel about listing your home with me?"

If the sellers respond that they're not sure or they need to think about it, you'll need to use your objection handling abilities to determine the cause of the objection and how best to deal with it.

Presenting the Price

Once, and only when, the sellers have agreed that they're satisfied with your marketing and services and can see the value in using your services to sell their home, is it time to present the CMA and discuss pricing their home for sale. At this point, your next task will be to educate the sellers on how you price homes, and then, on how you specifically priced their home.

Probably the most common mistaken belief held by sellers is that REALTORS® are responsible for setting the price of homes. You'll need to demonstrate how the price of homes varies with supply and demand and relate that to the current market. The sellers will need to understand that a market in which there is more supply than demand (a buyer's market) will result in lower or decreasing prices and, conversely, a market which has a greater demand than supply (a seller's market) will cause home prices. You'll have to provide data regarding the type of market in which they find themselves, and how it will affect the pricing of their home. This will substantiate your proposal. A thorough review of the prices of comparable properties that have sold in the area, as well as the properties that have expired, will help to reinforce the price range in which buyers are willing to purchase similar homes.

Charts and studies available from the National Association of REALTORS (NAR) or Canadian Real Estate Association (CREA) can be used to demonstrate how buyers find and purchase homes.

Bringing recent newspaper articles to substantiate what the market is doing at any given time may be helpful. If the market has slowed down because of increased inventory, then the newspapers will have written a story about it. Sellers tend to believe what the media reports and if you're unable to convince them that the market has changed since their neighbours sold a month ago, they're going to be more inclined to expect the same result.

The next step will be to review how positioning their home in relation to others on the market will affect their ability to sell it in the time frame they require. A simple tool to assist in this is the "Buyers' Triangle". Once the average market value for similar homes has been established, the Buyer's Triangle can be used to demonstrate how pricing their home, even marginally above the market, can reduce the number of buyers willing to view their property.

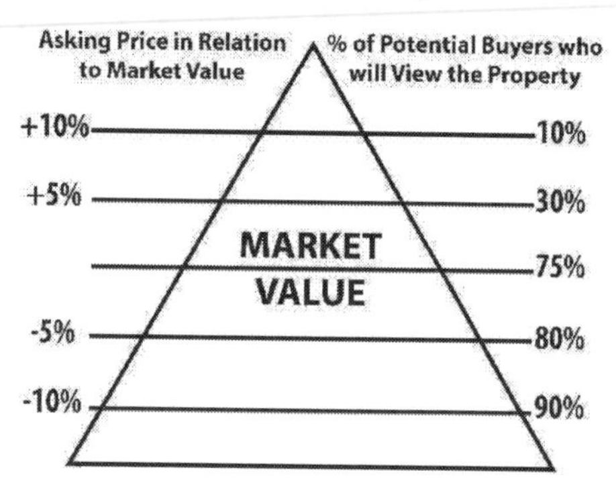

Another tool is known as "The Window of Opportunity". This chart demonstrates that when a property is first exposed to the market, the maximum number of buyers view the home in the first two to three weeks and then the

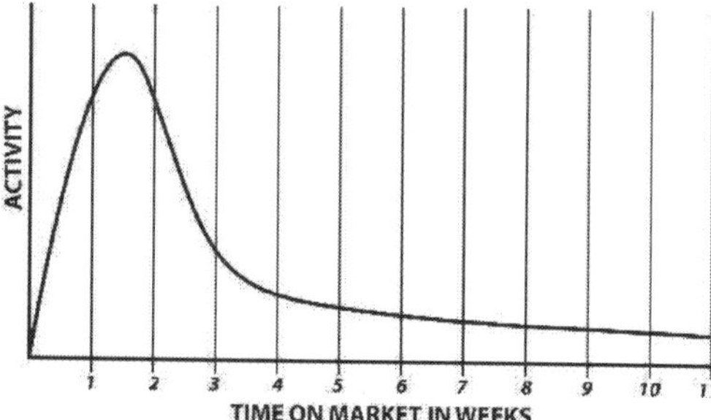

number of showings traditionally tapers off. You'll need to explain that, by pricing their home too high, or trying it high for a few weeks, the number of qualified buyers exposed to their home will decrease and will result in a delay in getting their home sold.

One of the most effective tools you can show the sellers to reinforce this concept, without breaking privacy laws, is to bring a printout of the showing activity of any of your or your brokerage's recent listings that have been on the market for four weeks and show them how the activity has declined week by week. If they ask you why your listing has been on the market for four weeks, hopefully the answer will be "that the seller did not take my pricing suggestion".

Once you've established the necessity of pricing the home correctly, it's time to review the comparable homes and discuss the appropriate price range for the sellers' home. Your CMA must be thorough and accurate. You'll have seen the properties against which the sellers will be competing, so you can speak intelligently about any comparisons and adjustments you may have made. It is important, before proceeding with the CMA, to establish whether the time it takes to sell the property, or the price at which it sells, is the paramount consideration for the sellers. This will assist you in helping them decide where in the price range they may want to price their home.

By reviewing the comparable properties that have sold and those that have expired, you'll be able to clearly define the range in which the sellers should consider pricing their home. It's important to remind them that the properties that are currently available are the "wish list," the prices other sellers would like to get for their homes. However, the Solds are the prices which buyers are prepared to pay for similar homes (the reality). Once this range has been established, it's vital that the sellers understand that you're not there to tell them what price to set for their home, but to work with them to help set a realistic price within that range.

> *"Mr. and Mrs. Seller, you've seen what the comparable properties have sold for and what buyers are prepared to pay for similar homes. It's my job to work with you, so that together we can set a realistic price that will help get your home sold. Do you have any questions about the information we've discussed so far?"*

By ensuring that the sellers understand your role and by dealing with any questions they may have at this point, you will greatly reduce the likelihood of having to deal with objections to the price range you're suggesting and, ultimately, to the final price that will be set for the home.

Price Perception

A study conducted at Cornell University in 2007 by Thomas, Simon and Kadiyali, entitled *"Do Consumers Perceive Precise Prices to be Lower than Round Prices? Evidence from Laboratory and Market Data"*, determined that buyers judge precise prices ($654,345) to be lower than prices of similar magnitudes rounded to the nearest thousands ($654,000) and, as a result, found that buyers are willing to pay higher sale prices when list prices are more precise and also will agree to pay prices that are closer to the list price.

This means that the traditional method of rounding list prices to the nearest thousands could actually end up costing the sellers money in the end. When discussing the final list price for your sellers' home, you may want to take this study into consideration.

The Transition and the Close

At this point, it's time to close for the listing. The first stage in the close is to ensure that the sellers see the value and are in the right frame of mind to sign the listing. The transition should remind them of what you've discussed, the fact that they feel they're comfortable with your marketing program and that they understand the price range you've discussed with them. It should then encourage them to take action, namely sign the listing contract.

"Mr. and Mrs. Seller, let's take a moment to review. We've discussed the marketing that you feel is critical to getting your home sold and how I'm going to deliver that. We've reviewed the properties that you're going to be competing against, the properties that have sold and what buyers are paying for them as well as the homes that haven't sold because they were priced too high. And we've determined a price range that should get your home sold in the time frame you want. Does that all make sense to you?"

When they say "Yes", you can now close for the listing with a simple assumptive close. Take out the Listing Contract, put your pen on the paper where you input the List Price and ask them,

"OK, so how much do you want to list your home for today?"

The Bridge to the Close

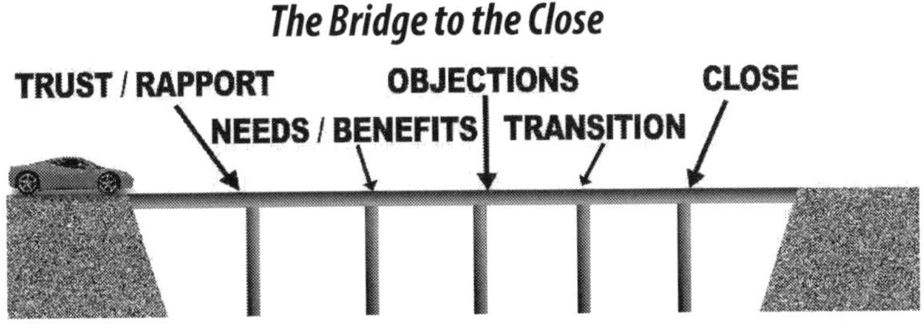

Business Building Exercise

Develop your Listing Presentation (you can find loads of them by speaking to your colleagues and checking online) and **rehearse it at least 5 times.** You may also want to **role play it several times with another REALTOR®** so you can get some constructive critiques.

CHAPTER 2

It's All about Systems

Now that you have the listing, it's time to take the necessary steps to completely and consistently provide the kind of outstanding service expected by your sellers. A consistent approach to all activities involved in managing the marketing, offer and follow-up processes will be required to ensure that nothing is missed throughout the entire sales cycle. This consistency comes from being highly organized and following the same process and procedure every time, for every person and ensuring that your listing system covers every contingency possible.

The Listing File

The first component of your Listing System is your listing file. This file, which must be complete and cover everything you do and plan to do, during the life of the listing. It will be your primary reference whenever you need to discuss the property with anyone. In order to fulfil this requirement, the listing file should contain the following items:

1. A copy of the listing contract to be used as a reference for any future activity occurring with this property.
2. A copy of the MLS Listing Input Form.
3. Copies of Working with a REALTOR and FINTRAC Identification Forms.
4. A Listing Task List, or Checklist, which specifies every activity to be taken from the time of the initial contact with the seller to when an offer is registered.
5. A copy of the original CMA which can be used in the event that a price adjustment is required or if justification of the price is needed when dealing with offers.
6. A copy of the Survey, if available.
7. A copy of the Geowarehouse, MPAC or GeoJet Reports or Title.
8. A Feedback Form which details the feedback received from buyers' Agents and potential buyers and which will be used as the basis for the Weekly Activity Report (detailed later).
9. The Seller Questionnaire from the Informed Seller's Guide, which will provide much of the information about the home to be used for marketing purposes.
10. Copies of any offers received and their disposition, whether accepted or not.
11. Copies of any deposit cheques received.
12. Copies of all notices, waivers, amendments, releases and any other documents relating to any offers received.
13. The Deal Tracking Form, a detailed list of everything required to be completed once an offer has been accepted, including:
    a. The offer date

b. The closing date

c. The Buyer's name

d. The Buyer's REALTOR® name and contact info

e. The Seller's lawyer name and contact info

f. The Buyer's lawyer name and contact info

g. The amount of the deposit, the date it was received and when it was delivered to the office

h. Any conditions, when they are to be removed and the dates when they are actually removed

i. Any additional terms of the contract

j. The date that the contract is submitted to the lawyers

14. Copies of any correspondence between yourself and the sellers as well as any between yourself and any other REALTOR® regarding the listing.

15. Copies of all of your marketing material, such as ads, websites, highlight sheets, flyers, Walkscore reports, etc.

16. Copies of all the Weekly Activity Reports sent to the sellers.

17. Copies of all showings scheduled.

18. A copy of the Commission Cheque stub in case it's needed for CRA.

It's advisable to have a paper or electronic copy of this file with you at all times during the listing period, so you have a ready reference in the event that anything occurs, such as an offer being presented or a price adjustment required.

The Listing Board

Any effective listing system has to include a means of visually tracking the progress and status of all listings. Traditionally that would have included the Listing Board, a white board hung on a wall at the office. However, as we move forward with the increasing use of technology, the more traditional methods have become outdated in favour of more mobile media. For the purpose of this book, we'll discuss the format of the traditional board, as the incredibly rapid transformation and proliferation of CRM systems is worthy of an entire book of its own.

In order to ensure that the board allows you to see where the listing is in the sale process, it should include the following pertinent information:

1. MLS Number
2. Address
3. Sellers Name
4. Initial Contact date
5. When the Informed Seller's Guide has been sent
6. Listing Appointment Date
7. Listing Date
8. List Price
9. Offer Date
10. Conditions and Removal Date
11. Date of Receipt of Deposit
12. Closing Date

Many CRM systems also offer this kind of tracking program and a REALTOR would be well advised to spend some time reviewing these systems. For a much more exhaustive examination of different CRM systems and their relative merits, I highly recommend viewing Gary David Hall's website, www.garydavidhall.com.

Business Building Exercise

Set up a number of Listing files with all the paperwork required by your brokerage, the New Listing Task List, Seller Questionnaire, Feedback Form, Marketing Checklist and Deal Tracking Form.

A Silver Bullet

You can find a copy of the forms and checklists in this chapter at www.foundationsforsuccess.ca.

New Listing Task List

NEW LISTING TASK LIST

MLS#:		Lockbox Code:	
Address:			
Client Name:			
Residence Phone:		Cell:	
Business Phone:		Business Fax:	
Email Address:			
Lawyer's Name:			
Phone:		Fax:	

ITEM		ATTACHED TO FILE	
Listing Contract signed		Listing Contract	
Taxes Confirmed		Listing Input Sheet / MLS Feature Sheet	
GeoWarehouse / MPAC Search Completed		Title	
Mortgage Verification Form signed		Tax Assessment Form	
Mortgage Verification Form sent to bank		Survey, if available	
Mortgage Verification Form returned		GeoWarehouse / MPAC Printout	
MLS Data Input Sheet Completed		Property History	
Listing Broker Loaded (if applicable)		Photos	
Listing Contract and Input Sheet Submitted		Mortgage Verification Form	
New Listing Checklist Completed & Submitted		Copy of Highlight Sheet	
Lockbox Installed		Seller's Ad Questionnaire	
Sign Ordered		Copy of each Flyer	
Photos Taken		Copy of each Ad	
Office & / or MLS Tour Date Set		Copies of Activity Reports	
Host Office & / or MLS Tour		Trade Record Sheets	
Ads written & submitted		Communications Record	
Design and Print Flyer for Home Office		Feedback Form	
Design and Print Flyer for RE Offices		Transaction Activity Record	
Design & Print Flyer for Neighbourhood			
Design & Print Highlight Sheets			
Distribute Flyers			
Place Highlight Sheets in Home			
Public Open House Scheduled			
Design & Print Open House Invitation			
Distribute Open House Invitation			

Showing Instructions			
Keybox Location:			
Alarm	Y	N	Code:

Features / Upgrades

Seller Questionnaire

SELLER ADVERTISING QUESTIONNAIRE

NAME: ____________________

ADDRESS: ____________________

Why did you buy this property?
Special qualities, location, amenities, etc.

____

____

____

____

____

What do you love about your home?
Features, special times, memories

____

____

____

____

____

What will you miss about the home / location?

____

____

____

____

____

What renos/ improvements did you do?

____

____

____

____

____

What would you have done, given the time?

____

____

____

____

____

Deal Tracking Form

DEAL TRACKING FORM

MLS#:		Address:	
Offer Date:	DD / MM / YR	Closing Date:	DD / MM / YR
Seller's Name:			
Buyer's Name:			
Buyer's REALTOR Name:		Cell:	
Business Phone:		Business Fax:	
Email Address:			
Seller's Lawyer Name:			
Phone:		Fax:	
Buyer's Lawyer Name			
Phone:		Fax:	

DEPOSIT

Amount:	$	Date Received:	DD / MM / YR	Handed in to Office: ☐

CONDITIONS

Financing	Removal Date:	DD / MM / YR	Removed	Y	N
Inspection	Removal Date:	DD / MM / YR	Removed	Y	N
Status Certificate	Removal Date:	DD / MM / YR	Removed	Y	N
Lawyer's Review	Removal Date:	DD / MM / YR	Removed	Y	N
	Removal Date:	DD / MM / YR	Removed	Y	N
	Removal Date:	DD / MM / YR	Removed	Y	N
	Removal Date:	DD / MM / YR	Removed	Y	N

ADDITIONAL TERMS

Date Offer Submitted To Office: DD / MM / YR

OTHER PERTINENT INFORMATION

The Listing Board

MLS	Address	Sellers Name	Contact Date	Informed Sellers' Guide Sent	Listing Appt	Listing Date	List Price	Offer Date	Deposit Received	Conditions	Closing Date
C123456	123 Any St	Joe Smith	May 3	May 4	May 6	May 6	$655,299	Jun 2	Jun 3	F- Jun 8 I – Jun 8	Jul 2

Your Communication System

It's no secret that the biggest knock against REALTORS® and the most common reason complaints are made to regulatory agencies and boards is a lack of communication with clients. So, it's obvious that a consistent approach to maintaining communication with your clients is imperative both from a service provision perspective as well as from a regulatory standpoint.

Your communication system must ensure an easy, smooth transmission of information in both directions between you and your client. The sellers should know that you will be contacting them regularly to keep them informed of:

- any showings,
- feedback from the showings,
- any Open Houses,
- any changes to your marketing plans,
- changes in the market conditions and
- any advice required regarding any changes in the market that may affect the marketing or price of their home.

They should know and understand what they can expect in terms of the response times for you to return their calls, texts, messages and pages. They should understand that you are available, within certain limits, to deal with any issues they may have regarding the sale of the property and that, as their real estate go-to-person, you encourage them to contact you with any questions, concerns or issues that may occur.

On the other hand, as communication is a two way street, the sellers must also make sure that they stay in touch with you should anything change about their status, such as the sellers going away for any extended period of time, the arrival of a new addition to the family, relocation or anything that may create a change in their contact information.

Any communication you have with the sellers, potential buyers or other REALTORS® should be documented in writing and attached to the listing file, so that any questions that may arise involving communication can be verified by your notes.

A weekly report should be provided to your sellers so that they are continually informed of everything that's occurring in regards to the sale of their property. The report should detail:

- the number of showings scheduled for the week,
- any feedback, both positive and negative, from other REALTORS®, buyers and anyone who attended the Open Houses,
- the marketing performed during the previous week and scheduled for the following week,
- any changes in the neighbourhood market conditions
- any advice you can provide that may affect the sale of their home.

This weekly report can be emailed or delivered to them but should not be used to replace the ongoing verbal communication that is essential to the outstanding level of service with which you intend to provide the sellers.

Activity Report

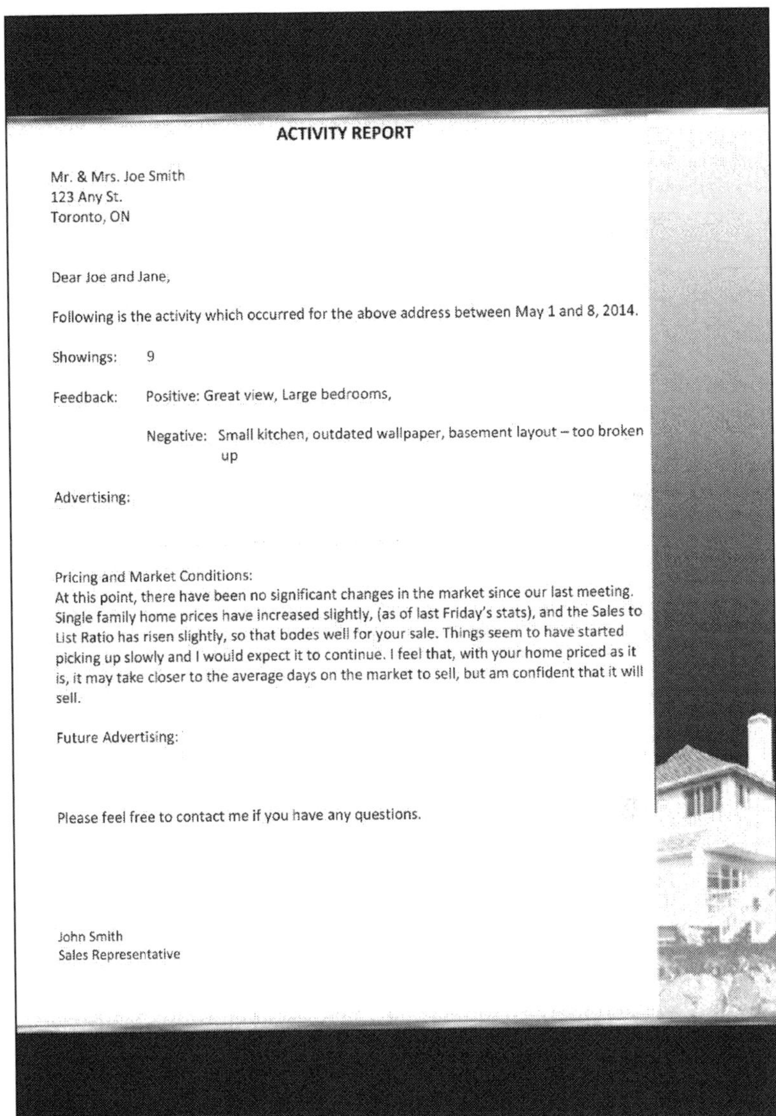

ACTIVITY REPORT

Mr. & Mrs. Joe Smith
123 Any St.
Toronto, ON

Dear Joe and Jane,

Following is the activity which occurred for the above address between May 1 and 8, 2014.

Showings: 9

Feedback: Positive: Great view, Large bedrooms,

Negative: Small kitchen, outdated wallpaper, basement layout – too broken up

Advertising:

Pricing and Market Conditions:
At this point, there have been no significant changes in the market since our last meeting. Single family home prices have increased slightly, (as of last Friday's stats), and the Sales to List Ratio has risen slightly, so that bodes well for your sale. Things seem to have started picking up slowly and I would expect it to continue. I feel that, with your home priced as it is, it may take closer to the average days on the market to sell, but am confident that it will sell.

Future Advertising:

Please feel free to contact me if you have any questions.

John Smith
Sales Representative

Exposing the Client

As with any system, there must be a set process to follow which is fully repeatable and clearly defined. A Marketing Checklist, in which all of the marketing and advertising is spelled out, will help keep you on track and on time.

We'll review the process of writing ads and marketing in "I'm Just Sayin'."

Location, Location, Location

So, where do you place ads? Traditional advertising utilizes print media, such as local newspapers and home sale magazines as well as electronic media, including radio and television advertising. These methods of advertising, however, tend to be expensive and, with the dramatic proliferation of less costly and more widely accessed sources on the internet, show a diminishing return on investment.

Internet advertising provides a huge range of opportunities to promote your sellers' properties from free advertising sites such as Kijiji, Craigslist, Backpage and many more, through social media such as Facebook, Twitter, Instagram, Pinterest and more to personal, corporate, franchise and property-specific websites. The choices are continually expanding and the chances to advertise have never been greater.

Expose their best side

One of the secrets of truly successful REALTORS® is having their listings professionally photographed. In a recent NAR study (2014 National Association of REALTORS® Home Buyer and Seller Generational Trends) 83% of potential buyers indicated that they considered the photographs of the home to be very useful in their decision to view homes. In many discussions with potential buyers, I've found that the quality of the photographs also played a large part in the buyers' decision to view the property. And yet, there are still REALTORS® who insist on taking their own photos with their phones' cameras, resulting in shots of corners of bedrooms, windows in living rooms and toilets in bathrooms. Professional photographers have the skills and equipment to show the home in its best light thereby increasing the opportunities to have more potential buyers consider viewing the home.

Minimize to Maximize

Many sellers confuse staging with home decorating services. In reality, staging is a comprehensive review of a seller's home with an eye to transforming it so that potential buyers can easily picture it as their future home. While your sellers may absolutely love the flocked wallpaper and green velvet curtains, they may not appeal to a wide range of buyers. It's important that sellers understand that despite their personal preferences and predilections, a buyer needs to be able to see themselves living in the home and staging gives them the opportunity to make the changes necessary to attract as many potential buyers as possible.

Staging also involves reducing the clutter we all have in our homes. Clutter, the things we just can't or won't get rid of because we never know when they'll come in handy, is just another culprit which distracts the buyer from seeing the house itself. More importantly, your sellers' clutter may be sending a message that there isn't enough space, which makes the home seem small in the minds of the buyers.

Most importantly, staging has been shown to help sell homes faster and for more money than homes that haven't been staged.

According to NAR, staged homes sell 80% quicker and for up to 11% more money than non-staged properties. One of the major factors is that, with the majority of buyers seeing homes on the internet, staged homes have that additional WOW factor, making them stand out from the rest of the crowd.

There are many different options for you to take advantage of in staging your clients' homes. You could pay for the initial consultation only or pay for the consultation and stager's work while the client pays for any additional work required or pay for the complete staging including any rental items required. The cost to benefit ratio must be examined to determine which route you plan to follow.

Hey look at Us!

The use of Just Listed flyers for marketing the home is an integral part of the process, and a part of marketing yourself (which we'll discuss in a later chapter). The delivery of Just Listed flyers to homes in the community affords you the opportunity to promote the home to neighbours and have them notify any friends who may be considering a move into the neighbourhood. The flyers should also be delivered to other real estate brokerages in the community as well as in your home office, which will give the area REALTORS® a 'heads up' about the property.

To obtain the maximum effect from Just Listed flyers, they must include a description of the home, the features, and the benefits of living in it. As with any advertising, it should be designed to evoke an emotion, encourage the recipient to imagine themselves living there and have a clear and definite call to action.

Highlight the Home

One of my pet peeves is the use of the MLS Listing Sheet as the Highlight or Feature Sheet for a home. Highlight Brochures should be something that portray and augment the quality of the home, something that the REALTOR® can be proud of and that can be used in listing presentations to demonstrate the quality of work utilized by the REALTOR® when marketing a client's home.

Highlight brochures must take the prospective buyer on a pictorial and descriptive tour of the home. They must be of high quality with professional photographs and have descriptions of the features and benefits of the home that are well thought out. Imagine yourself guiding a buyer through the home. Write the brochure with the descriptions and photos in the order in which you would normally show them through it. For example, first the foyer, then the living room, dining room, kitchen, family room (if there is one), then upstairs to the bedrooms, ending with the master bedroom, next the basement and then out to the back yard. This ensures that nothing is missed and you are creating a clear picture in the buyers' minds.

You may also want to add a page to describe upgrades and unusual features of the home as well as additional information about the neighbourhood. Sixty-three percent of buyers surveyed (2014 NAR Home Buyer and Seller Generational Trends) indicated that the quality of the neighbourhood played a significant part in their decision about where to buy a home. With the advent of Walkscore (www.walkscore.com), prospective buyers now have the chance to review neighbourhood amenities and transit, so it's advisable to include a copy of the home's Walkscore with the Highlight brochure.

Come Take a Peek

Video marketing and Virtual tours are becoming more and more important in the marketing of a home, to the extent that, in the 2014 NAR study, forty-three percent of buyers described the use of a virtual video tour as a very useful tool in helping them decide to view a home. Most professional photographers now also include the production of a virtual tour as part of their service. In Toronto, you're able to attach virtual tours to the MLS listing as long as it is not branded. Check with your local board regarding their rules on the use of branded virtual tours on their MLS.

Creating powerful videos, which once used to be extremely prohibitive due to the cost of production, has become increasingly available to every REALTOR® due to the changes brought about by technology. What used to take hours of time and expertise to create is now as simple as using the video camera on smartphones or tablets to record and inexpensive or even free applications to convert and edit the recording. Two of the experts in this area are Mark Arnstein, who works in the North Toronto area and Vivien Sharon, whose niche is the Yorkville community. They have both embraced video marketing as a means not only to market the properties they sell but has also to inform potential buyers about the communities in which they sell.

Vivien credits video marketing with helping develop leads, gain recognition and build her business.

> *"A video introduces the audience to a real person who is caring, trustworthy, and committed to their client. The connection is personal and viewers appreciate that my priority is their success and happiness. This tool has proven very effective as my business continues to grow and expand. It has helped me establish credibility, build leads, and introduced me to a new and growing audience using social media and online tools to hire their REALTOR®."*

It's been shown that using videos will significantly increase the likelihood of your site's presence on Google's first page and that there is a 40 percent increase in click through rate on those results. This means that more people will see the video of the home and then click through to your site to investigate it further. An Australian real estate group reported that real estate listings with videos generated 4 times as many leads as those without videos.

Increasingly, people are interested, not just in the house, but in the community into which they're considering moving and community videos allow customers to see what kind of amenities are around them (like public transportation and restaurants). It also lets them get a feel for the neighborhood and the community.

Including video marketing and virtual tours will help develop increased interest in both your product and in your marketing services, thereby making your personal branding more powerful.

Marketing Checklist

MARKETING TASK LIST

MLS#:		**Address:**	
Client Name:			
Residence Phone:		**Cell:**	

ITEM		ATTACHED TO FILE	
Just Listed Flyers Designed		J/L Flyer	
Just Listed Flyers Delivered		Listing Input Sheet / MLS Feature Sheet	
Home Office		Copy of Highlight Sheet	
Neighbourhood RE Offices		Seller's Ad Questionnaire	
Neighbourhood		Copy of each Flyer	
Websites:		Copy of each Ad	
Personal		Copies of Activity Reports	
Company site		Communications Record	
REALTOR.ca		Feedback Form	
Backpage			
Kijiji			
Craigslist			
Property Address Site			
YouTube			
Blog			
Twitter			
Facebook			
Other			
Sign Ordered			
Curbside Marketing Signs Ordered			
Sign and Curbside Installed			
Staging Consultation			
Photos Taken			
Virtual Tour Completed and Posted			
Ads written			
Ads placed:			
Real Estate Magazine			
Newspaper			
Other			
Other			
Design & Print Highlight Sheets			
Highlight Sheets Placed in Home			
Host Office and / or MLS Tour			
Public Open House Scheduled			
Design & Print Open House Invitation			
Open House Invitations Distributed			
Host Open House (VIP Event)			
Host Public Open House			
Just Sold Flyers designed			
Just Sold Flyers delivered			
Sold Rider Placed on sign			
Just Sold Calls made			

The Offer Management System

"I've got an offer for you." Lovely words indeed...words that create a wide range of emotions and signal the start of a truly interesting and, if handled correctly, easily managed sequence of events that lead your listing to becoming a sold property. However, if handled in a sloppy or haphazard way, the sequence of events can create many difficulties and headaches for you, your sellers and the parties on the other side.

Your Offer Management System must ensure that all registered offers are dealt with in a consistent and logical sequence and they are dealt with in a manner that is clear and beyond reproach. There must be clear communication between you and your sellers, as well as between you and the buyer's agent.

In both single and multiple offer situations, the first step, after notification is received of a signed offer, must be notification of the sellers and the establishment of a time for the offer presentation. Once the time has been set for presentation, the buyer's REALTOR® is notified and the presentation arranged.

Your next step in managing offers is to arrive at the site of the offer presentation early, whether it be the sellers' home or your office. You need to review the offer process with the sellers. They should understand that they have three options in dealing with offers; they can accept the offer outright if it has everything they want; reject it (not an advisable option), or they can make a counter-offer.

They need to be aware that a good offer is composed of many parts: price, conditions, dates and terms.

They should be advised that, in order to not hinder the negotiations, they need to keep their emotions in check, and to not give anything away during the negotiations. Should they have any questions, they should wait until the buyer's REALTOR® is finished and has left the room, at which point they can ask the questions through you. It's important that the sellers understand that negotiations are a process and that counter-offers (sign-backs) may also be countered and it may take time to reach a satisfactory conclusion. They should also understand that negotiations should be viewed as an opportunity to work to achieve a beneficial result for both parties, not to beat the other party into submission - the concept of a win-win result is the central factor in any successful negotiation. By negotiating to achieve a win-win situation, the offer presentation and subsequent negotiations become an actual negotiation and not a confrontation.

Single Offer System

Management of single offers, while easier than multiple offers, still requires a set series of procedures to reduce the likelihood of errors, omissions and miscommunication.

Unlike a listing presentation in which you turn your phone off, an offer presentation is a whole different kettle of fish. In this instance you'll want to keep your phone turned on. Let the sellers know that you're keeping it on in the event that another offer is registered, or something happens that could generate a higher price for the seller.

When presenting a single offer, it's important to follow a consistent sequence during the presentation. The first step is to invite the buyers' representative to tell the sellers a little about their client. This allows them to personalize the offer rather than have it be nothing more than a piece of paper and will aid in the negotiation, as the sellers will, hopefully, see the buyers as people who are sincerely interested in purchasing the property. Once this is complete, it's your job to take over presentation of the offer.

Sellers want to know the bottom line, what the buyers are proposing as the purchase price. If the price is provided right at the beginning, they tend to focus on the price, to the exclusion of all the other details which go into making up a reasonable offer. So that they understand all the terms and conditions of the offer, it should be presented in an order which allows them to hear the entire offer before the price. As each component is presented, it gives you the opportunity to obtain their agreement or counter to each of the elements.

If price is disclosed first, you risk having them hear nothing else from that point onward other than Charlie Brown's teacher (*wah, wah…wah, wah, wah*). To avoid this, an offer should be presented in the following order:

1. Completion Date
2. Conditions and removal dates
3. Terms and finally,
4. Price

Multiple Offer System

The process of managing multiple offers can be much more difficult than that for a single offer. But, like presenting any offer, it must be 100% fair and above board, especially if a salesperson has their own offer as one of the multiples.

A deadline for offer presentation is set and all offers must be submitted by that time. As new offers are registered, each previous REALTOR® is notified of the new offer, the number of offers and which position they will be in for the presentation and the time for offer presentation.

In order to be as neutral as possible, the listing REALTOR® should avoid seeing or evaluating the offers before the presentation. Each buyer's REALTOR® should be given the choice to either present the offer personally or submit their offer in a sealed envelope. In the event it is faxed or emailed, the offer should be sent to the listing REALTOR's® office and the front office staff should seal it in an envelope with the buyer's REALTOR's® name and brokerage written on the outside. They should be time stamped and assigned a number, in the order in which they were registered.

At the presentation, each envelope is opened in sequence and the merits of each offer discussed. If the REALTOR® is to present the offer personally, they present it in the order of registration.

In order to ensure there are no questions about the process, once all offers have been presented, the seller signs an Offer Presentation Acknowledgement, naming the brokerages and REALTORS® and the order in which they were presented.

In the event that the listing REALTOR® has their own offer, every representative must be notified that there will be multiple representation. Depending upon your region's legislation, should a collateral agreement exist with the sellers regarding a reduction of the listing broker's commission in the event of a double end, each representative must be notified of the existence and details of the agreement before they present their offer. In order that the listing REALTOR® can be free to present their own offer and there can be no apprehension of bias, their broker or manager should sit in and act as the sellers' REALTOR® for all offers.

In the event that a significant number of offers have been submitted and presented, each offer is reviewed with the seller. Initially, the offers with conditions attached are reviewed first and the seller can decide if any should be held for further review. If not, they are eliminated and the representatives notified.

The next review takes into account the closing date, purchase price and other factors of the remaining offers. At this point, the seller has the option of accepting one, rejecting them all or sending them all back for a revision of the price, date or any other component. Should the sellers opt to have the offers revised, a specific time will be set for the reps to have their revised offers back to the listing REALTOR®. Once all offers have been received, the review process will resume and one offer will be accepted. In order to expedite the process and to be fair to all parties, requests for revisions should be kept to a minimum.

Next Steps

Once the final signatures have been affixed, the sellers should know what the next steps will be, when they'll occur and who's responsible for managing each step. Since there are many opportunities for problems to arise during the time the property is sold conditionally, it's important to keep the sellers' expectations at bay. You'll need to let them know there may be problems with condition removal, but that you're there to help deal with them so that condition removal occurs as smoothly as possible.

Those Pesky Conditions

Now that you have an accepted offer, it's time to deal with the conditions that may have been included. As with anything to do with managing a listing, it's important that you have a system in place that ensures thorough follow up on all conditions and that all waivers and/or notices are received and managed properly and on a timely basis. Should a problem occur with removal of a condition, you'll need to discuss possible options for resolution with the buyer's REALTOR® and when a solution has been reached, let the sellers know about the problem and the possible resolution and then confirm that they agree. You'll want to advise the sellers to never assume there will be another offer and that it's always better to deal with the one you have until it's no longer possible to reach a successful resolution. In this chapter, we'll review some of the common issues faced when managing conditions.

In my opinion, the inspection condition is one of the most stressful events of the purchase process. There are many occasions in which things can, and occasionally do, go wrong during the inspection.

Perhaps one of the most stress-creating occasions occurs when the seller refuses, or is unable, to leave the home during the inspection. I had the bad luck to have this issue many years ago. I had been in the business for less than a year when I listed a home owned by an elderly couple who had built the home in the 1950's. It was in a very desirable area and was only on the market for about three or four days when we received and accepted an offer which was subject to financing and inspection.

The inspection was scheduled and on the day before the inspection, I spoke to the sellers and told them I would come by to take them out while the inspection was being held. They declined to leave the home due to medical reasons, so I informed the buyers' REALTOR® that the sellers would be in the home and that I would be there as well to try to keep them from interacting with the inspector. Since I was going to be there, the other agent asked if I could keep an eye on the inspection as they had another offer to deal with. I agreed and on the day of the inspection, I arrived at the home early so that I could explain the process to my clients. The buyers and the inspector arrived at the agreed time and started the inspection while I stayed on the back deck with my clients.

As the inspection proceeded, despite my warnings and requests, my client (the husband) would occasionally drift off the deck and look in on the inspection. About half-way through the inspection he didn't return, and when I found him, he was following the buyers around and arguing with the inspector. Finally, as the inspector was removing the electrical panel cover, my client exploded and threw the inspector and the buyers out of the house. As you can imagine, this effectively terminated the deal. It's an inspector's job to find issues with the home so the buyers are aware of exactly what they're purchasing. Sometimes the sellers have a hard time hearing that their much beloved home has problems. This is definitely not the place for the sellers. Get them out of the house.

Another stress-creating issue occurs when buyers use the inspection to create an opportunity to try to reduce the agreed upon purchase price. When this occurs, it's your responsibility to review with your clients, the issues raised by the buyers and determine if they are valid reasons for any price adjustment. You'll need to reinforce the fact that they have the same three options available to them as when the offer was first presented; accept, reject or counter the proposal. They also need to understand the possible consequences of each action. Once they've been apprised of the options and potential results, it's up to them to instruct you on how to proceed.

The biggest challenge and most stressful occasion occurs when an inspection takes place on the condition removal date and there are issues which need to be dealt with at the last minute. This places tremendous stress on both the sellers and the buyers (not to mention the REALTORS®) and should be avoided if at all possible. When I was selling real estate, my partner and I made sure that no inspection was allowed on the day of condition removal. By this simple expedient, we were able to greatly reduce the stress on our seller clients.

One of the other common issues around inspections is the question of whether or not to use a pre-listing inspection. I think the following article written by Josie Stern and reproduced here with her permission, is one of the best explanations of why a pre-listing inspection is so important.

> *"It's common in today's market for the seller to provide the buyer with a home inspection of the property before exposing it to the market. The inspector usually makes himself available, during the marketing of the home, to answer buyer questions eliminating the need for a buyer to do their own home inspection. You might be asking yourself "what is the advantage for me to do this and why should I incur the cost of the home inspection?" There are numerous advantages for you especially in a market where multiple offers are common:*
>
> - *if a buyer has done a home inspection on another house but lost it in competition, the buyer may be reluctant to spend more money on another home inspection, fearing they may not be the highest bidder once again, and pass on your house instead of making an offer*
> - *if a buyer does not have time to do their own home inspection before the offer date they may also pass on your house*
> - *you have the chance to fix any problems before you put the house on the market instead of buyers walking away because their inspector found a problem you weren't aware of*
> - *you choose the inspector based on reputation and credentials instead of relying on the buyer who may*

use a friend or a company who may not be qualified to inspect your house

- *it avoids having a parade of home inspectors through your home before a multiple offer situation by all interested buyers*

- *it helps you comply with full-disclosure real estate laws because it guarantees you haven't overlooked a defect or material fact for which you could later be held liable*

The objective is to set the conditions that will attract as many offers as possible on your house and/or to eliminate any possibility the buyer will walk away from a deal because they have found deficiencies with the house that you were not aware of. No surprises.

***Case study**: Seller A puts his house on the market and does not provide a pre-list home inspection. There are 3 offers on the property, 2 from buyers who have done a home inspection before the offer date and submit unconditional offers and 1 from a buyer who submits a conditional offer upon a satisfactory home inspection. The highest bid, by tens of thousands of dollars, is from the buyer who submitted the conditional offer. Although you understand the risks of accepting a conditional offer versus a firm offer, the price is too tempting to pass up. The next day the successful bidder has buyer remorse concerned they overpaid for the house. They perform the home inspection and find a reason to either renegotiate the sale price or walk away from the deal. The buyer asks for an exorbitant price reduction that, if you agree to, will result in the sale price being lower than the price on the firm offer you* *rejected. Your choices are to agree to the price reduction or go back to the second highest bidder and see if they are still interested in your house. Most of the time, the second bidder will no longer be interested or will offer you a lower price than they did before. Making the matter worse is recording the transaction as "having fallen through on a home inspection" on the Toronto Real Estate Board system which may threaten your deal with future potential buyers. This is not a good place to be "caught between a rock and a hard place".*

We are much too experienced to compromise OUR client's position in this way, but sadly, we know it has happened to clients represented by less experienced and less thorough agents. The unfortunate part is this could be avoided by providing a pre-list home inspection costing no more than $500. The lesson is to not be penny wise and pound foolish but to "line all your ducks in a row" to ensure a smooth transaction and as many offers as possible to achieve the highest sale price." ***(http://josiestern.com/selling-home-toronto/pre-list-home-inspection/)***

Another issue commonly faced nowadays is the presence of rental items, such as hot water heaters, furnaces, security systems and others, which carry a rental contract with them. Some of these contracts can carry onerous cancellation or transfer provisions in them. In order to minimize the impact these contracts may have on a purchase, you may want to consider having the sellers review them prior to listing the home, so they're fully aware of any provisions which may create issues.

Status Certificates (Condominium Documents) are yet another issue that crops up. Issues around them consist of:

- when they have to be produced,
- how long they remain valid once ordered and
- trying to set a date for condition removal.

Depending upon the provincial legislation, condominium corporations have a specified time period to provide the documents. In Ontario, condo corporations have 10 days following a request and payment of the fees for the document to produce the documents.

"76 (3) The corporation shall give the status certificate within 10 days after receiving a request for it and payment of the fee charged by the corporation for it." Condominium Act, 1998, c. 19, s. 76 (3)."

As a listing agent, I've found that it's always easier to have the documents available once the property has been listed rather than waiting until an offer is accepted. This eliminates any lag time or delay in getting the condition removed in that the 10-day period to actually receive the certificate will prolong the conditional period. This could make it possible for another condo to come onto the market which may derail buyer interest in your unit or for the buyer to find another unit elsewhere. When an offer is presented containing a clause with the condition removal date specified as a certain number of days, to protect the sellers and ensure complete clarity, you may want to consider amending it to read:

"This offer is conditional upon the Buyer's lawyer reviewing the Status Certificate and attachments and finding the Status Certificate and Attachments satisfactory in the Buyer's Lawyer's sole and absolute discretion. The (Buyer/Seller) ___________ agrees to request at the (Buyer's/Seller's) ___________ expense, the Status Certificate and attachments within _____ days of

acceptance of this Offer. Unless the buyer gives notice in writing to the Seller personally or in accordance with any other provisions for the delivery of notice in this Agreement of Purchase and Sale or any Schedule thereto not later than 5 p.m. on __________________, that this condition is fulfilled, this Offer shall be null and void and the deposit shall be returned to the Buyer in full without deduction. This condition is included for the benefit of the Buyer and may be waived at the Buyer's sole option by notice in writing to the Seller as aforesaid within the time period stated herein."

Sold!

Conditions have been removed and the deal firmed up. Now comes the waiting. However, this is your opportunity to shine in your clients' eyes as you demonstrate your commitment to customer service. Many REALTORS® use this time to simply sit back and wait for the deal to close and the commission cheque to roll in. But now you have an opportunity to show your clients how committed you are to helping make their transition as easy and smooth as possible by assuring them that you will do everything you can to make sure everything proceeds in a timely and efficient manner.

The first issue you'll need to address, excluding providing outstanding service should they wish to purchase a new property, is the initial onset of sellers' remorse. This happens for a number of reasons and can become a real concern if not treated with compassion and understanding. It's important to let the sellers know that you understand that selling a family home is never easy and that the emotional tie can be very difficult to overcome; however, once the deal has been finalized, it's just as important to let go and move forward. You may have to do some emotional handholding during this period, but you'll also have to be firm and remind the seller of the potential consequences of reneging on the deal.

The next issue that may crop up during the run up to the move is the issue of any repairs that may be required as a result of the inspection. In this case, you'll need to be ready to provide your sellers with referrals to any trades which may be required to fulfill the terms of the agreement. It's always a good idea to prepare the trades you're going to recommend so that they're aware that the sellers may be contacting them and that you'll need them to provide priority service to the sellers. Also, you'll want to make sure the sellers keep a copy of the bills for the repairs, as well as any warranties and guarantees so they can provide them to the buyers in the event of a dispute. You may also want to consider some of the home warranty programs available so that the buyers are covered for anything that may go wrong in the first year after they move and to protect your sellers from having to deal with any issues later.

The largest hurdle for many sellers, according to several of my past clients, is packing for the move itself. What to take, what to get rid of, what to do with the things they may want. These are some of the many things that cost sellers sleep. Having a reliable moving company to help them with this stage can make the difference between a frustrating experience and one that eases the transition to their new home. Your advice on a trustworthy mover can make this part of their journey smoother and will greatly increase your reputation in their eyes.

As you move closer to the closing date, you'll need to contact the seller to ensure that they're on track for their move and that they've spoken with their lawyer to arrange an appointment to complete any paperwork still required. I've always found that it's a good habit to contact the clients' lawyer to confirm that they have received everything they require in order to move forward with the sale. You'll also need to remind the sellers that they need to be ready to have the buyer take their last inspection of the property. They should be reminded to notify their utility services and other services of their move approximately three weeks prior to the move.

Your role up to and including the day of the move is to assist your sellers so that everything goes smoothly and that you're there to answer any questions and to provide or refer any services that they may require that will ease their transition. Of course, bringing lunch by on the day of the move is always welcome.

Don't forget to get a testimonial from your client as soon as the sale occurs, or they may forget and move on. In many cases you may want to ask them if they'd like you to write the testimonial for them, send it to them and they can then reword it as they feel appropriate.

It's also important to have permission in writing from both the buyer and seller allowing you to market the sale including the sold price.

Prospecting the Listing

One of the most important factors in having listings is the ability to prospect for more listings using the existing one. In order to maximize these opportunities, you'll need to have a system that allows you to get the listing out to as many people as possible in the quickest timeframe.

The first step in the system is the use of Just Listed flyers. These provide you with the chance to knock on the neighbours' doors, introduce yourself and attempt to develop some rapport. We know that when a property lists in an area, there tends to be a Domino Effect, whereby another one or two properties are listed within a short period of time. You can take advantage of this by meeting potential sellers and showing them your commitment to customer service. If you're not inclined to knock on doors, you can make warm calls to the neighbours.

This is also an opportunity to contact your Sphere of Influence, remind them that you're always looking for referrals and to mobilize them. And the best way to let them know is to make a few phone calls and invite them to your VIP Open House.

Holding Open Houses is yet another very effective method of prospecting for buyers and sellers. See "Exposing the Client" for the Open House system.

Ad and sign calls, while a passive form of prospecting, can be effective in developing leads. However, it's important to ensure that you qualify callers before spending time meeting and showing them properties. In order to give yourself the best opportunity to convert the caller to a prospect, you must have your dialogue memorized and personalized.

One of the most common mistakes made, which costs REALTORS® leads, is to answer the caller's questions and leave it at that. This is a give-and-take opportunity; answer their question but follow it immediately with a question of your own.

> *"That house is priced at ____________. What price were you looking at?"*

It's very important to build rapport with the caller. One of the best ways to do that is to mirror the caller's tone and speed of conversation and to try to find common ground so you can create a connection with the caller. Once you've built some rapport and provided them with some information, it's time to close for an appointment so that you can discuss your services, find out exactly what the caller's looking for and whether they're a buyer or seller.

Once the property has sold, there's another excellent opportunity for you to market yourself to the neighbourhood. Immediately after the conditions have been removed and the deal has been firmed up, you can begin your post-sale marketing program which consists of the following steps:

1) Place the sold header or rider on your sign. This is a great opportunity for a photo op with your sellers gathered around the sign, which can then be used as a photo testimonial; "*Another happy family moving on, courtesy of...*"

2) Your Just Sold flyers should be distributed within forty-eight hours. These can be used as an opportunity to knock on the doors in the community, giving you the chance to discuss the market and sales in the community with the neighbours and prospect for new listings.

3) Warm calls can be implemented to around two hundred homes in the area as well.

4) Emails to your Sphere of Influence should be completed announcing the sale.

5) Notice of the sale can be distributed via the internet and social media.

The major purpose of having a listing, other than making money of course, is as a tool to get more listings. You need to take every opportunity and advantage offered by having a listing to develop more leads for more listings. By following a consistent system to prospect your listings, you can help ensure that you have a steady supply of leads and future business.

SUMMARY

In this volume, we discussed how to manage listing presentations that focus on providing value to prospective clients, based on what the prospect is looking for, rather than on what you believe your value is. By breaking the listing presentation down into the four parts and spending more time on the inquiry phase, thereby gaining better insight into the prospect's views of the value they're looking for, you'll be better able to demonstrate how you can provide that value and differentiate yourself from the other agents.

However, a great listing presentation is of no value if you fail to provide the outstanding service you promised to the client. That service will depend on having a system in place that allows you to perform a consistent sequence of tasks for each and every listing. A sequence which must include the information which needs to be collected from the seller, processes that will ensure that the listing is managed the way in which it should, and routines to ensure that you are able to prospect the listing so as to get more listings and buyers.

On the Right Foot

And now, your task will be to complete the Business Building Exercises in the Workbook; developing your Pre-Listing Package, Listing Presentation, and your Listing Management systems. You'll need to spend a significant amount of time role-playing your presentation, objection handling skills and your closing skills, but by investing the time now, you'll save yourself significant missteps and be that much closer to getting your career started off on the right foot. Good luck!

FOUNDATIONS FOR SUCCESS

BUYERS, BUYERS, BUYERS

Finding and Managing Buyers, The Buyer's System

BUYERS, BUYERS, BUYERS

"Owning a home is a keystone of wealth - both financial affluence and emotional security."

Suze Orman

CHAPTER 1

Buyers, Buyers, Buyers

In the last volume of the series we examined how to find and work with listings. As a new Sales Representative, it's very likely that your first few deals will come from working with buyers. In this volume we're going to take a look at how best to service those clients. Before beginning to discuss the Buyers' System, it's important to understand where buyers come from, why they buy and why, as a new Sales Representative, it's important to work with them.

The 2014 NAR Generational Trends Report found that Millennials (people aged 22 – 35) made up the largest share of home buyers at 31 percent, 76% of whom were first time buyers, followed by people aged 35 - 50 (Gen X) and the Baby Boomers each at 30 percent. Seniors only accounted for approximately 9 percent of total buyers.

"About half of millennial buyers primarily purchased a home just for the desire to own a home of their own. Gen X placed a high importance on owning a home of their own, but many needed a larger home and needed to move for a job-related relocation. Older Boomers and the Silent Generation are more likely to move for retirement, the desire to be closer to friends, family, and relatives, and the desire for a smaller home."

Millennial buyers place a high priority on convenience to both their job and lifestyle options as well as the affordability of the homes they're viewing. They also try to stay close, usually within 10 miles, to their previous residence, while older generations tend to move longer distances, typically up to 30 miles from their previous home. Boomers and seniors place a higher priority on convenience to friends and family, convenience to shopping, and convenience to health facilities.

Younger buyers tend to be willing to compromise on many factors in the home they purchase, such as the price of the home, distance from job, size of the home, and condition of the home purchased. However, the older generations are usually less willing to compromise on the features of the homes they purchase, as they want to avoid the additional costs and headaches associated with renovating.

When looking for a home, it's no surprise that all generations begin their search process by looking online; however, Millennials tend to spend more time online researching the homes, communities and the REALTOR® before making contact. Older buyers are more likely to be more occasional users during their home search and tend to contact a REALTOR® once they've done some research.

An interesting factor that became clear in the NAR study was that the search time for a home was different for the various age groups, with older buyers tending to take a shorter period of time to find their next home than younger buyers. The study demonstrated that younger buyers (under age 59) tend to search for a home for 12 weeks. Buyer aged between 59 and 67 tend to look for 10 weeks and older buyers (68 to 88 years of age) search for just 8 weeks.

Why work with buyers?

I know, everyone, including me, says that in this business, you need to list to last. You have to focus on getting listings. And I firmly believe that. However, you're more than likely going to find that, for the first year or two, you'll work with more buyers than sellers. And that's OK, because working with buyers gives you many different opportunities to develop critical success factors that will stand you in good stead in the future, not to mention an income.

You'll get the chance to develop and hone skills, such as prospecting and objection handling, asking the right questions and active listening, recognizing and adapting your client handling skills to different personality types, writing and negotiating offers and many more. You'll develop time management and prioritization skills.

And even more importantly, you'll have the chance to develop your reputation, both with clients and with your colleagues. You'll learn how to build and maintain trust with your clients and how to avoid the many traps which can create roadblocks to that trust and reputation.

What's your role?

A good buyer's agent is able to carry out a series of essential tasks that reach far beyond just searching for properties. They must:

- Know how to ask the questions needed to uncover the buyer's needs and wants as well as their major motivating factor in the purchase.
- Become a trusted adviser and supporter during the entire home buying process.
- Help buyers understand the buying process and educate them on current market conditions
- Help buyers to both understand that they will need to balance obtaining, and help them find, as many of their needs as possible, within the constraints of dealing with the realities of the market and / or their specific financial constraints

- Help buyers achieve their lifestyle needs with a different set of features than originally anticipated (this is particularly useful when dealing with financial constraints)
- Uncover and disclose any information that will help buyers make informed choices as to which properties to view and ultimately purchase.
- Help buyers in narrowing their search until they have identified their top choices through testing their criteria during the Buyers' Interview process.
- Advise buyers of clauses and pricing and help them understand the implications of the offer during the offer preparation phase.
- Manage the negotiation and counteroffer process so as to provide the client with the best possible advice in order for them to make the most informed decision.
- Provide oversight and follow up on any conditions to ensure the process proceeds as smoothly as possible and provide references to any service personnel that may be required.

What's your value in all this?

So what are buyers looking for from their REALTOR®? Since younger buyers are more likely to have never purchased a home before they're more likely to need assistance with understanding the process. According to the NAR study, all buyers benefit from their agent pointing out unnoticed features and faults in a property and all buyers most want their agent to help find the right home to purchase.

The study found that younger buyers valued the agent's honesty and trustworthiness as a significant factor and it's been shown as a result, that millennials tend not to be willing to sign Buyer

Agreements with a REALTOR® until they've had the time to develop that trust.

Older buyers, however, rated the REALTOR's® reputation and their knowledge of the neighborhood as a higher factor. The study speculated that this may be due to older buyers tending to move longer distances and not necessarily knowing the neighborhood.

Referrals were the most common way that clients found their REALTOR®. Younger buyers predominantly used an agent that had been referred by a friend, neighbor, or relative, while older buyers were more likely to use an agent again that they previously used to buy or sell a home.

The study found that:

- Fifty-two percent of buyers found finding the right property the most difficult step.
- Twenty-four percent found understanding and completing the paperwork the most difficult part of the process.
- Fifteen percent of buyers had the most difficulty with understanding the complete process and what the next steps were
- Twelve percent found obtaining a mortgage the most difficult step.

The study went on to say that what buyers want most from their real estate agent is:

- Help finding the right home to purchase
- To help the buyer negotiate the terms of sale
- Help with the price negotiations

As can be seen, your value to this process is multifaceted and can be significant. Your involvement in the process, your skills and the team of support personnel you build, and to whom you can refer, will enable your buyer clients to find the right home, at the best possible price, with the best possible terms with the best guidance and information possible.

Who are they and where do they come from?

Buyers may come from many different sources. You can convert leads developed from ad and sign calls. Open houses, if well run, can be a great source of buyers. The most preferred source of leads is through referrals while prospecting is a necessary source of business. Sellers can also be a source of buyers. Running buyer or investor seminars is another outstanding opportunity to create buyer leads as are trade shows. In other words, buyers can be found wherever you decide to look for them.

When converting leads to buyers, you must have your lead follow-up system up and running and be ready to act immediately. It's important that you've developed and internalized your script so that you can easily convert a call to a lead and then to a buyer. Your script must allow you to qualify leads as you speak with them, as you don't want to waste time or gas with suspects or unmotivated people.

Ask and ye shall be given

Give and ye shall be broke! When speaking to a prospect, it's a give and take opportunity; you give them a little information, but it's critical that you get some back as well. As you're building rapport, remember to mirror the caller's tone, speed and volume. Answer their question then ask an open ended question to elicit some information that will help you grow your insight into what they're looking for and their motivation. Avoid closed ended questions. All you end up with is a yes or no answer.

"How much is the house?"

> *"It's $__________, is that the price range you were looking in?"* Yes / No

Instead, try:

> *"It's $_________. What price range were you looking in?"*

This leads them to provide more information and allows you ask more open-ended questions as a follow up.

> *Caller: I'm calling about the house you're advertising for $____________. Can you tell me about it?"*

> *"Sure. It's a 3 bedroom, 2 bathroom bungalow on a 50 by 150 lot. Can you tell me a little more about the kind of home you're looking for?"*

> *"Can you tell me more about the specific community you want to move to?"*

When describing the home, one of the key factors in getting buyers to become more interested in viewing it is to focus on the benefits of owning the home not just the features. People buy on emotion and then justify the purchase with logic, especially when the object is in demand. In order to appeal to that emotion, you need to be able to demonstrate to the prospect that there's some benefit to them of owning the home.

> *"It's a 3 bedroom, 2 bathroom bungalow on a 50 by 150 foot lot. Do you have kids? It's a great home for kids. They can play in the huge backyard. It's fully fenced so it's safe for them and there's plenty of room for them to run around. It's got a nice deck off the back so you can entertain and watch the kids play as well."*

When I first started working as a REALTOR®, a trainer and coach in Edmonton named Lyndon Sommert demonstrated a great tool to use to pique the interest of potential buyers. It's called the Red File. Because that's what it is. It's a red file folder with a list of properties that you've previewed and believe are special due to their price or appeal. Having this file will allow you to maintain the conversation should the lead not find the home they're calling on appropriate for them.

"OK. It sounds like that house isn't for you, but I have a list of houses that I've seen that I think are great buys. Would you like to hear about them?"

This gives you the opportunity to create more curiosity, build more rapport with the caller and creates openings to close for an appointment.

Many times there is one consistent objection which crops up.

"Can you give me the address, I just want to drive by and take a look."

At this point you have a choice to make. You can give them the address and then hope they call you after they've looked at the house, or you can decide not to give them the address and close for an appointment. The first option leaves things to chance, the second eliminates it. They'll either agree to an appointment or they won't. If they don't, I would argue that they weren't serious in the first place and you're better not to have wasted your time.

Always try to close for the appointment using your objection handling skills, but if they insist on just getting the address, your answer should be, *"I understand that you would really like to drive by the home, but I only give out addresses to my clients."* Many times that answer will motivate them to agree to the appointment.

Informed Buyer's Guide

Once the prospect has agreed to the meeting, the next step in your lead follow up system must be to send them your Informed Buyer's Guide. This guide provides then information about you, such as:

- Who you are
- What you stand for (your Mission Statement) and what differentiates you from other agents
- Information about your brokerage
- Current market statistics
- The agency relationship
- The buyers' services you provide
- The buying process
- Testimonials
- A Buyer's Questionnaire
- Plain language versions of the contracts they'll encounter.

Once you've sent this, you then have an opportunity to follow up with them to find out if they've had a chance to read it, if they have any questions and can then reconfirm the meeting.

Business Building Exercise

Write out a list of qualifying questions you can use when you receive an ad or sign call and role play them with a colleague until you're comfortable with them.

Set up your Red File and begin previewing new listings.

Set up your Informed Buyers' Guide.

The First Meeting

Now that you've had the prospect agree to meeting with you, you can either bring them into the office or meet them in a public place such as a coffee shop. From a safety standpoint, it's much more preferable to meet where there are other people as opposed to having your first meeting with someone you don't know at the property or at their home.

At this meeting, your main task will be to find out about them. Using open ended questions, you'll want to determine their needs and wants, their lifestyle and most importantly, their motivation.

You'll also want to demonstrate, by utilizing your Buyer's Presentation, how you can assist them throughout the buying process.

The Kick-Butt Buyer's Interview

Just as with the Listing Presentation, your Buyer's Interview has 4 key components:

The Inquiry

When working with buyers this component will likely be the most significant and lengthiest part of your Buyer's Interview. Here's where you get to find out as much information about the buyer as possible and, at the same time build rapport and ultimately find out how you can best serve the buyer's needs.

A Silver Bullet

You can find a sample of the Informed Buyers Guide and Buyer's Presentation at www.foundationsforsuccess.ca.

What kind of service are they looking for? The 2014 NAR Study revealed that the most difficult thing buyers faced was finding the right home, followed by understanding the paperwork involved. The majority wanted their REALTOR to help them find the home and then negotiate the terms and price for them. How involved do they want you to be in helping them through the process?

How do they want to communicate? It's important to know not just their method of communication, but how often they want to hear from you. How often do they expect to be in touch with you and what kind of information would they find most helpful?

What kind of buyer are they? Buyers come in many different shapes and sizes. There are first time buyers who are looking for a property to get them started on the road to a larger home. Others may want an investment that will appreciate after three to five years. They may be repeat buyers who may be looking for a house to meet their needs for the next ten to twenty years or investors looking for a good investment property with decent cash flow potential and an infinite number of other variables. Your job will be to ask the questions you need to in order to help you determine how to best serve their needs.

What kind of home are they looking for? Here again there's an infinite number of variables and this will be one of your major challenges. Unless you plan on spending a tremendous amount of time in your car, showing them every new home that's listed, you'll have to get them to be very specific about their ideal home. It's at this point in the interview where you'll utilize your Buyer's Questionnaire.

The Buyer's Questionnaire is designed, as part of the Buyer Management System, to help you ask the questions you need to in order to get the answers that will help point you in the right direction. It helps you clarify their Determinant Buying Motivation

(DBM); what their main criteria for choosing a home is and what will sell them on a particular home. It assists in defining which houses to show them and which can be eliminated. However, the questionnaire is just a guide and doesn't include all the questions you'll need to ask. When you've asked a "What" question, it needs to be followed by a "Why" or clarifying question that will give you a better understanding of their true requirements.

"So, it sounds to me like you're looking for...is that right?" Can you tell me a bit more about why that's important?"

For example, someone with an elderly parent and a couple of older children living with them may tell you that they need a bungalow, so the parent doesn't have to use any stairs. However, by asking the following clarifying question, you may gain more understanding of their true needs.

"I understand that you want to make sure your father doesn't have to use stairs. If I could find you a two storey home with a bedroom and bathroom on the main floor, would that work for you?"

Another situation that could arise would occur when a buyer tells you they want four bedrooms in the home. By asking the following question, you may be able to help them gain a better understanding of their options, which will ultimately help determine the homes to show them.

"You've said that you want four bedrooms. Would you consider a home with two or three bedrooms above grade and one or two in the basement?"

These questions may lead to further discussion and will ultimately help you home in on the right group of homes to show the buyers.

Once you've determined the right series of homes to show, your next major task will be to determine their motivation. This can best be determined by asking some key questions. These questions will help you determine if there is an urgency, an ability and a readiness to buy. If you have two of these three components in place it's fairly safe to say that you're dealing with a motivated buyer.

"Why are you thinking of buying?" This will help you better understand if there's there a compelling reason for the move or if they're just thinking about making a move. If there is a compelling reason, you've likely established that there's some urgency to the purchase as well as a readiness.

"Have you been pre-approved?" When potential buyers have taken the time to meet with a lender and gone through the paperwork required to be approved for a mortgage, you know they're serious about buying. If they're pre-approved, the ability to buy exists, you know how what price range they're looking in and that they're indeed ready to buy.

"How long have you been looking?" "Have you seen anything you really like?" Motivated buyers generally don't take a long time to find a home. If your prospect has been looking for several months, they're probably not motivated enough for you to commit the one thing you can't waste, your time.

"When do you want to move / How soon do you plan on moving in?" This is similar to the previous question, in that it goes to a time frame for the move. However, where the first question asks how long they have been looking, this question seeks to find out how long they plan on looking. If they're not thinking of making a move within the next six months, it might be a better use of your time to put them on a drip email campaign and touch base with them every so often to see if their motivation has changed, rather than taking them out to homes that they're just not going to buy.

"If you found the right home today, would you be ready to buy it?" This is the ultimate qualifier question. If they answer with a yes, there's urgency, ability and a readiness to purchase.

"Are you working with a real estate agent?" While this doesn't have anything to do with their motivation, it's a critically important question to ask. Since you want to get paid for your work, asking this question will ensure that your efforts will be rewarded if you work with the buyers.

Some additional questions you may want to ask to assist in qualifying them are:

"If you could design the ideal moving situation for your family, what would it look like?"

"Do you need to sell your current home before you can buy?"

"Have you bought a property in the past?"

"Have you met with a lender yet? What Price Range are you looking in?"

"What can I do to make it easier for you to get the kind of real estate information you are looking for?"

"Tell me the process you typically use to make decisions like this?"

"What is the most important service you want from a real estate agent like myself?"

The Buyer Questionnaire – Page 1

BUYER QUESTIONNAIRE

Name: ______________________________

Address: ______________________ Phone: __________

______________________ Cell: __________

Email: ______________________ Fax: __________

Type of Property Wanted: Single Family House ☐ SF w/ Suite ☐ Condo ☐

Townhouse ☐ Detached ☐ Semi-Detached ☐ Attached/Row ☐

Area: **Central** ☐ **North** ☐ **East** ☐ **West** ☐ **Out of Town** ☐

Neighbourhoods Desired ______________________________

____

Style: ______________________ Year: __________

Minimum Bdrms Up: __________ Minimum Bdrms Down: ________

Minimum Washrooms Up: __________ Minimum Washrooms Down: ________

Basement Development: P-Fin _____ F-Fin _____ Suite: _____ Suiteable: _____

Price Range: __________ Down Payment Available: __________

Garage: Yes ☐ No ☐ Single ☐ Double ☐ Larger ☐

Amenities Desired: ______________________________

____

Pre-approved: Y N Bank: ______________ Int. Rate: ________

Willing to do upgrades: Y N How Much: ______________

Other Important Info:

The Buyer Questionnaire – Page 2

ADDITIONAL QUESTIONS

Is the age of the home important? ____________________

What are you looking for in a kitchen, family room? ____________________

____

Do you want a separate dining room? ____________________

What is your preferred layout? ____________________

What are your high priority features: appliances, ensuite, fireplace?

____

____

What other types of rooms do you need? A main floor laundry, a home office?

____

____

What about storage space? Basements, lockers?

____

____

Is energy efficiency important? Newer windows or a high efficiency furnace?

____

____

What other landscaping features are important: a fenced yard, play areas, pool, gardens?

____

____

Is the direction the home faces important? ____________________

Educate the Buyer

There's a wide range of misinformation about the market, what REALTORS® do and a multiplicity of other issues. As part of your Buyer Interview, it will be your responsibility to find out what information the buyer has and what they don't. You'll need to spend some time reviewing that information and correcting any misunderstandings they may have. You'll also need to educate them on the information they don't have; provide them with answers to the things they don't know that they don't know.

They'll need to be shown the realities of the overall market for the area as well as the community in which they wish to live. You'll need to explain how the inventory levels and seller expectations may affect the prices and potential for multiple offers.

There's a commonly held misconception that, should the Buyer work with the listing representative, they may get a break on the price due to a possible reduction in the agent's commission. It's important that you educate them on the roles, responsibilities and fiduciary duties of the Seller's Representative vs. the Buyers' Representative.

Since the Listing Sales Representative is under contract with the seller to market and sell their property for the best possible price the buyer needs to understand that the Seller's Representative's primary responsibility is to their client, the Seller. When a buyer contacts the Seller's Representative, they should be aware that a listing agent can only be expected to:

- Arrange a showing.
- Help arrange financing.
- Provide details about the property.
- Explain all the forms and agreements related to buying the property.

They should not, therefore, expect the listing representative to discuss anything related to the sellers' motivation to sell or the price that the seller will accept.

They should also understand that the amount of the commission is between the Sales Representative and the seller and that any break in the commission will benefit the seller, not the buyer. In other words, the buyer is not assured of getting a reduced price if they work with the listing representative; rather, the seller will likely end up netting more.

However, when the buyer engages the services of their own personal Sales Representative, someone who is under contract to work solely in their best interest, they get all of the same services listed above plus:

- A Sales Representative that will look after their needs first.
- All the applicable fiduciary duties with no possibility of any conflicts of interest.
- Access to all available listings rather than just the one they called on.
- Expert advice, when writing an offer, on including clauses which will provide the best protection for the client including home inspections, financing and many others.
- Expert negotiation of the offer to purchase so as to achieve the best possible price and terms for the buyer rather than the seller.
- Expert advice on market value and pricing, as well as helping them decide when they should consider walking away from the negotiation.
- Discovery and disclosure of any available information about the property including liens, warranties, disclosures, seller's purchase price, and market and planning activity in the area.

Part of educating the buyer is also to review the buying process from start to finish. In doing so, you can ensure that they understand each step, who is responsible for what and what the next step will be.

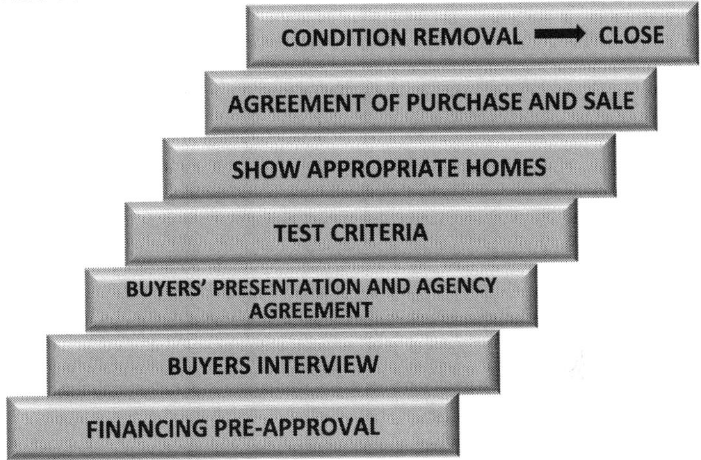

Now that they've been pre-approved and everyone is aware of the price range in which they should be searching, the next stage is to really determine the type of home and location to look at. You'll need to educate them on the Buyer Representation Agreement (or whatever the Buyer Contract is called in your jurisdiction) and how it can ensure that you're acting in their best interest. If they're ready, you can then get them to sign it at this point.

Testing, Testing...

The next step will be to search for the homes they've described and "test" their criteria, by conducting a search on MLS for the homes that match those criteria. This will allow you to confirm that the type of home, with the features, in the price range and the area they've described, is available. This will also allow you or the buyer to make any modifications to their criteria based on having viewed the homes online, and will save both you and the buyer time, by eliminating the need to drive around to view homes that wouldn't have matched their wants and needs. The next step will be to actually schedule showings of homes that do match their criteria.

Pricing will also be one of the major items upon which you'll need to educate the buyer. How home prices are determined and what factors affect the pricing will all need to be discussed at this point so that the buyer has a realistic concept of the price of homes in the areas in which they intend to buy.

The next item you'll want to make sure the buyers understand are the contracts and supplemental forms they'll come into contact with. It's helpful to review the contracts thoroughly with them so there are no surprises along the way.

It's also advisable to let them know how negotiations work and what kind of expenses they can expect to incur, including legal costs, deposits, land transfer taxes, and adjustments. Remember, the better educated your clients are, the fewer problems there can be with the sale process.

And the final aspect of the process will be educating them on the different conditions that they may encounter when writing a purchase agreement, what they mean and how they can affect the buyer. Explaining who will be involved in managing them and how they will be removed will also help reduce the possibility of issues cropping up at a later stage.

Demonstrate Your Value

This is the part where you get to distinguish yourself from the other REALTORS® they may have been speaking with. Here's where you get to talk about the benefits of your services, and how you're going to meet the needs they expressed in the inquiry phase of your meeting and how you can do that better than anyone else. It's not about the number of services you can provide, it's about the benefits the client will receive from using your services and the value they perceive that you bring to the table.

The simplest way to do that is to review each of their needs and then explain how you will meet them.

"Mr. and Mrs. Buyer, we spoke about how important responsiveness was to you. Here's how I provide that kind of service to my clients...."

"Mr. and Mrs. Buyer, you said that working with someone who has knowledge of the buying process was very important. Let me show you how I can provide that to you."

Overcome Objections

Throughout the inquiry phase, by asking loads of open ended questions, you're going to find out what kind of concerns the buyers may have. This phase of the buyer's interview allows you to review those concerns and deal with them before they crop up as actual objections. As you move through the interview it's important to check back with the buyers and make sure they understand each step.

"Mr. and Mrs. Buyer, now that we've had a chance to discuss...How does that sound?"

"Does that make sense?"

"Do you have any questions about what we just discussed?"

Asking these questions and then providing them with the answers to their concerns now, will save you many headaches when it comes time to try to help them make the decision to write an offer later.

A fully educated buyer, who understands the value that you bring to the transaction, is one who is able to make better informed decisions, who will recognize that you're the REALTOR® they want to work with and who will, ultimately, be an easier client with whom to work.

CHAPTER 2

The Buyers' System

The very first step in managing a complete buyers' system has to be working with buyers who are motivated and ready to buy. We've all had the experience of working with buyers who aren't at that point yet, and it becomes a sequence of taking people out to homes that don't truly fit their needs or aren't the "right house" over and over again.

This goes back to your lead follow up system and your ability to qualify leads. Are they a true lead, a warm or a cold prospect?

Without a comprehensive system which ensures a consistent approach to all the activities involved, it becomes very easy to inadvertently miss something that may at first seem trivial but can eventually become a major issue. For example, when writing an offer, it may seem like overkill to pull the title on a property to confirm who the sellers are. After all, the listing agent would have done that, right? However, what happens if there's an error in the listing information and the spelling of the sellers' name is incorrect? That little error, if not corrected, will become a major issue later on. By following the same process and procedure every time, for every person, you can safeguard yourself against even minor slips.

A thorough buyers' system begins with the buyer's file. Once you've established that the prospect is a qualified, motivated buyer, their information is placed in a file which will include the following:

- The Buyer's Task List, which includes:
    - The buyer's complete contact information
    - The contact information of their mortgage broker and lawyer
    - The dates of any offers and conditions relating to it
- The Buyer Questionnaire and any supporting notes, which will provide the criteria the buyer has used to determine the homes to be considered.
- Copies of all the listings you've shown them
- A copy of any Purchase Contracts, whether accepted or not, and supporting documents such as:
    - Schedules, Amendments, Waivers and / or Notices of Fulfillment, Mutual Releases, etc.
- A copy of the title for any purchase contracts written
- A copy of the deposit cheque and receipt for any accepted offers
- The buyers' CMA which can be used to help justify the purchase price offered when dealing with offers.
- The signed Buyer Representation Agreement (BRA)
- All necessary FINTRAC forms
- Any correspondence with the client and any other REALTOR® regarding the purchase
- The Deal Tracking Form, a detailed list of everything required to be completed once an offer has been accepted, including:
    - The offer date
    - The closing date
    - The Seller's name

    - The Seller's REALTOR® name and contact info
    - The Seller's lawyer name and contact info
    - The Buyer's lawyer name and contact info
    - The amount of the deposit, the date and time it was delivered to the listing office
    - Any conditions, when they are to be removed and the dates when they are actually removed
    - Any additional terms of the contract
- A copy of the commission cheque stub in case it's needed for tax purposes.

This file should be carried with you, in either a paper or electronic format, so you have it readily at hand should any issues crop up.

The Buyer's Task List

BUYER'S TASK LIST

MLS#:	**OFFER DATE:**	**CONDITION DATE:**
INSPECTION DATE:	**POSSESSION DATE:**	
Address:		
Client Name:		
Residence Phone:	**Cell:**	
Business Phone:	**Business Fax:**	
Email Address:		
Lawyer's Name:		
Phone:	**Fax:**	
Mortgage Broker:	**Phone:**	**Fax:**

ITEM		ATTACHED TO FILE	
PURCHASE CONTRACT:			
Purchase Contract signed		Accepted Purchase Contract	
Purchase Contract presented		MLS Feature Sheet	
Purchase Contract accepted		Tax Assessment Form	
Initial Deposit cheque copied		Survey if available	
Initial Deposit cheque to Listing Realtor		GeoWarehouse Printout	
Purchase Contract faxed to Mortgage Broker		Property History	
Receipt confirmed		Copy of Initial Deposit	
Trade Record Sheet Submitted w/ copies of: • Purchase Contract • Deposit Cheque • MLS Feature Sheet • BRA • Working with a REALTOR • Confirmation of Cooperation & Rep. • Individual Identification (FINTRAC) • Receipt of Funds (FINTRAC)		Copy of Additional Deposit (if needed) Copy of Trade Record Sheet Buyer's Representation Agreement Working with a REALTOR Confirmation of Cooperation & Representation Individual Identification (FINTRAC) Receipt of Funds (FINTRAC)	
CONDITIONS:		**FOLLOW UP:**	
Inspection Booked		1 day	
Inspection Condition Removed		1 week	
Check with Mortgage Broker 2 days prior		1 month	
Financing Condition Removed		Clients transferred to Database	
Review of Status Certificate Removed		Set up on Newsletter	
Condition Removal faxed to Listing Realtor		24 Touch System instituted	
Additional Deposit copied (if needed)			
Additional Deposit to Listing Realtor			
1 WEEK PRIOR TO POSSESSION:			
Call Lawyer to confirm			
Call Listing REALTOR to confirm possession			
Call Clients			
Schedule final buyer's walkthrough			
DAY OF POSSESSION:			
Call Lawyer to confirm Key Release			
Call Listing Realtor to confirm Key Release			
Call Clients – Meet at new home for walkthrough			

A Silver Bullet

You can find a copy of the forms and checklists in this chapter at www.foundationsforsuccess.ca.

Business Building Exercise

Set up a number of Buyer files with all the paperwork required by your brokerage, your Buyer's Task List, Buyer's Questionnaire and Deal Tracking Form and have them ready for when you begin taking buyers out on showings.

On the Road Again

The next component of the buyer system is your method of managing showings. When showing homes, I've found it helpful to provide the buyers with basic guidelines of how I handle the showings, using the following **"Rules of the Road"**.

1. Each time we view homes, I'll prepare a list of the homes along with a map for you to follow from one home to the next. (Thank goodness for Google Maps). You'll also get a copy of the listing information for each home.

2. I try to book our showings in one hour sessions for each home. This is done so that we have the time to spend viewing each house and allows us to run a bit behind schedule, without creating any inconvenience for the homeowners at our next showing.

3. Please be on time for the first showing. This will help us stay on schedule. Remember, the home owners will have had to leave the home and we want to make sure we don't create any more disruption to their routine than we have to.

4. If you are going to be late, please give me at least 15 minutes' notice so I can notify the listing agent who can then inform his clients.

5. When going through homes, please be prepared to remove your footwear. After all, we don't want to track stuff through someone's house.

6. As you go through each home, feel free to open any closets, cupboards and behind every door. If this is going to be your home, you need to know what everything looks like.
7. I would suggest that as we view the homes, you may want to make notes about each one for future reference. That will help you distinguish the homes you like from the ones you don't.
8. Please stay together as you go through the home, especially if you have children. That will reduce any chance of accidents or injury to anyone.
9. If you need to use the washroom during the visit, please check with me first. We may occasionally encounter a home where the water will have been shut off and we don't want to have that kind of problem, do we?
10. Please hold any negative comments until we get out of the home. We don't want to take the chance on anything getting back to the seller which we don't want them to hear.
11. Most sellers want to know what you thought of the home. I believe in providing feedback that will help people get their home sold, even if not to you. Please let me know what you like and don't like about the homes we view so I can give those comments to the listing REALTOR® when they ask.

Home Showing System

In order to ensure you don't create confusion for your buyers it's advisable to show a maximum of four to five homes each time you take them out. Since you don't want to waste their time or yours, the homes MUST be compatible with the requirements decided on at the first meeting.

When booking showings, call the listing REALTOR®'s office at least one day prior to the scheduled showing to ensure that you get confirmation of the showing. This is absolutely necessary when the listing requires 24 hours' notice. The method of booking showings varies widely across the country and is beyond the scope of this book.

Business Building Exercise

Check with your broker or manager for the specifics of booking showings in your area.

In order to avoid wasting time when showing properties, it's advisable to use a mapping system such as Google Maps or the one built into your MLS system to map out the homes. Arrange the showings in a logical sequence and then book the showings based on the travel time between each. The system I've always found that works best is to book each showing for one hour but stagger the showings by half an hour. In other words, home 1 is scheduled between 2:00 – 3:00, home 2 between 2:30 – 3:30, home 3 between 3:00 – 3:30, etc. I provide the clients with a copy of the map with the directions between each property as well as the client view of the MLS listing sheet in the order of the showings with the showing times on each.

Once you've arrived at the property, try to find something small that's wrong with the property while you and the clients are walking to it. This tends to go a long way in demonstrating that you're on their side.

When entering the property, ring the doorbell and, when you open the door, announce your presence. Many years ago, I was showing a home to a female buyer and had to take my younger daughter with me. I had booked the showing the day before and it had been confirmed that no one was going to be home during the showing. When we arrived and based on the information I had received that no-one would be home, I skipped my usual habit of opening the door and calling out "Hello!" a couple of times. I opened the door and we proceeded down the hall. As we did, the door to the bathroom at the end of the hall opened and out stepped a very naked young man. Needless to say, everyone was somewhat startled and embarrassed and I learned a valuable lesson.

When touring the home, part of my system is to have the clients wait at the front door while I turn on the lights and then follow them through the home, so as to allow the clients to discover the home themselves; to have that "WOW" moment. By not leading them, it also prevents you from introducing them to the various rooms; *"This is the living room, this is the kitchen ..."*. Honestly, if they don't know that the room with the fridge and stove is the kitchen, they probably shouldn't be buying a home.

As you proceed through the home, an important part of showing buyers through the home is to relate what they told you they were looking for to the benefits of the home. *"Didn't you say you wanted... Would this home would work well for that?"* Should they have any questions about the structure or concerns about the house, remind them that, *"That's why we're going to have an inspection done."*

One of the key things to remember about any questions the buyer may ask is to know what you know and what you don't. Don't assume, don't try to bluff; answer their questions honestly. It's OK to let them know you don't know the answer, but that you will find out the answer for them.

Once you've finished the showing, ask for feedback, don't give it. The last thing you want is to do is to talk yourself out of a sale. Despite your belief that this is definitely not the home for them, let the buyers make up their own mind.

In order to help determine the buyer's feelings about the home, use trial closes throughout the showing and listen for clues in what they're saying. If she turns to him and says, "*You know, our living room furniture would look really good in here,"* it's a great indication that this is one of the homes under serious consideration. You may, at this point, want to test the waters and find out what they're thinking.

"So folks, let me ask. What do you think about this home?"

"So, how does this home stack up?"

"Can you see yourself living here?"

After you've completed the showing, one of the most important steps you'll take is to ask for the sale. This is the point where many REALTORS® get cold feet and lose out on possible sales. Your trial closes will indicate if they've found a home they like and if you don't ask for a decision, they may not make one. Sometimes, the buyer is actually waiting for you to ask for the decision and won't make one without you asking. Always ask them for a decision. As Wayne Gretzky once said, *"You miss 100 percent of the shots you don't take."*

"It sounds to me like this is a home you really like. So what do you think about writing an offer on it?"

"Would you like to sit down and discuss the purchase of this home?"

"If you feel this is the home for you let's go back to my office and I'll do a Comparative Market Analysis so you'll have some information to base an offer price on."

At this point you have three possible options, depending on the buyers' response. You can write the offer. If they haven't found the right home, you can have them sign a Buyer Representation Agreement and continue to work with them or, if they aren't prepared to sign a BRA, you can either continue to work with them on the chance they won't sign an offer with another REALTOR® or you can let them know you only work with people who have signed a BRA and let them go.

The Buyers from Hell? It may not be them

Many years ago, I had the opportunity to work with a client who, it seemed, was bound and determined to do everything they could to frustrate every deal I wrote for them. There was always something wrong with the way the house was priced, or the layout of the home was wrong, or something on the inspection was too serious for them to move forward with the purchase. During the American Revolution, Thomas Paine wrote, "These are the times that try men's souls." And this was the client who tried my patience, to the point that I finally gave up on them, only to later learn they had then bought a home with another REALTOR® on the first time out.

We've all had the "Buyer from Hell"; the client who, no matter how hard you work, no matter how many homes you show them, no matter how many offers you write for them, just don't seem to get the concept of what it's going to take to actually buy a home. Or they complain about everything and seem to throw up roadblocks at every turn in the process. Well, maybe it's not actually them.

It's important to remember that, many times, these folks may not be sure of the process, what's involved, who's responsible for what and what to expect when they go out and look at homes with a REALTOR®. They're probably under some stress and that generally doesn't bring out the best in people. Your job will be to help them, for the most part, alleviate that stress.

In order to accomplish that, you're going to need to understand them and to empathize with them; to put yourself in their place. Since, as REALTORS®, looking at homes, writing and negotiating offers and understanding the process is old hat to us, it's easy to overlook or miss the uncertainty and stress that can cause even the calmest client to lose their equanimity. Our responsibility goes far beyond simply finding and securing them a home. We need to understand who they are, how they communicate, to understand their concerns, where they're unsure, what their motivation is and to make sure we've educated and advised them so as to reduce or eliminate any of the issues which can cause them discomfort throughout the process.

I would argue that, in many cases, the buyer from hell is simply a reflection of our own failings in the communication, empathy and objection handling departments. All too often we try to "sell" something to our clients, whether it be ourselves and our services or a property; in essence, we try to provide solutions to them.

Where we tend to get it wrong, though, is when we try to offer a solution we think will resolve the problem, without actually spending the time to find out what the real, deep down, pain actually is. We know that, for the most part, people buy because of pain. They either want to eliminate it or avoid it. It used to be a statute of sales that to sell something we had to offer a solution to the problem. I would suggest, instead of offering up solutions, we need to look at sales as if we are doctors. We need to find out about their pain. In my previous career, I learned a really helpful mnemonic that used to help me ask questions about my patients' problem. That mnemonic was WOCSNOR and it goes like this:

W What's your WORST pain? In other words, what's the most important issue they're facing in their current situation? Is it money, space, location or something else?

O What OTHER pain is there? Is there something else that's creating an issue for them in their current location? What's the next most important thing?

C Is it CONSTANT or INTERMITTENT? In other words, is this something that's a constant problem they need to get away from right now, or does it create problems on an occasional basis that they would like to move away from?

S How SIGNIFICANT is the pain? Is this situation untenable or can they live with it if they have to?

N What's the NATURE of the pain? What is the actual pain that the client's experiencing and feel needs to be resolved? This is where your ability to ask questions and actively listen will earn you the respect and trust of the client.

O Are there any OTHER symptoms? These are things other than the pain that are creating issues for them and that they feel need to be resolved.

R What's the RELATIONSHIP of the pain and the symptoms? If the pain gets worse, do the symptoms?

A simple example of this may be that the client has a problem in keeping up with their current mortgage (their worst pain). As a consequence, they are having to work longer hours which is placing a strain on their family life (other pain). Since they feel under stress all the time, the problem is constantly with them and is taking a significant toll on them and their family. They believe that the large mortgage is just too much for them to continue to support and that having a smaller mortgage will remove the issue (the nature of the pain). They feel that, since there is an increased strain on the family, they're seeing more behavioural difficulties for the kids in school (other symptoms) and as the issue becomes worse so do the resultant behaviours.

Now, I know this sounds a lot like pop psychology, and in this example, it probably is. And the solution for this, from our perspective, is easy; sell the current house and buy a less expensive one. However, if you take this kind of approach to finding out what the problem is, then explore different lines of inquiry, and finally, help them understand that the cost created by the problem exceeds the cost of making a change, you can then offer your clients different solutions to the problem. For example, they may be able to refinance the existing home to ease the mortgage pressure. They may be able to take in tenants to defray some of the costs. And perhaps, they may want to consider the sale and purchase option. In any case, by finding out about the pain, giving them options and then helping them to deal with the solutions, you eliminate a significant portion of the fear, confusion and pain that leads them to become the buyers' from hell.

Let's Write an Offer

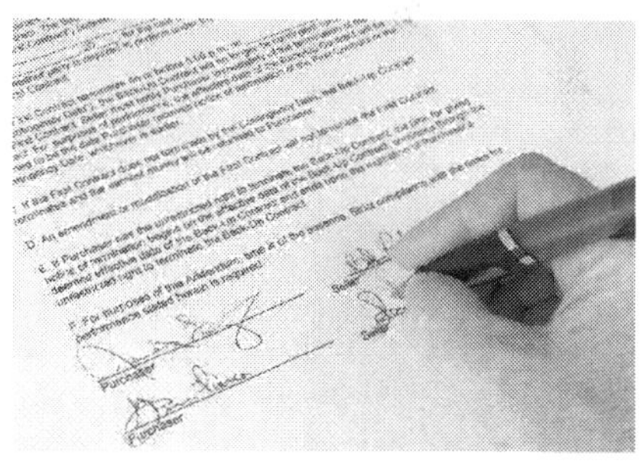

What a wonderful phrase! But, now comes the real challenge. It's at this point that your knowledge of contracts, the market, objection handling, offer presentation and negotiation gets put to the test.

The first step in the whole process is to explain the different types of representation. In Ontario, these are single, multiple representation and customer status. Make sure you familiarize yourself with the ones in your area, so you can explain them thoroughly to the buyer.

If you haven't already got them signed, the next step is to have the buyers sign the applicable representation agreements and any other required forms (if applicable).

The next step is to prepare a buyer's Comparative Market Analysis so that the buyers can understand the way homes are priced in the area. You'll also want to have as much market information, such as past and present trends and patterns, as possible to back up the CMA when you explain it to your client and when it comes time to negotiate for them.

One of the most common questions you can expect to get is *"What do you think we should offer?"* You can offer information based on your experience and expertise but should avoid advising the client on the actual price to offer. Provide them with a price range, but make sure they're the ones to name the price they want to pay. In this way, you can avoid any question of misrepresentation of the price.

When writing the offer, explain the forms, clauses and schedules as you go. This will ensure your client fully understands the entire contract and has the opportunity to ask any questions they may have about what's involved. Offers to purchase are made up of five major factors:

- Price
- Conditions
- Terms
- Chattels and Fixtures
- Possession date

You'll need to explain how the structuring of each component can help or hinder the buyers' chances of getting the offer accepted with as few changes as possible. Ensure that they understand the possible consequence of writing a low offer. These may be to alienate the seller, resulting in an outright rejection of the offer or a counter offer at, or close to, the list price. The seller may refuse to deal with another offer from the buyer, should they decide to write another one and they take the risk of another offer coming in, forcing them into a multiple offer.

You'll want to ensure the chattels and fixtures specified in the offer match those in the listing and that all exclusions are identified as well.

We'll Take It If...

Our most important task, our primary duty, is to protect the interests of our client. Many times clients will rely on your knowledge and advice on what to include in an offer; however, there will be occasions when they want a property so much that they're willing to forgo some of the protections offered by including specific conditions in an offer. It's your responsibility to advise them of the desirability of having a condition that protects them and the consequences of not including that clause.

While this section is not meant in any way to be a comprehensive guide to the conditions which should be included in an offer, there are certain conditions which, if ignored, can have serious consequences for both the buyer and their REALTOR®. Your job will be to determine which will best protect your client and help them make the best possible informed decision about which to include. As a new REALTOR® you're strongly advised to seek the advice of your manager or Broker about which conditions you may want to include in any offers you write. It's in your best interest, and your clients', to have your manager check the first few offers you write to make sure you've included everything you need and everything's in order before having the clients sign them.

Review and ask for agreement on each condition and term. In the event the buyer chooses not to include a recommended condition, you should have them sign a form which acknowledges that you've advised them to include it, but they have chosen not to. In Ontario that form is the Acknowledgement re: Conditions in Offer (Form 127).

One of the most important conditions is that of financing. The potential consequences of not including a financing condition are extreme. Imagine someone who buys a home without such a condition, only to find out later that they can't actually afford the home. Not only will they lose their deposit, but they could potentially be on the hook for any damages incurred by the seller when they have to resell the home again. These damages could include the difference between the price the buyer agreed to pay and the new sale price if it's less, the carrying costs for the home over the period of time it takes to resell, and many more.

The next and, in my opinion, equally important condition is that of the property inspection. Failure to include this condition has the potential for very serious consequences. While we're all very aware about the necessity of disclosing latent defects, there are times when even the seller may not have knowledge of issues which could create a problem. Should your buyer purchase a home without having an inspection completed, they're putting themselves at risk for some nasty surprises. Buying a home is expensive enough without having to come up with even more money as a result of any unpleasant surprises.

Another issue commonly faced nowadays is the presence of rental items, such as hot water heaters, furnaces, security systems and others, which carry a rental contract with them. Some of these contracts can carry onerous cancellation or transfer provisions in them. In order to protect your buyer from accepting what could be onerous terms, the inclusion of a condition in which the buyer has the opportunity to review the rental agreements is one which must be considered.

Business Days vs. Date and Time

One of the most common ways in which condition removal can become an issue is the use of the term 'business days' when defining a date, a condition is to be satisfied. In most contracts, business days are specified as any day, other than Saturday, Sunday or statutory holidays in the applicable Province. Sounds pretty clear, doesn't it? Let's take a closer look at the term and the possible implications.

The "Business Day" is typically considered to cover the period from 9 a.m. to 5 p.m. However, this is simply a convention and may cause some uncertainty as to when a condition must be waived or fulfilled. Another concern which may arise is when the term of days is to begin. Let's assume an offer has a condition that requires removal within five business days. If the offer is accepted at 10 pm, it makes sense that the five days would begin on the following morning, as no business could reasonably be transacted for the remainder of the day. If the offer was accepted on a Monday, the conditions could reasonably be expected to be removed on the following Monday. However, if the offer was accepted at 9 am on the Monday, it could be argued that there was a reasonable expectation that business could be transacted throughout the remainder of that day, leading to an expectation that condition removal should occur by Friday of the same week. This could, therefore, lead to an issue if both parties are not of the same mindset.

In order to eliminate the possibility of this uncertainty arising, it's advisable to clearly define when the condition must be waived or fulfilled. This can best be done by using a specific date and time for condition removal.

> *"Unless the Buyer gives notice in writing delivered to the Seller personally or in accordance with any other provisions for the delivery of notice in this Agreement of Purchase and Sale or any Schedule thereto not later than ___________ p.m. on _________________, that this condition is fulfilled, this Offer shall be null and void and the deposit shall be returned to the Buyer in full without deduction."*

While this may require a few changes and initials during the negotiation process, the little extra work involved will eliminate the possibility of even more work being required if there is uncertainty about removal date as well as the possibility of the transaction failing as a result.

One thing to remember when writing an offer is that the possession or closing date should not be on a weekend or a holiday. I've also tried to avoid setting the closing on a Friday or on the last day of the month. I avoid Fridays in case there's a delay in getting the funds transferred. If that happens, the buyer could end up not having a home to move into over the weekend, which could make for very unhappy clients. Also, try booking a mover for the last day of the month, unless you've booked four months in advance.

Make certain that all the chattels and fixtures your clients want, as well as the exclusions listed, have been clearly stated, don`t take anything for granted. If you're not certain what constitutes a fixture or a chattel, my colleague and friend Brian Madigan has a simple solution. He says to, *"Imagine picking up the property and turning it upside down. Anything that falls out is a chattel and anything that doesn't is a fixture."* That's the best description I've heard yet.

Once everything has been completed, your next task is take a few minutes and review each page of the offer to make sure that all the signatures and initials are in place. Time spent now will more than make up for the time you'll have to spend running around to get a missed signature or initial.

Request an appropriate deposit and explain how it will assist in demonstrating to the seller that the buyers are serious about purchasing the home and in getting the offer accepted.

Throughout the offer process you may, if they're going to occur, encounter some objections from the buyer. We'll discuss handling these objections in the section titled "I'm Just Sayin'"

In the event that your offer is part of a multiple offer, you'll need to advise your client on the multiple offer process and how they can best position their offer for success.

The Offer Process

Whether you're in a single or a multiple offer, your primary responsibility is protect your client's best interests.

Remember, and remind the buyer, you're there to advise, but the decisions are theirs to make, not yours, and that you are bound by their lawful and ethical instructions.

When dealing with a single offer, your offer management system must ensure, once the offer has been signed, you inform the listing REALTOR® that you have an offer for them. This may take different forms in different jurisdictions. For example, in Ontario, this means calling the listing office and registering the offer. However, no matter which format is used in your area, the most important component is to speak directly with the listing REALTOR® so as to ensure that there's no opportunity for miscommunication. Once that has occurred, a time for the offer presentation should be established.

Never discuss the offer over the phone. This only provides the opportunity for the listing REALTOR® to begin preparing to counter your offer and weakens your position. At the time of the offer presentation it may be beneficial to have the buyers close by so that any counter offers can be dealt with rapidly. I've had clients sitting outside the property in their car or at a nearby coffee shop.

At the offer presentation, your job is to try to build rapport with the Sellers, so as to help them better understand your clients and to help your clients obtain the best possible terms. Provide some information about the buyers. What are their motives for wanting the house? What have they said about the house to show that they appreciate its features and benefits? Respond to questions and concerns from the sellers and be prepared to handle any objections which may occur.

Remember that facts and figures are persuasive; arguing and too much talk are usually ineffective. Very often sellers and buyers are ready to accept the terms of an offer but need a rationale and this is where all the work you have done in the building trust stage and determining needs will pay off. Make sure you are prepared to offer the objective support that they need.

If you obtain a counteroffer from the sellers, you have another offer to sell and it becomes the buyers' option to accept, reject or counter. When negotiating the counteroffer, your objective is to help the buyers understand the changes and why they're important to the sellers. This will help your clients make an informed decision about what they want to do with the counteroffer. Finally, be patient. Don't push. Ask questions, watch the buyers' body language, let them sell themselves on the counteroffer.

Once the offer has been accepted, make sure any changes have been initialled and final signatures have been completed.

Your next task will be to make copies of the agreement, the deposit cheque and the receipt for the deposit and provide a copy to your buyers and the office, as well as place a copy in your buyers' file.

Multiple Offer Management

Dealing with multiple offers can be frustrating and challenging. Your job will be to give your client the best chance to win the war. There are six key factors to success in this, including:

- Mindset & Preparation
- Price
- Conditions
- Terms
- Dates
- Deposit

Mindset & Preparation

Clients may face the specter of entering into multiple offer situations many times, which can become a frustrating experience; one which may actually deter some buyers from proceeding further with their plans to purchase. In an effort to reduce this frustration, it's important to explain the multiple offer process to prepare them for the possibility and educate them on what it takes to win.

Should you find yourselves in a multiple offer, you'll need to explore their motivation and determine what their mindset is regarding the price they're offering.

> *"You said that your best offer is $X. If the house sold for $X plus $2,000, would you be okay with that or would you have paid the extra $2,000 to get the house?"*

Price

Of course, one of the major factors affecting a seller's decision about which offer to go with is the price. You'll need to help your client establish their top dollar and not let them fall into an auction mentality. Set your target and don't go beyond it. The most important thing you can do to assist them with this decision is to do your homework; provide them with a complete CMA. You must have your facts and figures ready and review current sales. Prior to showing homes, and definitely before writing an offer, it's necessary to speak with their financing person and find out their maximum approved price. This will help ensure they understand their limits and avoid the auction knee jerk reaction.

Conditions

While price will play a major part in the decision, winning in a multiple offer is not just about the price. It's also about conditions; the number and content of them.

Remember, your job is to protect your client's interests, so including conditions will certainly accomplish that. However, try to keep them to a minimum and as simple as possible, with as short a period for removal as possible. Your clients may elect to write the offer with no conditions. In this event, you'll need to discuss this with them and make sure they understand the potential consequences of having no conditions in the offer. Should they choose to continue, ensure you've had them sign the form discussed earlier.

When including a financing condition, you'll want to ensure the client is pre-approved and that both you and they know their maximum limit.

Including an inspection condition is extremely important in order to protect your client. However, you may be able to eliminate it by having an advance home inspection completed. This will allow your client to completely understand the issues in the house and to determine if they want to continue with the offer. This, however, can become expensive, since the inspection may cost your client around $400-500, with no assurance that they may want to move forward or that, if they do, they'll actually end up winning the multiple offer.

One option to consider was suggested to me by Brian Madigan. It's to include an inspection condition in which the buyer will "absorb" the first $X of any deficiencies found on the inspection. This clause states that the buyer will accept any minor flaws in the home, up to a specified amount of repairs, but that should anything serious be found, they have the right not to proceed.

> *"This Offer is conditional upon the Buyer, at the Buyer's own expense, having the relevant building(s) inspected by a bona fide home inspection firm to determine that the building(s) are in sound structural and mechanical condition and that the electrical system is safe and adequate, and that, in the written opinion of the home inspection firm, all deficiencies can be remedied at a cost not greater than ____________________ ($__________). Unless the Buyer gives notice in writing delivered to the Seller personally or in accordance with any other provisions for the delivery of notice in this Agreement of Purchase and Sale or any Schedule thereto not later than 8:00 p.m. on the _____ day of ___________ 20___, that this condition is fulfilled, this Offer shall be null and void and the deposit shall be returned to the Buyer in full without deduction. The Seller agrees to co-operate in providing access to the property for the purpose of this inspection. The Seller agrees this condition is included for the benefit of the Buyer and may be waived at the Buyer's sole option by notice in*

writing to the Seller as aforesaid within the time period stated herein."

Terms

Keep any terms to minimum and make sure there's nothing onerous in them that may create an issue for the sellers. Don't ask for random items, such as the lawnmower or snow blower. Include the chattels and fixtures as shown on the listing.

One of the most common terms included is that of having the seller leave the house in a clean and broom swept condition and remove all debris from the house and yard. When going into a multiple offer, you may want to consider changing that to say the "Buyer will clean the house". This can be very appealing, as sellers want to concentrate on packing and moving and don't want to have to worry about having to take the extra step of having the home cleaned.

Dates

The simplest option here is to give the sellers their closing date. If there are conditions present, keep the dates as tight as possible.

Deposit

Try using a larger deposit to demonstrate to the seller that the buyer is serious about completing the transaction. It's easier to walk away from a $5,000 deposit than it is a much larger one. Here's an example:

Offer 1	Offer 2
$450,000 offer	$450,000 offer
80% financing = $360,000	80% financing = $360,000
5% deposit = $22,500	Deposit = $90,000
Cash to Close = $67,500	No cash to close

No conditions	No conditions

Offers 1 and 2 provide the same price and terms, however, offer 2 demonstrates much more commitment to completing the transaction and may help sway the sellers.

Buyer's Letter

The use of a Buyer's Letter may help to sway the sellers. Sellers are often emotional about selling their home and will often identify with a buyer who loves their home for the same reasons that they do. Have your buyers write a cover letter to the sellers telling them a little something about every member of the family, including the children and what it is about their home that makes them want to buy it. They can also explain why their offer is the one that is most likely to close. Include anything that would help the seller feel confident that your deal will close on time.

Present in Person

In all multiple offers, try to present the offer in person. You're much more powerful when you're at the presentation. You can pick up on the sellers' frame of mind and build rapport with them.

You have the opportunity to speak with the sellers and may be able to assess the possible pain points of the sellers and modify offer to "ease their pain". You have an opportunity to make a positive impression on the sellers and make the case for your clients. It also means you have more of an opportunity to discuss possible options with the listing REALTOR®, such as closing date, condition date (if any), chattels, etc.

Make sure you have your clients on standby at a convenient location such as a local coffee shop or outside in their car. That way you can make any changes or sign off on counters immediately rather than waiting.

Service, Service, Service

Servicing the buyer doesn't end once you've shown them some homes and written and negotiated an offer. It's when your time to shine truly begins. Everything you've done to this point is just a foretaste of the kind of service you're going to provide that's really going to wow your clients.

As with everything, a systematized approach to the management of the purchase is a must. The Buyers' Task List details each step to be taken in making sure everything progresses as smoothly as possible.

Going, Going...

Your first task, should there be a financing condition, will be to make sure a copy of the purchase contract and supporting documentation is sent to your buyer's financial institution. However, simply assuming that they've received it and that they are aware of the condition dates involved can lead to many headaches. It's advisable to request that they confirm that they've received the information and then reconfirm the condition removal date and then document your conversation with them.

Staying on top of this condition is an absolute must if you're committed to outstanding service. It's never a good idea to leave the information with the financial institution and then wait to hear from them.

Several years ago, I had a transaction in which I had sent the purchase agreement and listing information to the mortgage broker the night it had been signed. I checked with him in the morning to confirm that he had received it. The condition date was seven days after acceptance, and as part of my buyers' system, I called him two days before the scheduled removal date. When I spoke with him, he had no idea what transaction I was talking about, so I reminded him of the client's name and the fact that the conditions had to be removed in two days. I could hear him shuffling paper on his desk. Suddenly he gasped and said he had just found the transaction. It turns out he had put it on his desk and had inadvertently piled other papers on top and forgotten about it. As a result, I had to go back to the sellers and get an additional two-day extension; a pain, yes, but at least it avoided something which could have had much more serious consequences. Had I simply waited to hear from him, it's likely that the deal would have collapsed. Part of your system should be to have a quick check back with the financial institution at least two days prior to the condition removal date to help ensure things are progressing smoothly or to take any remedial action necessary.

The next component of your system is the management of the home inspection. If your offer contains a home inspection condition, your next conversation should be with the home inspector. You'll want to confirm the date and time of the inspection and coordinate this with your client.

You may consider calling the inspector when you write the offer and tentatively book a date and time while the clients are with you. You can then reconfirm with everyone once the offer has been accepted. This also has the advantage of being able to let the listing REALTOR® know that your buyers are serious and have already booked the date for the inspection, which may help in the negotiations.

When booking the inspection, it's a good idea to have scheduled it at least one day prior to the condition removal date. In the event that there are some issues that need to be resolved, it becomes incredibly stressful on the buyers, the sellers and both REALTORS® should any negotiations required have to be conducted at the last minute. I've had the experience of trying to negotiate having the sellers repair or replace items that were found on the inspection in the final hours before condition removal. Needless to say, it is challenging and stressful in the extreme and your clients won't thank you for putting them through it.

Managing the inspection will involve confirming the inspection with the listing REALTOR® and the inspector the day before it's scheduled. On the day of the inspection, you'll want to show up early so you can meet with the inspector and introduce them to the client. During the inspection, you'll find it helpful to follow the clients around. Be prepared to ask questions to clarify and help your clients understand what the inspector is pointing out to them as well as to help you grow in your knowledge of household systems. I fully believe that a great inspector will point out both the trivial and the serious to the clients but will explain it in a way that the client understands the difference and helps them make as informed a decision as they can.

I once used an inspector who wasn't able to help the clients distinguish the difference between a deficiency and normal wear and tear; serious issues and those that simply required some spackle and paint. Most of the problems encountered were simple wear and tear items and were easily repaired with a minimum of expense to either party. Without having asked him to clarify how much each of the repairs would cost, the clients would have lost the home they loved, and I would have lost the transaction. I never used that inspector again. It can be a challenge, as a new Sales Representative, to find this kind of inspector, but by asking your more experienced colleagues, you'll find it easier to determine the inspector with whom you'll feel comfortable.

One of the issues that crops up occasionally as part of the removal of the inspection condition is that of renegotiating the purchase price due to defects uncovered during the inspection. It's important to educate your buyer so that they understand that unless there are major problems, there is small likelihood of a major price reduction. Every home will have some flaws in it. Minor issues, such as holes in the walls, leaky faucets, light switches installed upside down and others of this nature are best dealt with by having the sellers repair them. However, when the issue becomes more serious, such as a furnace that needs replacing, or a serious crack in the basement wall, your client can expect to have some wiggle room to renegotiate the price. Your major task will be to help them understand that they can't expect to buy a home without any issues, and therefore they can't expect to either decrease the price by the total of the cost of repair or replacement of the problem item or to have the sellers pay for the total cost of replacement. They need to be prepared to accept that they may have to negotiate a deal where the seller and the buyer each pay for a portion of the cost.

When dealing with the condition regarding the Status Certificate or Condo Documents issues that crop up often are,

- when they have to be produced,
- how long they remain valid once ordered and
- trying to set a date for condition removal.

Depending upon the provincial legislation, condominium corporations have a specified time period to provide the documents. In Ontario, condo corporations have 10 days following a request and payment of the fees for the document to produce the documents.

When writing an offer with a clause regarding the Status Certificate, to ensure complete clarity, it is strongly advised it be worded to include a specific date for condition removal, which includes the 10 day waiting period. Should the listing REALTOR® obtain it earlier, you can always amend the date.

"This offer is conditional upon the Buyer's lawyer reviewing the Status Certificate and attachments and finding the Status Certificate and Attachments satisfactory in the

Buyer's Lawyer's sole and absolute discretion. The (Buyer/Seller) __________ agrees to request at the (Buyer's/Seller's) __________ expense, the Status Certificate and attachments within _____ days of acceptance of this Offer. Unless the buyer gives notice in writing to the Seller personally or in accordance with any other provisions for the delivery of notice in this Agreement of Purchase and Sale or any Schedule thereto not later than 5 p.m. on _________________, that this condition is fulfilled, this Offer shall be null and void and the deposit shall be returned to the Buyer in full without deduction. This condition is included for the benefit of the Buyer and may be waived at the Buyer's sole option by notice in writing to the Seller as aforesaid within the time period stated herein."

The uncontrollable and therefore most frustrating part of managing the Status Certificate condition is the wait for them to be delivered. Part of your management of this period will be to stay in contact with the listing REALTOR® to make sure you receive the documents as timely and as smoothly as possible and to keep your clients calm during the wait. As before, it's important to check with the client two days before the condition removal date to ensure things are on track.

Gone

Condition removal is a time of both relief and stress for the REALTOR® and the client. It can be extremely stressful if there are unexpected delays or should issues crop up at the last minute. That's why your Buyer Service System must ensure that you've stayed on top of all the conditions and been in communication with everyone involved in the transaction.

Notices, Waivers and Amendments

So, the conditions are ready to be removed and the sale will be firmed up. One of the most common faux pas occurring at this point is the use of the incorrect form for condition removal. Many people are confused about when to use a Waiver, a Notice of Fulfillment and an Amendment. In order to better understand when to use these forms, it's necessary to understand what each form actually means.

A Waiver allows a party to a contract to proceed with the agreement without actually fulfilling the specific terms of the condition. This would occur in a situation where circumstances arise which are different from those envisioned when the conditions were drafted. In these instances, the condition has been met, but not in accordance with the exact terms expressed in the agreement.

For example, I want to buy a condo and include a condition of review of the status certificate as shown previously. However, I've worked as a property manager and understand how to review the status certificate and therefore don't need my lawyer to review them. When I'm ready to remove the condition, since I haven't actually fulfilled the terms of the condition by having my lawyer review the documents, I would have to use a Waiver.

A Notice of Fulfillment is used when the actual terms of the condition have been met, such as in the following instance. I have included a financing condition whereby my financing has to be met to my approval. Once the financial institution has provided the financing to my approval, I would then remove the condition using a Notice of Fulfillment.

The major issue that occurs is the use of an **Amendment** to remove the condition. Unless it is both parties' intention to actually remove the condition from the agreement, this form should **never** be used. This misstep most frequently occurs in cases in which a property inspection has revealed some problems with the home and both parties have either negotiated a price reduction or the seller has agreed to complete some work required to repair the issues. In these cases, the issue arises where an Amendment has been used to delete the condition of inspection and also insert a clause stating that the sellers will complete the work required or that the price has been adjusted. This is the **wrong** use of the form.

The correct method of handling this issue would be to use this form to **amend the contract** by inserting the clause regarding the work required or the price adjustment and have the buyer sign the form. They would also sign a Waiver since the condition is being fulfilled, but not to their satisfaction since the inspection revealed concerns. The Amendment would then be sent to the sellers for signature and once it has been received back from the seller, the Waiver would then be transmitted. In this way, the contract is modified only to include the new terms and the condition is waived.

Since this chapter is not meant as a comprehensive guide on forms, but merely as a review of the most common conditions, it's your responsibility and in your best interest, any time you have a question about which form to use and when, that you consult your Broker or Manager.

Business Building Exercise

Here's another business building exercise, and one I think is critical to your long-term success. **Find a number of available listings of all different kinds (single family, condo, multifamily, properties with tenants, etc.) and write offers for each of them. Use different conditions and terms to make them as real as possible and have your broker or manager check them to make sure they're accurate and realistic.**

After the Sold Sign Goes Up

Now that you've removed conditions and the deal is firm, there are a number of things you can do to reinforce yourself as the REALTOR® to whom your clients will want to refer their friends and family. This is where your Buyer's Task List and Deal Tracking Form will help guide you through the paperwork jungle. Your post-sale service system will need to ensure that your clients are kept informed of the next steps they'll need to take on the way towards closing the sale, including preparing for the move, ensuring they've spoken with their lawyer and any additional inspections have been scheduled. Your main task through this period will be to act as a point of reference or guide to ensure they understand each step and that things are able to progress smoothly.

It's always handy to be able to provide the buyers with a moving guide so they're aware of what steps to take to ensure their move proceeds smoothly. I've included the one I put together from various companies, but you may want to consider using the one that your moving company uses.

On closing day, I ask my buyers to let me know when they plan on being at the new house. That way I can do a walkthrough with them to ensure that the property is in the shape they expected and to deal with any issues which may have occurred. After all, you want to know the problems so that you can deal with them. That's how you can provide the stellar customer service your clients expect and become known as the REALTOR® that goes the extra mile for their clients.

One of the many questions I get is what to get the buyers when they take possession of their new home. There are many different options, including gift cards, but one of the best that I've heard is to provide them with a catered lunch on moving day. That could be as simple as bringing in sub sandwiches and drinks, a box of fried chicken with sides or anything else that they don't have to prepare. I've heard of an agent who stocks their clients' fridges with essentials like milk, bread, eggs, butter, veggies and fruit. While going to the store and picking up the groceries and then delivering them for each client could be a big time commitment, some of the large grocery chains now offer delivery options that make organizing something like that simple, time- and cost-effective.

However, it's not just the closing gift you give them that will make you stand out in their minds and keep you in their thoughts when they meet someone who's thinking about buying or selling. It's your after-sale service system that solidifies you as a "rock star".

The 1, 1, 1 System

Your system should include a method of staying in touch with the client once the sale has closed and they've moved into their new home. You'll want to make sure you speak to them:

- On the day after they've moved in, to find out if everything has gone smoothly and if there are any issues that may have cropped up overnight, so you can deal with them.
- One week later to ensure things are still going smoothly and to answer any questions they may have about the property or the neighbourhood.
- One month later to reconfirm that there are no issues and to let them know that should they have any need for service people or contractors that you have access to a wide range of providers.

At this point you'll need to transfer them from your active clients list to your database and set them up on your Referral Management System.

Business Building Exercise

Set up your post-sale Buyer's Service System.

SUMMARY

In the previous volume, we discussed how to manage listings. As a new Sales Representative, it's often easier to find and work with buyers. However, the principles of making presentations that focus on providing value to prospective clients, based on what the prospect is looking for, rather than on what you believe your value is remains the same as it does for listings.

Of significant importance, when working with buyers, is the necessity of qualifying them for motivation and the ability to purchase properties. You'll need to ask loads of open ended questions to get them to open up in order for you to find out just how motivated they are. In a later volume, we'll discuss the skill of actually closing for the offer.

Once you have the buyers committed and you've found them a home, your major task will be to shepherd them through the purchase process. This will require that you have a comprehensive system to follow that will ensure that everything runs smoothly and that you provide the outstanding service you promised to the client. Just as for a listing, that service will depend on having a system in place that allows you to perform a consistent sequence of tasks for each and every buyer. A sequence which must include the processes that will ensure that the offer is written correctly, conditions are managed in such a way as to reduce the potential for issues to arise and are removed within the timeframes required by the offer in which it should, and routines to ensure that you are able to prospect the listing so as to get more listings and buyers.

On the Right Foot

And now, your task will be to complete the Business Building Exercises in the Workbook; developing your Informed Buyer's Guide, Buyer's Presentation, and your Buyer's Management systems. You'll need to spend a significant amount of time role-playing your presentation, objection handling skills and your closing skills, but by investing the time now, you'll save yourself significant missteps and be that much closer to getting your career started off on the right foot. Good luck!

FOUNDATIONS FOR SUCCESS

I'M JUST SAYIN'

Communication, Objection Handling, Negotiation and Advertising

I'M JUST SAYIN'

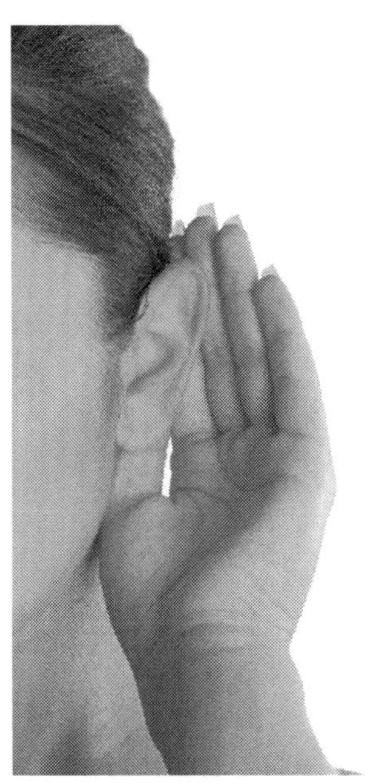
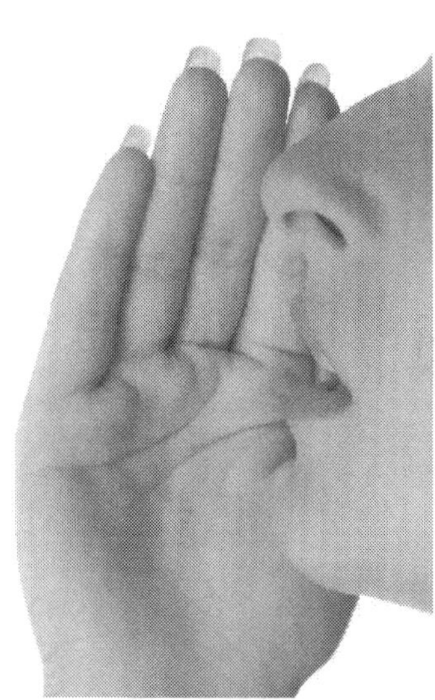

"The biggest communication problem is we do not listen to understand, we listen to reply."
Zig Ziglar

CHAPTER 1

The Art of Communication

"Wise Men speak because they have something to say. Fools, because they have to say something" - **Plato**

One of the single most important skills we need to have, as REALTORS®, is the ability to communicate clearly and effectively with our clients, colleagues and support people. This, though, goes far beyond the simple exchange of words. Communication is much more than just the transfer of information from one person to another. Effective communication is composed not only of the information itself, but also takes into account the medium through which the transfer of the information occurs, such as books, magazines and letters, electronic media, including radio, TV, email, and "simple" conversation. As well, the purpose behind the transfer, the non-verbal communication between the parties, including body language and gestures, how we dress or act and the ability of the person on the other end of the transfer to clearly hear and understand the information will all affect the effectiveness of that transfer.

Communication Styles

There are four styles of communication which you'll come across during your career, Passive, Aggressive, Passive-Aggressive and Assertive.

Passive

The Passive communicator avoids expressing their opinions or feelings, protecting their rights, and identifying or meeting their needs. They accept the communication, but don't provide feedback or encourage discussion. They don't feel comfortable expressing what they think or feel because they're afraid that it won't make sense to people or that it may make other people angry. The passive communicator's stance is one of *"You're right and my opinion doesn't matter."*

Aggressive

The Aggressive communicator expresses their feelings and opinions and promote their needs in a way that violates the rights of others. Their communication style is one in which shouting, arguing and speaking over people are typical traits. They can be verbally and/or physically abusive. This type of communication is generally born of low self-esteem, unhealed emotional wounds, and feelings of powerlessness. The aggressive communicator is clearly saying, *"I don't care how you feel or what you say, I'm right and you're wrong. You have to listen to me!"*

Passive-Aggressive

The Passive-Aggressive communicator appears passive on the surface but is really acting out their anger in a subtle, indirect, or behind-the-scenes way. They usually feel powerless, stuck, and resentful and feel incapable of dealing directly with the object of their resentments. They tend to express their anger by subtly undermining the object (real or imagined) of their resentments. The passive-aggressive communicator conveys the message, *"I understand what you're saying and I don't want to argue. But I'm going to show you that you're wrong."*

Assertive

The Assertive communicator clearly states their opinions and feeling and firmly advocates for their rights and needs without violating the rights of others. They value themselves, their time, and their emotional, spiritual, and physical needs as well as those of others. Assertive communicators sound like, *"I hear and understand what you're saying. Here's what I believe. Does that make sense to you?"*

Obviously, each of these styles require a different approach to communication when dealing with them.

When dealing with a Passive communicator, you need to be assertive and clearly state what it is that you want / need / feel. As you demonstrate that you value their opinion and views they may begin to feel more comfortable and may learn to trust you and become more open and assertive themselves. You'll need to build confidence with that person before he/she begins to communicate openly with you.

Because the Aggressive communicator's style can be overwhelming, it's extremely important to avoid getting caught up in their manner. You'll need to be assertive and clearly state what it is that you want/need/feel, without allowing yourself to get into a confrontation. One simple way to avoid allowing this type of communicator to trigger a confrontation is to speak softly. The louder they become, the calmer and quieter your responses should be. This compels most aggressive people to reduce the volume of their voice and lowers the "testosterone" level of the communication. It's important, right from the start, to communicate directly to them that the manner in which they are addressing you is unacceptable and to ensure that you maintain that stance throughout the entire conversation.

Because Passive-Aggressive communicators don't provide much feedback and it's difficult to get a grasp on where they are in the conversation, you need to ask clear, direct questions. Ask them to clearly explain how they feel about specific points throughout the conversation. If you suspect that they're hiding their anger or disagreement, it may be necessary to confront them. If their behaviour doesn't match their words, you'll need to point out that disconnect. Let the person know that while they're telling you one thing, you're confused because they've just done something completely different. Set limits and let them know that certain behaviors will not be tolerated.

Dealing with an Assertive communicator will be fairly easy. Maintain an assertive stance and allow them to express their opinion and acknowledge their concerns and feelings.

Get the message out

There are three components to an effective communication; delivery, reception and response.

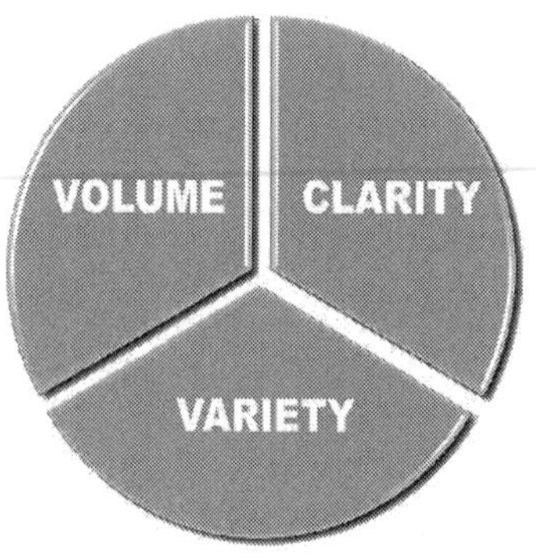

Effective delivery of a message also relies on three components. Volume, which must be appropriate for the situation and the person receiving the communication. The clarity of the message. Is the message understandable to the receiver? This includes the speaker's ability to enunciate both the words and the message itself, the pace at which the speaker is speaking and the avoidance of any distraction from the message or the use of any jargon, slang, or idioms which may cloud the message. And the final component is variety. The pace, variety of inflections and pauses highlight different aspects of the message, which serve to convey meaning and importance of different components of the message.

Listen, Ask, Listen Again

Reception of the message is every bit as important as the delivery of the message. Listening is not the same as hearing. It's an active process in which a conscious decision is made to listen to and understand the message of the speaker. It involves observing both verbal and non-verbal cues and ensuring that the listener understands the message. The diagram below demonstrates how a typical message is heard by most people. What's being said only amounts to a small amount of the actual message and what's being heard is even less than that, the tip of the iceberg.

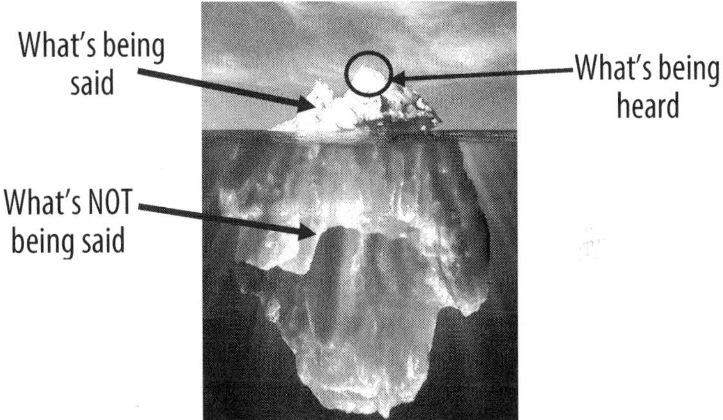

The job of a good communicator, and therefore a good REALTOR®, is to find out and understand what isn't being said and how that relates to what the client is looking for.

Key Principles of Active Listening

The Three Levels

I've always appreciated the saying, "We have two ears and one mouth, so we should listen twice as much as we speak."

When carrying on a conversation, pause and truly listen to what the other person is saying. There are three levels of listening.

In level one listening, the listener hears what the person is telling them, but is not focussing on it. They may be distracted, trying to figure out what the person is getting at or just not really interested.

It's not really about what the speaker is saying, it's about the listener and their thoughts.

In level two listening, the listener is paying close attention to what the speaker is saying, focussing on not just what's being said, but how the other person's body language, facial expressions and tone all covey the deeper meaning. At this level, the listener doesn't interrupt, talk over the speaker or try to finish their sentences for them, but really focusses on the true message.

In order to reach this level of listening, you have to actually prepare yourself to listen, to be relaxed and ready to fully engage the speaker. You need to be open minded and focus on what's being said, listening for ideas, not just words. Avoid jumping to conclusions or assuming anything about the conversation. Encouraging the speaker through the use of gestures, such as nodding, leaning in toward the speaker, and holding eye contact, the use of appropriate supportive phrases, such as *"I see," "I understand," "OK,"* etc., will inspire them to continue, while paying attention to pitch, tone and volume will help the listener to understand the emphasis of what's being said.

And finally, level three listening takes in not just the speaker, but the entire environment, what's happening around the conversation, the feeling in the room. An example of this would occur when you walk in to a room where something big has just happened. You can sense the tension or electricity in the room without anything being said. That's level three listening.

Reiterate and Listen

Once the speaker has concluded, you need to ask open ended questions and listen to the response. It helps to reiterate and clarify the message. This may be easier if you paraphrase the message and clarify any ambiguous or unclear points and then ask for confirmation.

"So, Mr. and Mrs. Seller, how do you see us managing our communication during the listing?"

Then wait for them to answer.

"OK. So what I'm hearing you say is that you'd like to ...., is that right?"

This should continue until the message or the clients' intention is completely clear and understood.

And the final piece of the communication puzzle is the response. Once you've ensured that you understand the issues, pause and reflect on how that impacts you and what you're trying to achieve. This decreases the chance of responding with something that may be regretted later. When you do respond, avoid using antagonistic sentences, such as "That doesn't make sense." Make it a conversation, not a confrontation. Acknowledge the other person's issue and then offer suggestions for a resolution. Once you've responded, it's important to ensure other that the person understands what you're saying and gauge their reaction to it.

"Does that make sense?"

"How do you feel about that?"

So, where can active listening be used? When working with clients such as at the Buyers Interview, it can help better understand their wants and needs.

"I want you to picture yourself three months from now. You're in your new home. Can you describe for me exactly what it feels and looks like to you?"

"OK, so I hear that you'd like to have 4 bedrooms, right? Do they all have to be on the same floor, or would it be ok to have one in the basement?"

"OK, so what I'm hearing you say is that schools are a really important element in the decision. Can you tell me more about that?"

When at a Listing Presentation, the use of active listening techniques allows you to ask questions and dig down to find out what the sellers believe is of value to them, focussing on their interests, rather than yours. It begins the process of building trust and respect and helps you determine what information or reassurance the client needs.

"So, Mr. and Mrs. Seller, what are you looking for from the REALTOR® who's going to help you sell your home?"

"What do you see as the most important things your real estate agent can do for you? What criteria will you use to select your agent?"

In summary, it may be helpful to understand that there's actually a formula for carrying on an effective communication. Once you've had the chance to listen to the speaker, the first step is to ask confirmatory questions.

"So, what I hear you saying is...Is that right?"

"Am I correct in understanding that you what you're saying is...?"

On receiving a confirmation, the next step is to ask inquiry questions based on the information the speaker provided you in the conversation. These include the five W's; Who, What, Where, When, Why as well as How. I've found that one additional question is extremely helpful in drawing out more information; *"Can you tell me more about that?"*

These will allow you to craft a response that will help communicate your point. Once you've clearly articulated the information you wish to provide, the next step is to ask a confirmatory question to ensure that the other person understands your information and whether it makes sense to them.

"How do you feel about that?"

"Does that make sense to you?"

"Do you have any questions about that?"

Following these simple steps will dramatically increase your ability to better understand and build rapport with the people with whom you'll deal.

CHAPTER 2

I'm Not Ready Yet!

One of the biggest challenges you're going to face throughout your career is the ability to handle objections. And most of that challenge will come from within yourself, not, surprisingly, from the objection itself. Handling objections is every bit as much about your confidence to deal with them as it is actually dealing with them. I hear you saying, "How can I have confidence in handling objections, if I don't know how to handle them?" One of the things I've learned, is that confidence comes from experience, understanding what creates an objection and lots of practice.

Managing objections isn't about memorizing specific scripts or having a series of rote answers at your fingertips. It's about asking the right questions, listening carefully to what the client is telling you and then giving them the answers they need to help them make an informed decision. Ask lots of open ended questions when speaking with people and they'll actually tell you how to handle their objection. Let me say that again. If you ask people what they're concerned about, they'll tell you.

Let's begin by defining the term objection. Unlike in a court of law an objection is not a formal protest to disallow evidence. It's simply a statement that the client hasn't understood something or hasn't been given the information they need to make an informed decision. They're just not ready to move forward, because they have a concern that hasn't been addressed. To get them to take the next step, whether it's signing a listing contract, agreeing to work with you or paying a reasonable price for a home, your job is to find out what's behind the curtain, the objection, and then deal with it.

There are, however, two other matters that can be confused with an objection. You need to be aware of what they are and how to deal with them. These are:

- A stall, which occurs when the client isn't prepared to make a decision at that moment. Instead they hide the actual objection behind a statement that allows them to avoid the decision, such as, "We need to think about it," or "We need to talk to someone about this." Statements like these give away the fact that there's still some doubt in their mind which you haven't satisfied. Often, they feel like they're being pressured to make a decision when they haven't had the opportunity to review and understand the facts.
- A condition, which prevents a client from moving forward and is beyond the client's control. An example of this occurs when a buyer has to wait for their three-month probation period at work to expire before they can be approved for a mortgage.

Where do they come from?

There are three main reasons for an objection to occur, both when dealing with sellers or buyers;

Concern

A lack of complete information, when clients are asked to make a decision, will be reflected as anxiety or worry and clients will resist proceeding until that worry or concern is satisfied. It may also be due to an unresolved fear about making the decision and making a move from what they perceive to be a "safe" position. *"Are we really ready to go ahead and buy this house?" "Are we making the right decision about selling, right now, in this market?"*

Managing their concern by providing any missing information will help reduce their anxiety. Helping them focus on the benefits of taking the action and reviewing their needs and wants will also help them make a more clearly defined decision. A major part of our job is to listen to, provide answers for and calm our clients' fears.

Uncertainty

Uncertainty arises when the client has a disbelief about a specific fact or mistrusts some of the information with which they're presented. They may also not see the value in taking the action as opposed to staying where they are.

Eliminating this objection is a matter of providing the proof of the information you've presented them, backed up by solid evidence, such as the raw data, charts or the completed Comparative Market Analysis (CMA). You may also want to show them other homes that have sold in the area so they have a more firm grasp of the values and realities of the market.

If they have an uncertainty about a particular aspect of a home they're thinking about buying or are unsure about the value you've proposed for the home they're selling, and are hesitating about moving forward, you can bring in a neutral party to provide an independent opinion, such as an inspector, engineer or appraiser.

Lack of Motivation

These are the most challenging people with whom to work. Objections are usually raised due to the client not having or seeing the need to make a move. "I'll buy something if you find me the right place, but I'm in no hurry," or "If we get the right price, we'll sell, but we're in no rush. We don't want to give the house away."

Dealing with this kind of client is a matter of asking the right questions to discover their level of motivation and then deciding whether to work with them or not. However, every so often, you'll encounter a client who starts off with a high level of motivation and then, for some reason, who's motivation level drops. At this point it's important to review their motivating factors and the underlying reason they're buying or selling and see if that reason is still as important as it was when they first began looking. If it's not, then you have a decision to make as well. Do you want to continue to work with or not?

Early and Often

As you can see, the most common reason for an objection to rear its ugly head is due to the client not having or believing some information. So, the easiest way to deal with objections is to anticipate them, deal with them early and often. In other words, as you proceed through your Listing or Buyer's Presentation, you have to make sure you provide loads of information and data to reinforce your advice. Throughout the presentation, you have to ask for confirmation that they understand and agree with the information using trial closes.

When I was learning to speak in front of people, one of the key pointers I learned was that you have to tell people what you're going to tell them, then give them the information and make sure they understand it, and finally tell them what you told them. This holds true for dealing with clients. You need to give them the information many times, make sure they understand it and ask if they have any questions. And, as I said before, it's about asking the right questions, listening carefully to what the client is telling you and then giving them the answers they need to help them make an informed decision.

The BASIQs

All too often objection handling is considered something to either be avoided or dealt with by utilizing a series of standardized, pre-programmed phrases. It should, instead, be viewed as an opportunity to demonstrate your ability to provide information and data that will assist the client in making a well-reasoned, fully informed decision.

In this chapter, we'll examine a system which can reduce friction, improve communication, provide you with answers about the underlying cause of the objection and assist you in helping the client make a decision to move forward with the transaction.

In many cases, when confronted by an objection, the Sales Representative's first reaction is to take a defensive position and point out the errors in the clients' thinking.

Client: "I think we should try it at a higher price."

Sales Representative: "If we do that it may cause you to take longer to sell or even not sell at all."

This can result in the client becoming defensive and then both parties end up in what David Knox calls "the tennis match syndrome"; the discussion goes back and forth, back and forth, creating unnecessary friction between the parties.

The approach I use is what I call BASIQ. The BASIQ system has five components:

Step 1 - Breathe

Step 2 - Acknowledge

Step 3 - Sound it back

Step 4 - Isolate

Step 5 - Question

Breathe

When confronted with an objection, the first step in this system is to stop and breathe. In taking the time to take a few deep breaths, you may find that what might appear to be an objection may be simply an idle comment and not an actual concern. This step avoids creating an issue where one doesn't already exist. And it gives you time to think of how to handle the objection.

Acknowledge

The next step is to simply acknowledge the fact that the client has a concern. This lets the client know that you've heard them and also helps reduce the possibility of a confrontation.

Sound it Back

The third step in this process is to sound the objection back to the client.

"OK, so what I'm hearing you say is..."

This step ensures that what you're hearing them say is what they actually mean. It allows the client to clarify their position and perhaps provide more information for you to use to determine the best way to deal with the objection. It also allows the client to hear their objection from someone else, which may change their viewpoint.

Isolate

Step four is to isolate the objection.

"Other than that, is there anything else that's causing you concern?"

"If we could resolve that, would you be prepared to move forward...?"

"If it weren't for that, would you ...?"

In handling objections, there's nothing more aggravating than dealing with an objection and preparing to close when suddenly another one rears its ugly head. To successfully close the transaction, it's important to make sure that all the client's objections are known. Since most people present the most serious objection first, this allows you to deal with each objection in order of importance. Dealing with the major objection first often eliminates the need to deal with the ones of lesser importance.

Question

The final step is to ask questions of the seller to determine the underlying concern behind the objection. By using open-ended questions, you can elicit a tremendous amount of information which may provide valuable information on how to deal with the objection and help the customer resolve their own issues. What information or reassurance does the client need?

"OK, I understand you're concerned about...can you tell me more about that?"

"It sounds like you're not sure about...what would you like to know about that?"

Once the underlying cause of the objection has been discovered, it's necessary to find out if the client is prepared to move forward if their concerns are answered. This entails the use of a closing question; a type of question which requires a yes or no answer;

"If I could show you how...would you be prepared to move forward?"

Any answer other than yes means that the objection is not the actual reason they're not prepared to move forward. Answering it will get you nowhere. If, however, they say yes, then you get to deal with the objection and find a way to close the deal.

Questions, Questions, Questions

I find it helpful to think of asking questions in a specific sequence to help me remember what I need to ask. That sequence is as follows.

The first question is a Trial Close. This helps me ensure that if I can deal with their objection they're prepared to move forward and listen to the information I'm going to provide.

"If I can show you how...will help you understand...would that help you make a decision?"

The next sequence of questions are what I call the Inquiry phase. This is where you're going to ask all the questions you need in order to find out the underlying issue that's holding them back from taking the step of signing the contract. In this phase you'll ask the 5 W's; Who, What, When, Where, Why as well as How and my personal favourite, *"Tell me more about that."*

I've found that most objections are the result of four main issues; money, motivation, a concern, disbelief about some information or the client needs reassurance about a particular aspect of the transaction.

Where we tend to get it wrong, though, is that we try to figure out what the cause of the objection is from asking a few quick questions and then offering a solution that we think will resolve the problem, without actually spending the time to find out what the real, deep down, issue actually is.

Pain, Fear or Gain

We know that, for the most part, people make a change because of Pain, Fear or Gain. They either want to eliminate something that's creating a problem (causing them pain), avoid dealing with something that may cause a problem (fear) or are looking to improve the situation they're in (gain a better position). It used to be a statute of sales that to sell something we had to offer a solution to the problem. Instead of offering up solutions, we need to look at sales as if we are doctors. We need to find out about their pain. It's only by taking the time needed to dig deep and finding out the true underlying cause and also through determining how the client feels it can best be resolved, that the objection can be dealt with appropriately.

In my previous career, I learned a really helpful mnemonic that used to help me ask questions about my patients' problem. That mnemonic was WOCSNOR and it goes like this:

W What's your WORST pain? In other words, what's the most important issue they're facing in their current situation? Is it money, space, location or something else?

O What OTHER pain is there? Is there something else that's creating an issue for them in their current location? What's the next most important thing?

C Is it CONSTANT or INTERMITTENT? In other words, is this something that's a constant problem that they need to get away from right now, or does it create problems on an occasional basis that they would like to move away from?

S How SIGNIFICANT is the pain? Is this situation untenable or can they live with it if they have to?

N What's the NATURE of the pain? What is the actual pain that the client's experiencing that they feel needs to be resolved? This is where your ability to ask questions and actively listen will earn you the respect and trust of the client.

O Are there any OTHER symptoms? These are things other than the pain that are creating issues for them and that they feel need to be resolved.

R What's the RELATIONSHIP of the pain and the symptoms? If the pain gets worse, do the symptoms?

If you take this kind of approach to finding out what the problem is, then explore different lines of inquiry, and finally, help them understand that the cost created by the problem exceeds the cost of making a change, you can then help them discover and thereby offer your clients different solutions to the problem.

Go for the Close

There are two types of closing questions. The first is the ***Sharp Angle Close***. This type of question takes a direct approach in finding out if the client is prepared to take the next step;

"If I could show you how..., would you be prepared to sign with me today?"

The second type of closing question takes a more indirect and softer approach but still requires a yes or no answer. It's known as ***"Feel, Felt, Found"***.

"I understand how you feel."

This helps defuse the situation and avoids locking heads with the client. It lets them know that they've been heard and acknowledges the fact that they have a concern.

"A lot of people have felt that way."

This lets them know that they're not the only ones with that concern and can help reassure the client. It also lets them know that you've heard this objection and dealt with it before, thereby reinforcing your experience.

"But what I've found is..."

This says, "*In my experience,*" further reinforcing the fact that you've heard this objection and dealt with it before and that you have the experience to back it up. This then leads to the closing question. Put together, this style of closing question would look like this:

"I understand how you feel. A lot of people have felt that way, but what I've found is that if I can show you how..., many people find it helps them make a decision. Would that help you make the decision to move forward today?"

Listen, Ask and Listen Again

Once you've asked the closing question, stop talking and wait for the answer. Allow the client to think and respond. Once you've received an affirmative answer, you can then move forward and begin to ask the detailed questions that will give you the answers you need to be able to deal with the client's concerns. These must be open-ended and designed to elicit as much information from the client as possible. The key to maximizing the opportunity to get answers is to actively listen. Remember, listening is not the same as hearing. Listening is an active process in which a conscious decision is made to listen to and understand the message of the speaker.

The ability to actively listen depends on several factors. The listener must focus on the speaker, and concentrate on the messages that are being communicated. Try to understand the other person's point of view and look at the issues from their perspective. Don't interrupt, talk over them or finish their sentences for them. Nodding and the use of other gestures or words will encourage them to continue and paying attention to pitch, tone and volume will help the listener to understand the emphasis of what is being said. Once the speaker has concluded, this is the opportunity to reiterate and clarify by paraphrasing the message, clarifying any ambiguous or unclear points and then asking for confirmation. Once you've completely understood the client's concerns, you're then able to offer suggestions for resolution.

"OK, I understand you're concerned about...can you tell me more about that?"

"It sounds like you're not sure about...what would you like to know about that?"

"What information do you need that will help you make a more informed decision?"

When offering suggestions, it's important to avoid using stock, rehearsed answers. Your suggestions for resolution of the concern must be based on the concern itself and the answers you've gained from listening to the sellers and must be based on facts, statistics and any other hard data available. When providing suggestions to the sellers, there are many techniques to assist you in getting your point across. Tell stories and relate how other clients or colleagues have dealt with a similar situation.

"You know, Mr. and Mrs. Seller, I understand your concern. I had a similar experience with another couple just a month ago. They wanted to....so we went ahead and did that. Here's what ended up happening..."

Illustrate your points with diagrams. As the saying goes, "A picture is worth a thousand words." Most people are visual and will be able to better understand your point when it's illustrated.

The Specifics

Sellers' Objections

Sellers have many different reasons for providing objections. They can, however, be grouped into five main categories:

- Pricing
- Commission
- They want to fix it up first
- They want to interview other agents
- They have a friend or relative in the business

The Pricing Objection

"We think it should be priced higher."

In most instances, the pricing objection arises when a seller doesn't have or doesn't accept the information they need to make an informed decision and this is merely the opening salvo in the battle to help your sellers understand why pricing their property correctly is so important. Unfortunately, it's also the point at which many salespeople try to prove their sellers wrong without trying to understand the underlying concern.

Is it because they feel their home is worth more than the comparables you've shown them? Is it because they have a huge debt load and need more out of their home than your analysis shows it's worth? Have they spent a ton of money on renovations and believe they should get their investment back, plus a bonus? Do they want to try it high because it's a hot market? Or are they just dipping their toe in the water, trying out a price and not really serious about selling?

The method of dealing with each of these concerns will be as varied as the concern itself and can only be determined by asking questions which require the seller to explore their own issues which will allow you to learn how best to advise them. That means that your next question must be:

> *"OK. I understand that getting the most for your home is important and that you feel your home should be priced higher than what the market says it should be. Can you tell me a little more about that?"*

Their answer to that single question will direct the remainder of your discussion with them and the information you will provide.

For example, if their answer is that they believe their home to be better than the other comparables, your discussion will then need to be about the comparables, a review of the data you've provided and the differences between their home and the comparables. You may need to take them out and play "The Pricing is Right" game. In this "game", you would take the sellers to several recently sold homes which closely match theirs and have them guess the sold price.

Many times they can be convinced that their home is worth more than they can actually obtain in the current marketplace. In order to reduce this possibility, you will need to be proactive and, as discussed earlier, bringing up the importance of proper pricing early and often. Spending time during the listing presentation, discussing and getting their agreement on who they are going to choose, the REALTOR® with the best services and marketing plan or the one with the highest listing price will help reduce the time you'll need to spend later.

You'll also need to spend some time finding out whether price is the key factor or if the time it takes to sell is more important to them.

Taking the time to completely review the current sales, market factors, inventory and absorption rate during the CMA component of your presentation and helping the sellers to fully understand these factors will greatly reduce the chance of having to deal with a pricing objection. It's important to remind the client that salespeople don't control the market and therefore the price you're suggesting is based on the price that buyers are willing to pay for similar properties. The Principle of Substitution, which states that a buyer will pay no more for a property than the cost of an equally desirable alternative property, must be clearly explained to the client.

If they've been told by another Sales Representative that their home is worth more than the CMA reveals, you'll need to explain how that may be misleading.

"Any agent who will list your property for more than the market says it's worth is just trying to get the listing now, but will quickly start working on getting you to reduce the price.

That's because they're afraid to tell you the truth right up front, something I'm not afraid to do and I assume you want me to tell you the truth.

So, if I can show you how listing your home in the price range I'm suggesting will actually get your home sold faster and for more money, would you be prepared to move forward today?"

In a 2014 National Association of REALTORS (NAR) study, it was shown that 47% of homes sold had reduced their price at least once before selling. This would have resulted in an increased amount of time required to get the home sold and would, in all likelihood, have resulted in the sellers netting less than if they had priced it properly at the beginning.

When dealing with the pricing objection, a common concern is the sellers wanting to list it high for a couple of weeks, or that buyers can always make an offer even though it's listed high. This objection can best be dealt with by reviewing the window of opportunity that occurs when a new listing hits the market and reviewing the sellers' time frame for getting the house sold.

"Mr. and Mrs. Seller, let me explain about the window of opportunity. When you sell a home, qualified buyers view the property right away and if it's priced right, it will sell. If it's priced too high, they either won't take a look or they won't bother writing an offer. By the time we reduce the price, we'll have missed that window of opportunity. If I could show you how taking the extra time, at the higher price, could result in you making even less than you want, would that help you move forward today?"

No matter what the concern is about pricing, asking probing questions and listening to the answers will provide you with the information you need to provide the sellers with the reasons to price their home correctly.

Clarifying their time frame for the sale and their motivation will be critical to your ability to deal with the objection.

"What's your time frame for selling?"

"What's more important to you, the price it sells for or the time it takes to sell?"

Sharp Angle Question

"If I could show you how taking the extra time, at the higher price, could result in you making even less than you want, would that help you move forward today?"

Feel, Felt, Found

"What I've found is that if you take the extra time, at the higher price, it usually results in you making even less than you want. If I show you what I mean, would that help you move forward today?"

The Commission Objection

Let's begin this discussion by understanding a simple truth; the more a client values something, the less likely it is that they'll object to paying for it. People have no problem paying more for something if they feel they're getting value. All standard family size cars have four wheels, an engine and a passenger compartment, and all are capable of getting a person from point A to point B. So why would someone who needs to get from point A to point B choose to pay $70,000 for one type of vehicle instead of $45,000 for another? Because, in the mind of the buyer, there is a perceived difference in **value** between the two brands. So it's incumbent upon you, throughout your listing presentation, to demonstrate that you have a value, perceived by the sellers, that justifies the commission you are charging.

Much like pricing, the commission objection has many possible causes which can be boiled down to three main themes. The first is that they believe we're overpaid and they don't have a real concept of what's involved in marketing and managing a sale.

"All you guys do is stick a sign on the lawn, put it on MLS and maybe run an Open House or two."

The second cause is due to the amount of competition and the willingness of other REALTORS® to undercut their colleagues.

"Another agent said they'd list it for less."

"You guys all do the same thing. Why should I pay you more?"

The final issue is that the sellers may have financial issues and need to make as much as possible out of the sale.

In order to effectively deal with the commission objection you must believe in your own ability to provide value and that the service you provide is worth the commission charged. You must also be willing to walk away from the listing if the commission isn't what you're prepared to accept.

As with any objection you need to discover why they feel the commission should be reduced.

"You obviously need to feel comfortable that the fee being charged is justified by the services being provided, am I right?

"Let me ask you, how do you feel about everything I've presented to you?"

In the event that they don't believe you're worth the commission or their objection is due to a lack of understanding of the responsibilities and intricacies involved in the sale of a home, you'll need to review the sales process, the marketing and services you're going to provide and ensure that they understand your commitment to providing them with the value which justifies the commission.

There are a number of stock rebuttals to the commission objection. I would, however, propose that these are nothing more than an attempt to shortcut the objection handling process. In no way do they deal with trying to understand the issues faced by the seller. If, during the listing presentation, you were able to demonstrate that the value you provide is worth the commission that you charge, you will, in all likelihood, not be faced with a commission objection in the first place. But, should it occur, you'll find it will be easier to deal with. However, until you have the chance to build your objection handling skills you may want to use them, so I've included some of the stock rebuttals in the Workbook.

Sharp Angle Question

> *"If we can resolve the commission issue, would you be willing to list with me today?"*

Feel, Felt, Found

> *"What I've found is that if we can resolve the commission issue, most people are willing to move forward. If we do that, would you be willing to list with me today?"*

An occasional commission objection you may encounter will be the seller asking if you'll reduce the commission if their home should sell quickly. In the event this question pops up, it's important to point out to the seller that real estate is actually a performance-based business; that the better we perform, the shorter time it takes to sell the home.

"Mr. and Mrs. Seller, I understand your concern. Let me ask you this. If someone does a great job, would you expect them to be paid more than someone who does a poor job? In this business, if I do a great job, it means that your home spends less time on the market and you get more for it. However, if I do a poor job, it means your home spends more time on the market and you end up getting less for it. So what you're suggesting is that you'd be prepared to pay me more for doing a poor job than for doing a great job. Does that make sense?"

"We want to Fix It up First"

This objection occurs when the sellers make the misguided assumption that by renovating their home, they will be able to recover not only the full cost of the renovations but also increase the value of the home significantly. In dealing with this objection, you need to ask the sellers what renovations they expect to do, how extensive the renovations will be and how much is involved in terms of financing and time.

Sharp Angle Question

"If I can show you how spending both the time and money involved in renovating before you sell could cost you thousands of dollars, would you be willing to list today?"

Feel, Felt, Found

"I understand how you feel. Many people I've dealt with have felt that way. What I've found is that if I demonstrate spending both the time and money involved in renovating before selling could cost you thousands of dollars, most people are willing to move forward. If we do that, would you be willing to list with me today?"

It's important to take time to review with them the cost of renovations versus the amount recoverable on the sale and to remind them that the renovations they undertake may not be to the liking of potential buyers and could potentially make it more difficult to sell.

"Mr. and Mrs. Seller, it would probably be more effective to take a more aggressive approach to pricing rather than investing more money in a house you want to sell. That way we can let the buyers decide on the renovations they want to do and avoid eliminating potential buyers."

You can also point out the fact that the renovations may take quite a bit of time and that they rarely proceed within the projected time frame, thereby costing them both time and money.

Demonstrating to them, using information from an appraiser, how much they can get back for specific renovations may help the sellers better understand the true effect that renovations can have on the value of their home.

You can find this information at Jackson Appraisals, Carson Dunlop Appraisals or Pillar to Post Inspections and at www.foundationsforsuccess.ca.

"We Want to Interview other Agents"

This statement can be both an objection as well as a stall. It's important that you determine which it is, as the method of dealing with each will be different. In either case, though, the first step in managing this is to ask the question:

"Mr. and Mrs. Seller, can I ask you whether you have any concerns about my marketing plan or the services that I provide?"

If their answer is that they don't, the next question will determine whether it's truly an objection or if it's a stall.

"I understand that you want to make sure you get the best agent to help you sell your home. Let me ask you then, what is it that you'd be looking for from the others, that you feel that we haven't discussed?"

If this is a stall, their answer will be that they don't know what the others offer and want to hear from them directly. This would require that you use a sharp angle closing question.

"It sounds to me like you still have some reservations about whether my services will get your home sold at the best possible price in the best time frame for you. If we take the time to review my services and discuss anything that you feel you would like to see, would that help you make the decision to move forward today?"

This will lead to either a yes, at which time you can lead them to a close, or a no, and you'll have to decide if you want to wait for them to interview the other Sales Representatives or move on.

"We Want to Wait until..."

One of the many real estate myths you're going to need to deal with is that it's better to wait until a certain time to list a home because that's when most people are looking.

"We want to wait until spring to list our home." or *"No one's looking during August, they're all away, so we want to wait until September."*

This is when you'll need to explain the theory of supply and demand to the sellers and how it can affect their sale. Prices in the real estate market are driven by supply and demand. The more properties available for buyers to choose from, the less likely it will be that prices will increase, and they may even decrease. And the reverse occurs; prices increase more rapidly when there are fewer properties available. If the sellers are waiting for a specific time to list their properties, they need to be made aware of how the supply of properties on the market will make a difference in the price they're likely to get for their home.

"I understand that you want to wait until there are a maximum number of buyers looking for homes. However, most people are doing exactly the same thing. The problem is that this could actually cost you money. May I explain?"

"By waiting until [date] to list, you're doing exactly what most of your competition will be doing. When you list your home at the same time as many of your competitors, buyers will have more options. This means that you'll to have to compete with more sellers and often prices become softer, which could cost you thousands of dollars. However, if you list now, when there is a shortage of homes on the market, you may get more for the home and sell it faster. Does that make sense?"

We have a family member / friend in the business

When dealing with this objection, you need to point out that the sellers' decision should be based on what's best for them, not their friend or relative.

"Do you absolutely have to sell this home, or are you just looking to do your friend a favour?"

You'll want to point out to the sellers that they'll need to look at all the services and marketing being done and decide who will provide them with the best opportunity to sell their home. As well, it's important for them to determine if they'd be comfortable expressing dissatisfaction or be prepared to fire their friend or family member if they're dissatisfied with their performance. I heard an objection handler for this that I thought was quite unique.

> *"Mr. and Mrs. Seller, let me ask you this. If you had to fire your relative, how well do you think Thanksgiving dinner would go?"* Too funny!

But, on a serious note, selling and buying a home is the largest financial transaction for many people and issues do arise. Many brokers spend a great deal of time defending ethics cases or dealing with lawsuits filed against their agents and brokerages. As a result, the client needs to ask themselves, *"Can our friendship withstand such an incident and will I have the courage to sue or complain if something goes wrong?"*

Buyers' Objections

Buyers' objections, in most cases, are the result of a lack of certainty or the presence of some confusion, a lack of motivation, a concern about money or they need the reassurance of someone that they're making the correct decision. They think the home's overpriced or they want to try writing a low offer, they want to wait to see if the price goes down or they want to look at more houses.

We think it's overpriced or We want to come in lower

> *"OK. I can appreciate that. If you were going to write an offer, what price would you like to pay for the home? ....*

Once they've answered this question, you'll need to determine if their intent in writing a low-ball offer is due to motivation, money or confusion and that can best be determined by the use of one of the closing questions discussed earlier.

Sharp Angle Question

"That's fine, but you need to understand that we should expect a counteroffer, so my question is, do you absolutely want to buy this home?"

Feel, Felt, Found

"I understand how you feel. A lot of people have felt that way. What I've found is that by writing such a low offer, you may alienate the sellers and not get the house, so my first question is, do you absolutely want to buy this home?"

If their answer is yes, then you'll need to ask some very specific questions to determine what their concern is and why they feel the price is too high. You'll want to know what they believe is a reasonable price and why.

"OK, so if I show you the comparable properties that have sold, it may help you to understand why they're at that asking price. Would that help you write an offer closer to the asking price?"

Once you've established their willingness to write an offer closer to the list price, you'll need to support your argument with statistics, review the CMA and by reviewing the buyers' needs and wants against the currently available properties. Another effective technique in helping the buyers get a better understanding of the prices of homes is to play the Pricing Game and take them to other comparable homes that have sold, then having them guess the price.

Discussing the potential dangers and end results of lowballing will also help them make a more informed decision. Alienating the seller can result in having them reject the offer outright, counter back at, or close to, the list price and also refuse to deal with another offer from the buyer. The buyer should also be made aware that they're taking the risk of another offer coming in and thereby placing themselves in a multiple offer, in which they'll have no choice but to write an offer closer to or even above the list price. It's always a good idea to ask the buyers to place themselves in the sellers' shoes. What would they do in the seller's place?

Establishing what's more important to them, the house or the extra money will help provide another method of dealing with this objection. By breaking down the cost of borrowing the difference between the list price and their offer, you can help them understand exactly what it will cost them. This is known as reducing to the ridiculous. For example, if they want to write an offer $30,000 below list, you can explain it this way.

"$30,000 amortized over 25 years at 3% equals $141per month, which ends up being $4.67 day. Is the house worth an additional $4.67 a day?"

We want to wait

This objection may come from a number of different sources. When dealing with this objection, your job is to determine whether it's an objection, a stall, if it's due to some uncertainty or due to a lack of motivation. And the only way to achieve this effectively, is to ask questions. What's holding them back? Do they need to discuss this with another party? Are they unsure about buying?

If it's an actual objection, you'll need to find out what their concern is. Many times it's because either they're under the impression that the market is slowing or dropping or it is in fact happening.

Sharp Angle Closing Question

"If I could show you that by waiting for the market to drop, you could actually end up in a position where it costs you more for this or a similar home, would that make it easier for you to make a decision about buying this house?"

Feel, Felt, Found

"What I've found is that by showing people how waiting for the market to drop could actually end up costing them more for a similar home, it makes it easier for them to make a decision about buying. Would that help you?"

If, at this point, they agree that it will help them make the decision, you'll need to spend some time reviewing the benefits to them of buying this house. The Buyer's Questionnaire (which can be found in the Volume 6 or at www.foundationsforsuccess.ca) will be of significant value in reinforcing the benefits they were looking for and comparing them to this home. You'll also need to provide them with the actual market trends and ensure the information they have is up to date and correct. Discuss the cost of buying versus the cost of remaining.

If the buyers are also selling their home, and especially if they're moving to a larger home, discussing the difference between the increase in value of their existing home when compared to the increase in the cost of their new home may help solidify the cost of waiting in the buyers' mind. For example, assuming home prices are increasing by 5% per month, a home priced at $400,000 will increase in value by $20,000 each month, while a home priced at $500,000 will increase in cost by $25,000 a month. So if the buyers wait 3 months to buy the $500,000 home, they will have made $60,000 on the sale of their home, while it will have cost them

$75,000 to buy their new one. This means that it will cost them $15,000 more to buy their new home.

The cost of buying the home versus the value they perceive the house to have could be another reason for the buyers wanting to wait. They may have difficulty grasping the relationship between what they're paying and what they're getting and may feel uncomfortable committing to a purchase as a result. It's critical to make sure you have a firm grasp of their needs and wants to manage this objection and therefore will need to review them with the buyers.

Sharp Angle Question

"If we take a few minutes to review what you've told me your needs and wants are and then see if this house truly meets those needs, would that help you make a decision about buying the home?"

Feel, Felt, Found

"Sounds to me like you're concerned about this house not meeting your needs. I understand how you feel. Many people have felt that way. But what I've found is that if we take a few minutes to review what you've told me your needs and wants are and then see if this house truly meets those needs, many people feel more comfortable making a decision. Would that help you make a decision about buying the home?"

Your questions will then have to take them through a review of the needs and wants you first established in the buyer's interview. You'll then have to have a conversation examining the costs and benefits to them of buying or not buying the home.

The same concern, which in some people may be expressed as an objection, can however, be hidden by a stall by other people. It's very much like the typical response you find occurs when you go into a big box electronic store and one of the salespeople asks if they can help you find something. What's your response? I know my almost automatic response is, *"No thanks, I'm just looking."* Classic stall for, *"I don't want to be sold anything."*

However, if the question is asked in a different manner, it usually evokes a much different answer.

"Hi, I see you're looking at TV's. Is there anything you'd like to know about this particular model?"

Change the question and you'll generally get a different answer. The stall is, in most instances, eliminated and if there is an objection, you can then follow up with specific questions designed to draw out the concern behind it.

When it comes to buying a home, two of the most common stalls are:

"We need to talk to our (someone) about it."

"We like to take our time to think things over."

This is simply the buyers saying that they have a concern but they're not ready to let you in on the secret, possibly because they're afraid you'll try to "sell" them. In managing this objection, you're going to have to determine the root cause of the concern by asking questions designed specifically to get behind the curtain they've thrown up in front of the issue.

"Buying a house is a big deal and I understand that you would want to think about it.

Let me ask you this, I get the feeling that you like the house, am I right? And it has what you told me you're looking for, doesn't it?

OK. So, there's something about the purchase that concerns you. Can I ask what that is?"

In dealing with a stall, your role becomes that of an advisor rather than a REALTOR®. You're going to have to determine the concern itself, provide them with the information they need and then ask the questions that will help them make an informed decision.

And finally, the objection may be due to an uncertainty about whether what they're looking for is the right thing for them. Younger buyers may experience this concern for a variety of reasons, including, whether the home fully meets their needs as they described them to you, the price of the home when compared with the benefits or simply a fear of proceeding with a purchase of this magnitude. Uncertainty about the suitability of the home or whether the home will fully meet their needs is a common experience for many older buyers as well. Your role in dealing with this kind of uncertainty is very similar to that of dealing with a stall.

Rather than just simply providing facts and figures, you'll need to spend time understanding their deeper concerns. You'll need to find out what their uncertainty is based on and what information they're going to need to help them reduce or eliminate it.

"What I'm hearing you say is that you're unsure about moving forward with purchasing this home. Is that right? May I ask what it is that's making you uncertain?"

Many times, this question will be difficult for them to answer as they may not immediately recognize the underlying issue. You may, therefore, need to ask some targeted questions such as:

"Are you unsure about whether this home has what you're looking for?"

"Are you concerned about whether you can afford it?"

"Is it the home itself that you're concerned about or is there something else that's holding you back?"

Helping them find the underlying answer will also help you determine what information or support you'll need to provide them so that they can make a decision.

We want to look at more houses

Uncertainty, lack of motivation or did you miss something during your initial buyers' interview? Figuring out which of these is the issue is going to be your challenge in dealing with this objection. The first question has to be directed at yourself. Did you ask enough questions, test the criteria they described and focus on finding out what they're really looking for? If there's a doubt in your mind, now's the time to sit down with your client and reaffirm that what you're showing them matches their criteria. It's extremely important that you review the Buyer's Questionnaire and confirm your understanding of what they want in a home.

"Mr. and Mrs. Buyer, can I ask you if the homes I'm showing you are really what you're looking for, or am I missing something?"

Once this possibility has been eliminated, your task is going to be to discover if the objection is due to a concern or a lack of motivation. And the only way to do this is to ask a direct question.

"Mr. and Mrs. Buyer, can I ask if there's something that you're unsure about in buying this property or are you rethinking buying at this point?"

If they're not sure the house is exactly what they want, then you can proceed to asking a closing question, which will help you determine how to deal with the concern.

Sharp Angle Question

"If we take some time to discuss what you like and don't like about this house, would that help clear things up for you and help you move forward?"

Feel, Felt, Found

"What I've found is that if we take some time to discuss what people like and don't like about the home, it generally helps clear things up for them. Would that help clear things up for you and help you move forward?"

However, if their motivation has changed, and they're no longer serious about purchasing a home at this time, you'll likely want to put them onto a drip marketing campaign and stop taking them out until they've recovered their interest.

No matter the objection, it's important to avoid getting into a back and forth exchange, trying to prove why the concern isn't valid. Taking the initial breath and acknowledging the fact that the client has a concern must always be the first step. Taking the time to make sure you understand exactly what their concern is will help you better gauge how best to deal with it. In order to avoid having more concerns pop up as you deal with one, ensure that there are no more objections other than the particular one with which you're dealing. And lastly, ask probing, meaningful open-ended questions to elicit the cause of the concern. And then listen to the answers you get, ask more questions and listen again. This will allow you to fully understand the objection and will give you the clues you need on how best to manage it.

Business Building Exercise

Role play your Objection Handling with a colleague for half an hour every day until you feel comfortable dealing with each objection.

CHAPTER 3

Negotiation 101

Say the word "Negotiation" and many people cringe. It can conjure up visions of two people sitting across a table from each other, each viciously trying to beat the other to a pulp to win a small concession. Not a pretty concept.

However, the reality is that we negotiate all the time; with our spouse, our kids, our coworkers and our clients just to name a few. Negotiation is about reaching a consensus, a compromise that's acceptable to all parties.

Unfortunately, many people see negotiation as a Win-Lose proposition. Who gets the biggest piece of the pie? How can I beat you into submission? This trend treats real estate negotiations as adversarial rather than competitive yet cooperative and creates a confrontational approach in which the parties end up feeling resentful, frustrated and dissatisfied with the experience and, ultimately, with the representatives on both sides. The losing party tends to feel their interests have not been looked after and their concerns ignored. This has the effect of creating a significant number of complaints and actions for commission recovery.

Negotiation must be viewed as a Win-Win proposition, a collaborative process, in which each party can achieve a result that's satisfactory to them. The question must be, "How can we work together and find common ground for both parties?"

Successful Negotiating = Good Planning

Being successful at negotiating is all about being prepared to negotiate. And good preparation is based on understanding the context and desired outcome of the negotiations as well as having and executing an effective game plan complete with specific strategies to achieve the desired outcomes.

Define the Context

Defining the context, or the circumstances that form the setting for an event, and the terms in which it can be fully understood and assessed is the first stage in preparing for negotiating. Whether it's buying or selling a home, having a firm understanding of the current market conditions is of critical importance. Is it a buyer's market, a seller's market or a balanced market? What's the current inventory and the absorption rate in the community? How do the renovations in the home affect the market value? These are some of the questions you'll need to wrestle with in order to have a grasp of the factors that will affect both the process and the outcome of the negotiation.

In preparing for negotiating, you'll want to obtain all the information you can about the home, the other agent, the other party and the neighbourhood. You must be able to support your assertion with relevant data such as market statistics, a complete and accurate CMA, historic data, renovation costs vs. recovery data, the number of months of inventory on the market and any trends which may be showing. Issues such as upcoming developments, like new condominium construction, traffic flow changes, zoning changes may all have an effect on the negotiation. Your ability to have these factors at hand during the negotiation will give you the opportunity to better understand not only your clients' position, but the other side's concerns and interests as well.

Define the Outcome

Before beginning to negotiate, establishing and understanding your clients' desired results is essential. What do they want to get from the negotiation? Is it all about price, or are there specific terms they're looking to achieve? Is there a specific closing date that they many need? There may be a laundry list of things they'd like to get, so it's always a good idea to make a list, in writing of all of their desires.

Next, have your clients prioritize the items in the list. They need to decide what their must haves are and what's negotiable. Prioritizing also means deciding what their ideal result is, what their "realistic one" is and what their bottom line is.

Set the Gameplan

Once you've defined what you're looking for out of the negotiation it's time to begin defining how you're going to achieve them. Prepare a scenario for the discussion, which will include anticipating the responses you might get and preparing answers.

When going into negotiations I would discuss, with my client, a plan of action based on the possible responses we might receive from the other party. Plan alternatives for any response. "If they offer this, then we can offer that."

It helps to understand what the client is willing to move on and what they'd like to get in return. It also helps to ask the client what it will cost them if they don't reach an agreement, as this can focus them on making sure the negotiations don't become confrontational and they work toward achieving the win-win for both sides.

Let the Negotiations Commence

One of the key factors in negotiating is being able to recognize and manage the communication styles of the other parties in the room. As discussed in Chapter 1, there are four communication styles, each requiring a different method of management.

Passive

Since passive communicators are inclined to use ambiguous language, when working on a negotiation with a passive communicator, your biggest challenge will be to draw out a precise response in order to fully understand the other side's position. You'll need to ask questions designed to probe further into each answer.

Aggressive

Aggressive communicators tend to attempt to hijack the negotiation and prevent the other side from expressing their interests or issues. You have two choices when dealing with them; you can either defuse the situation or ignite it. Through the use of some specific techniques, you may be able to turn the aggression into cooperation, and condescension into respect.

When dealing with aggressive communicators, it's important to try to deal with them one on one, outside the presence of others. Since aggressive communicators feel they need to appear to be in control of situations, and have an overwhelming desire to compete and win, avoiding disagreements with them in front of others, where they're more likely to be inflexible, will help defuse the situation.

You'll need to be assertive and professional in communicating with them. Clearly state what it is that you want/need/feel, without allowing yourself to get into a confrontation. Many difficult people respect those who communicate assertively and demonstrate strength without aggressiveness.

If there is an issue, avoid trying to work out a solution with them. The best method of dealing with issues is to go to them with solutions in mind, not just to discuss the problem. Difficult individuals are more willing to communicate and work with those who take the initiative and provide options.

Providing consequences to their actions is another valuable asset in "standing down" a difficult person. When properly presented, consequences can cause the aggressive person to pause and shift from taking an obstructive stance to one of cooperation.

"If we can't work this through, neither one of our clients is going to get what they really want. And that's really why we're here isn't it?"

Passive–Aggressive

Since passive-aggressive people get wrapped up in a lifestyle of never being straightforward, they may tend to carry on conversations which meander aimlessly and appear to have no real point. One of the reasons for this is that it is a means of acting out their frustration or disagreement with your position in a subtle or indirect way.

In order to deal with this during negotiations, it's your job to communicate back assertively and ask questions designed to get them on track and elicit the responses you need in order to move the negotiation forward.

"I'm sorry, but I'm afraid you've lost me. What is it you're getting at?"

"I'm sorry to interrupt, but I don't understand. I have a few questions before you continue."

"Hold on. I'm sorry, but I'm a little confused. In one sentence, what is it you want me to know?"

"That's all well and good, but before I make any promises or commitments, I need clarification in a few areas."

Assertive

Assertive communicators are the easiest people with whom to negotiate. Since assertive communicators clearly state their opinions and feelings during negotiations you'll never be in doubt as to where you stand.

When negotiating with an assertive person, express your needs clearly and directly. Stand up for what you believe your client needs and advocate effectively on their behalf. Offer options for handling problems work together to achieve consensus.

Focus on Interests not Positions

Roger Fisher and William Ury, in their book, *"Getting to Yes: How to Negotiate Agreement without Giving In"*, state that, "Your position is something you have decided upon. Your interests are what caused you to so decide." In positional bargaining, each side takes a position, argues for it, and makes concessions to reach a compromise. Unfortunately, this tends to produce agreements that may not meet the criteria of one party or the other, since when bargaining over positions, we tend to get locked into those positions and the more you defend that position against attack, the more committed you become to it. This ends up becoming a contest of wills and is inefficient as it usually takes a long time to reach agreement.

Rather than becoming entrenched in a position ("I have to get this much for the house."), try identifying what the other side is looking for in the transaction. What's most important to them;

price, location, amenities, a large yard, etc… This can easily be accomplished by asking the question, *"What's the most important thing you're looking for out of this transaction?" "Why is that so important to you?"*

Demonstrate that you understand the other side's situation and acknowledge their interests. This encourages the other side to be more responsive to your client's interests and needs.

Separate People from Problems

When negotiating, emotions, personalities and feelings can become interwoven with the substance of the negotiations themselves. People become so personally invested in the success of their assignment that they fail to separate the emotional and relationship issues from the substantive issues, such as the terms, dates, conditions or price, so it's very common for them to take responses to the issues as a personal attack.

In order to reduce this feeling, you must allow the other side to express their emotions but avoid reacting emotionally to their outbursts. In the event that the other party becomes aggressive or agitated, the use of symbolic gestures such as an expression of sympathy (nodding) can be used to defuse those strong emotions.

"You're obviously upset by this. Am I right? Tell me more about that."

"I hear what you're saying."

Put yourself in their place. Try to see the situation from the other side's perspective. While it's not necessary to agree with their position, understanding it is important.

One of the most frequent mistakes I see when people are in the midst of negotiations is assigning an intention to the other party that may actually be a reflection of the REALTOR®'s own fears.

"This guy's not calling me back. I think he's trying to force us into a multiple offer."

"She's not allowing me to present my offer in person. I think she wants to see what my offer is and bring in a better one of her own."

As human beings, it's natural for us to be suspicious, however, this sort of suspicious attitude makes it difficult to accurately gauge your opponent's real intentions; whatever they do you will assume the worst.

Don't play the blame game. Blaming your opponent will only make them more defensive and create a more significant roadblock to success.

Using the active listening techniques described in the previous chapter will help to ensure that you have a complete understanding of the issues, rather than just getting into a confrontation over them. Ask a question, listen carefully, not just to the answer, but to what's behind the answer and then ask more questions to elicit the deeper cause of the issue at hand. Summarize the speaker's points to confirm that you've correctly grasped their meaning.

"So, what I'm hearing you say is..."

Provide Options for Mutual Gain

One of the most effective means of reducing the likelihood of positional bargaining is to offer the other side options. This encourages flexibility and more open and reasonable discussions. All options should be considered – even unusual ones, as you never know what may appeal to the other side or create some discussion which could break a logjam. This could mean being willing to change possession dates, offer different terms or modify conditions. Don't be afraid to be creative. Look for options in which differences can be made compatible or complementary and are of low cost to you yet of high benefit to them.

Try to make proposals that would be appealing to the other side, since all parties to the negotiation need to be able to reconcile the agreement with their principles and self-image.

Use Objective Criteria not Emotion

Remove subjectivity from the negotiation, as the use of subjective information reduces the opportunity to dispute the facts and makes it easier for the parties to agree, since the facts reflect some fair standard instead of the arbitrary will of either side. When faced with some intransigence from the other party, ask questions designed to remove the emotion.

> *"I understand you feel this way, but let me ask you, what are you basing that on?"*

Establish your Bottom Line

What's the clients' worst acceptable outcome? Your client will need to decide, in advance of the actual negotiations, what they're willing to accept and at what point they'll reject any proposal below that line and walk away. The ability to walk away from negotiations if they don't ultimately meet the needs of the client is the ultimate power in a negotiation. However, in order to definitively identify that point, your client will need to understand their options. One of the important questions to ask your client, therefore, is what it will cost them if they don't reach an agreement.

It's about getting what they want

Ultimately, the purpose of the negotiation is to get what the client wants. Occasionally, agents lose sight of that fact and when they do, negotiations become bogged down in positional bargaining and end up going off track. Remember, it's not about how good you are, your success rate or your ego, it's about the client and your commitment to the client's best interests, to getting the deal done with a win – win result.

Make the Other Side Look Good

One of the key factors in negotiation is building a relationship with the other party. It's much easier to achieve a successful outcome with someone with whom you have a good relationship. Making the other side and the other agent look good goes a long way to establishing yourself as someone with whom people will want to do business. Always show respect and understanding for the other party.

Time equals Money

Patience, Patience, Patience. Negotiations sometimes take time and patience to achieve the best win-win situation possible. It's important to take the time needed to work on a deal and to give people time to think, rather than trying to get things done as quickly as possible.

Many years ago, I had an expensive condominium listed for sale. We received an offer on it that was lower than what the seller was going to accept, so he countered the offer. The buyer then countered that and we went back and forth for a couple of days. It looked like we weren't going to be able to put the deal together. About two or three days later, the other REALTOR® and I met and discussed some possible solutions including changing the way the financing was structured, some of the terms and eventually came away with a deal we believed our clients would agree to, and they did. After almost two weeks of negotiating, we were able to get the unit sold at a price and for the terms that, while they may not have been ideal for either party, allowed them both to get what they ultimately wanted. Sometimes, you've just got to slow down and let time work for you.

Participation

When people feel that they haven't been heard, allowed to participate or don't feel involved in the negotiation, it tends to create a lack of interest in the outcome. This, of course, creates a lack of commitment to the negotiation process and ultimately to a poor outcome. Giving your opponent a stake in the outcome by making sure they participate in the negotiation process makes it more likely that they'll feel that the process is, in part their process and are therefore more likely to accept its conclusion.

Negotiation Pointers

The following list contains some basic pointers for you to use when going into negotiations. It is a combination of negotiating skills and just plain good manners. While it may seem a little simplistic, it is designed to provide you with a basic framework upon which to build successful negotiations.

1. Always try to present or allow the other side to present the offer in person.
2. Face the other person.
3. Look them in the eyes when speaking to them.
4. Use a good voice tone (not too loud or whiny).
5. Use appropriate facial expressions.
6. Use good body posture (straight or relaxed).
7. Use active listening skills.

8. Ask for what you want.
9. State the reason you want it.
10. Thank the other person if he or she agrees to the request.
11. Suggest a compromise if he or she doesn't agree.
12. Thank them if the person agrees with your compromise.
13. Ask the other person for a solution if he or she does not agree with the compromise.
14. Say thanks if you agree with the other person's solution.
15. Suggest a different idea and keep on negotiating if you don't like the other person's solution.
16. If you need time to think about a solution, ask for it. Also ask the other person when you can talk with him or her again.

Case Studies

These case studies reinforce the concepts discussed in this chapter and will help you better understand the possible solutions. Take some time, and discuss them with colleagues, to see the possible solutions

Case Study 1

- Sellers - John and Marie S.
- Buyers – Mark and Sue K.
- They are in multiple offers.
- Mark and Sue have the highest priced offer but have included an inspection condition. They definitely want the home but want to make sure there's no major issue before finalizing the offer.

- John and Marie like the price but they want the home sold.
- There's another offer that has no conditions, but the price and terms are not as attractive.

Case Study 2

- Sellers – Zbignew and Rena W.
- Buyers – Margaret P.
- The home is priced $35,000 above the closest competitor.
- Margaret has offered $15,000 below the closest competitor, with conditions of financing, inspection and a review by the buyer's lawyer.
- She has asked for a closing date in 90 days.
- The sellers have countered $5,000 below their list price.

What are some options?

Take some time to review the possible options open to you in each of the case studies and then turn the page to see how you did. Discuss these scenarios with your broker or manager and see if they have other options as well.

Options

Case Study 1

1. Offer more money and shorten the condition days
    - This makes the offer more attractive to the sellers but costs the buyers more money.
    - It still protects the buyers from potential inspection issues.
2. Remove the condition from the offer
    - This keeps the money the same but the buyers lose the protection of the inspection
3. Offer the same money but include the "buyer will eat" clause (see page 247)
    - This still protects the buyer
    - The sellers get the amount they want and assurance that, unless there's something drastically wrong with the home, everything should go fine.

Case Study 2

As the Buyer's Representative

1. Use objective criteria not emotion
    - Use current statistics to validate the price being offered
    - This will reduce the discussion to a purely objective level
    - Review the stats with the listing agent to reach mutual agreement on the validity of the statistics
    - Avoid getting into nit-picking about specific comparables. You're looking for mutual agreement.

2. Focus on interests, not positions
    - What does the seller really want?
    - How can you adjust the offer to meet their needs?
3. Provide Options for Mutual Gain
    - Eliminate one or more of the conditions
    - Modify the closing date to better suit the sellers
4. Be prepared to walk away if the conclusion doesn't fit your clients' needs

As the Seller's Representative

1. Provide Options for Mutual Gain
    - Try to find a closing date better suited to the sellers' needs
2. Use Objective criteria not emotion
    - Review the stats with the buyer's agent to reach mutual agreement on the validity of the statistics and then use them to assist in educating the seller
    - Ask questions of the seller to eliminate their emotional viewpoint

"This is the best offer we have right now, isn't it?"

"We don't have any other offers, do we?"

"So, since this is the best offer / only offer we've received, isn't the market telling you that this is what the property's worth?"

"If we can get this deal done, that will help you move into that new home you want, won't it?"

CHAPTER 4

Get the Word Out

It's all about marketing, and marketing is all about having systems in place. Your marketing system must be structured so that nothing is overlooked and you have taken full advantage of every opportunity to market yourself.

Marketing and advertising are two very different aspects of your marketing strategy, but work alongside each other to help you spread the word about your services and build your name and face recognition.

We'll discuss both components in this chapter, but before we get there, let's define the two terms. Marketing is a long term, consistently applied strategy, designed to put your name or brand in front of a selected group of potential clients in order to create awareness, face and name recognition. Think of Home Depot sponsoring a NASCAR racing team. Now, car racing obviously has nothing to do with home renovations; however, by sponsoring the team, Home Depot gets their brand in front of more people than they could ever do just by running ads on TV or in the print media.

Advertising, on the other hand, is designed to promote a specific product or service and to encourage or persuade an audience to continue, or to take some action, such as buying that product.

Branding. It's a word very much in vogue right now. Experts will tell you to make sure you brand yourself, that your brand will be the thing that people will remember and that your brand will speak to your market. And to a certain extent, they're right. Before going any further though, I think it's critical to define what a brand is.

A brand, simply put, is the way you state that "This is MINE!" It's come to mean the commercial identity of a specific product, service or business, which has been designed to convey and create awareness of the virtues of working with or buying the product or service. A brand can be conveyed in many ways. It can be a logo, such as Nike's Swoosh or Starbucks' twin-tailed mermaid logo. It can be a slogan like Subway's "Eat Fresh". In either case, it's a means of differentiating the product or service from other similar products or services.

One of the frequent questions I get is whether a new Sales Representative should try to brand themselves right from the start. In real estate, the large franchise companies have spent millions of dollars and countless hours of manpower to define how they're different from each other.

It's my opinion that new salespeople should, at the beginning, take maximum advantage of the brand of the company for which they work, rather than spending the time and money it takes to develop one for themselves. With very few exceptions, new salespeople haven't had the time or gained the experience to decide which stream of real estate they plan on following. However, this shouldn't preclude them from working towards differentiating themselves from the other REALTORS® with whom they'll be competing.

When designing a marketing strategy, the first four questions a REALTOR® should ask themselves are:

- WHY should you Market yourself?
- WHAT do you want to Market?
- WHO is your Target Market?
- HOW should you Market it?

Why should you market yourself?

The simple answer is to develop and then increase your presence in the marketplace. But deeper than that, it is to create a long term, consistently applied strategy, designed to put your name in front of a selected group of potential clients in order to create awareness, face and name recognition.

So, how do you do that? A complete marketing plan is a five step process including:

- Identify & Define your Brand
- Establish a Marketing Strategy
- Establish a Marketing Budget
- Initiate your Marketing Strategy
- Track your Results and Adjust

Identify & Define your Brand

The first step is to identify and define your brand. What do you want your brand to convey to the public? Think of the characteristics you want your brand to convey, for example, how will you provide value to the public? Understanding that value is better defined as the market's perception of the benefits received for what's given, in other words, what's in it for me (WIIFM). Without a strong perception of value in the public's mind, it's unlikely a strong relationship can be built.

In the first chapter, you were asked to write a statement defining the characteristics of your business that you want the public to see; your Mission Statement. This will become a defining component of your marketing plan. Next, determine how you will interact with prospects and clients to convey those traits.

Your next task will be to identify your "Competitive Positioning Strategy or Value Proposition". This is how you'll "differentiate" yourself from other REALTORS and create value for your market. You'll need to determine where you can focus on your competition's vulnerable spots and identify services you can offer to meet the unmet needs of your market in a new and better way. This is best accomplished by doing some market research. Get out into your farm and meet people. You're going to have to do that as part of your prospecting anyway, so why not now? Ask them what kind of services they would like to see from a REALTOR®. Were they satisfied the last time they used a REALTOR®? What do they think was missing from the service?

Establish a Marketing Strategy

Who will buy? Why should they buy? And even more importantly, why should they buy from YOU?? These are the key questions you need to ask yourself when planning your marketing strategy.

Define your Target Market

The first of those questions will lead to you your next step, that of defining your target market. Deciding on who your target market will be will include an analysis of the market profile in the area, including the size of the market, whether it's growing or decreasing in size, the demographics, and any opportunities you can use to grow your presence. You'll also need to find out who your competitors are, their market share, and the services they provide. When considering the target market, put yourself in their place. What are they looking for? What's important to them? What are their general needs and wants? How do they think?

When deciding on who to target, you must also take into account the many different groups within a community, such as Generation

Y (also known as Millennials), Baby Boomers (50's – 70's), seniors, and new Canadians and understand what's important to each.

How to reach them

The second phase of defining your target market is how you will reach them. You'll need to understand how each group communicates and then devise a strategy that meets the needs of each. For example, we know that people in the Gen Y age group prefer communicating through social media and mobile devices, Boomers prefer electronic media such as TV, radio, email and Facebook while seniors prefer word of mouth educational seminars and workshops, print media such as newspapers, flyers and through networking.

Depending on your target market, your marketing program may rely on more traditional strategies, such as billboards, buses and bus benches, print media, flyers or newsletters, or it may rely more on non-traditional methods like outbound marketing, such as email, inbound marketing strategies, such as landing pages and online ads, social media or it may be a mix of traditional and non-traditional methods. You'll need to assess the requirements of your market and set a plan to meet those needs.

What do I say?

Phase three is to determine what you will say to your target market. Your goal is to meet their needs by identifying the unique needs of your potential audience and look for ways to tailor your product or service to meet them. Next, it's important to say the right thing, to "speak their language". To accomplish this, you'll need to understand the market's "hot buttons", the issues which are the most important to them and then ensure that you communicate with them as an understanding member - not an outsider.

When do I say it?

Establish a yearly marketing plan. This is a written overview of the marketing strategy you plan on using. It should specify each type of marketing being used, when each message is to be sent and how and should be tailored to match your desired target market's communication styles.

EVENTS						
	PRINT MEDIA	DATABASE	WEBINARS / SEMINARS	TRADE SHOWS	FACEBOOK ADS	CARDS
JAN	NEWSLETTERS (DATABASE) FLYERS (FARM)	"A" LIST LUNCH ANNIVERSARY CARDS	JAN. 15 - FIRST TIME BUYERS WEBINAR		HAPPY NEW YEAR	HAPPY NEW YEAR BIRTHDAYS
FEB	NEWSLETTERS (DATABASE) FLYERS (FARM)	"A" LIST LUNCH ANNIVERSARY CARDS	FEB. 19 - LIST IT TO SELL WEBINAR	WOMEN'S SHOW	START THE YEAR OFF RIGHT	BIRTHDAYS
MAR	NEWSLETTERS (DATABASE) FLYERS (FARM)	"A" LIST LUNCH ANNIVERSARY CARDS	MAR. 16 - FIRST TIME INVESTORS SEMINAR	HOME & GARDEN SHOW	EASTER GREETINGS	EASTER BIRTHDAYS
APR	NEWSLETTERS (DATABASE) FLYERS (FARM)	"A" LIST LUNCH ANNIVERSARY CARDS	APR. 16 - BUYING YOUR DREAM HOME WEBINAR		SPRING CLEAN UP	BIRTHDAYS
MAY	NEWSLETTERS (DATABASE) FLYERS (FARM)	"A" LIST LUNCH ANNIVERSARY CARDS	MAY 21 - COTTAGE BUYING WEBINAR	RENOVATION SHOW	MOTHER'S DAY	MOTHERS' DAY BIRTHDAYS
JUN	NEWSLETTERS (DATABASE) FLYERS (FARM)	"A" LIST LUNCH ANNIVERSARY CARDS	BBQ @ COMMUNITY HALL JUN. 18 - SUMMER SAFETY WEBINAR		KIDS OUT OF SCHOOL	FATHERS' DAY BIRTHDAYS
JUL	NEWSLETTERS (DATABASE) FLYERS (FARM)	"A" LIST LUNCH ANNIVERSARY CARDS	NO WEBINARS		NONE	BIRTHDAYS
AUG	NEWSLETTERS (DATABASE) FLYERS (FARM)	"A" LIST LUNCH ANNIVERSARY CARDS	AUG. 20 - BACK TO SCHOOL WEBINAR	C.N.E.	BE READY FOR BACK TO SCHOOL	RAMADAN / EID BIRTHDAYS
SEP	NEWSLETTERS (DATABASE) FLYERS (FARM)	"A" LIST LUNCH ANNIVERSARY CARDS	SEP. 21 - FIRST TIME INVESTORS SEMINAR		FALL CLEAN UP	ROSH HASHANAH BIRTHDAYS
OCT	NEWSLETTERS (DATABASE) FLYERS (FARM)	"A" LIST LUNCH ANNIVERSARY CARDS	CLIENT APPRECIATION EVENT OCT. 15 - HALLOWEEN WEBINAR		HALLOWEEN	THANKSGIVING (CA) BIRTHDAYS
NOV	NEWSLETTERS (DATABASE) FLYERS (FARM)	"A" LIST LUNCH ANNIVERSARY CARDS	NOV. 19 - WINTER TUNE UP WEBINAR		PREP FOR CHRISTMAS	CALENDARS BIRTHDAYS
DEC	NEWSLETTERS (DATABASE) FLYERS (FARM)	"A" LIST LUNCH ANNIVERSARY CARDS	NO WEBINAR		MERRY CHRISTMAS	CHRISTMAS CHANUKAH

Establish Your Marketing Budget

Unless you've had previous experience in marketing, this can be one of the most difficult issues to decide on as a new REALTOR®. A frequently asked question is "How much money should I be spending on my marketing?" And the answer to that is just as difficult. It depends on what you're trying to accomplish. During the early years you should expect to spend more on start-up marketing than you will later in your career, but that will also depend on your marketing strategy. In order to attract new prospects and retain current customers a good rule of thumb, but not an absolute, is to expect to spend around 4 - 5% of your projected gross revenue on marketing. However, this will vary depending on many factors, such as the overall type of marketing, the frequency of the marketing, the target market, the medium being used and other elements of the marketing plan.

Another frequent question many new Sales Representatives wrestle with is that of whether it's more effective to market to a large area or to run a niche marketing campaign. In order to best address this, let's take a look at the difference between the two. Mass marketing gives you the opportunity to communicate with the largest possible audience, and generally involves the use of mass media, such as TV or a massive flyer campaign. It's like throwing a net into the ocean and hoping to get a lot of the right fish. It can be expensive but may result in a larger number of leads. Niche marketing, on the other hand, focuses on marketing to a small group of people. It's generally less expensive and uses more personal marketing techniques, such as warm calls, flyers, doorknocking and others. It can be compared to fly fishing, where you select the lure and the location and then patiently draw in the fish you want to catch. So, the type of marketing you choose to use will depend on the effect and type of market you want to attract.

Get it going

The next step is to get your marketing up and running. In order to accomplish that you'll need to follow the Marketing Plan and budget you established earlier to the letter. Your marketing must be consistent in the content, the message and the timing. You need to consistently provide the public with information that is valuable to them, has the same message so they get to know who you are and what you stand for and that they can expect to receive at the same time. That lets them know that you're knowledgeable, concerned about what's important to them and reliable.

How am I doing?

The final step in successful marketing is to track your results and adjust your plan based on those results. All too often REALTORS send out marketing pieces and don't bother to find out from where they're getting their leads. Tracking allows you to ensure that you're spending time and money on the most effective marketing model possible.

When you get leads, ask them where they heard about you and enter that information into a database. Keep client records and track how the client heard about you and what prompted them to call. You need to know what parts of the plan are effective and working for you and what components aren't. Every quarter take some time and review your data. This will allow you to modify your plan as indicated. For example, if your flyer campaign worked very well, why wait until next year to do it again? If the results were poor, you can re-evaluate the process now.

If the results were not what you hoped for, rather than scrapping the entire plan, take a look at the components of the marketing piece. There are three elements that you'll need to analyze.

The first one is the content; what you said and how you said it. Was it appropriate for the target market and did it speak to their needs and wants?

The next factor is the medium. How did you deliver your message? Did you use the most effective medium for the target market?

And the final component is the follow up. Was the follow up as effective as it could be? Did you get back to people in the optimum period of time? Did you qualify them thoroughly?

Business Building Exercise

By this point you should have already determined who your target market will be; that will be your farm. Your business building exercise is to **plan the marketing you're going to use for the balance of the year to develop your name and face recognition in your farm. Set up your Yearly Marketing Plan and keep it where you can see it on an ongoing basis.**

Advertising

Advertising is an activity designed to promote a specific product or service and to encourage or persuade an audience to continue to act or take some new action. In real estate its purposes are to:

- Sell the property
- Create interest in genuine buyers
- Develop buyers for other properties through ad calls
- Help win listings, and
- Increase repeat and referral business

When planning the marketing for a property, there are a series of practises which must be taken into consideration. This chapter will review those practices with an eye to producing a series of advertisements designed to achieve each of these purposes.

Preparation

In most current real estate ads, a home is described according to its features. It is, however, a basic tenet in marketing that people purchase an item, not because of what it does, but because they can see themselves using it. When describing a feature of a home it is extremely important to describe the benefits of the feature, rather than just the feature itself. The description must be tangible; the audience must be able to feel it and see themselves using it, even if it's only in their imagination.

There's another basic tenet of advertising that states that people buy products or services on emotion and then justify the purchase with logic. Think of your car. Why did you buy it? For a great many people, it was purchased because they liked the look, how they felt driving it and how it looked in their self-image. And then they justified that with things like the fact that they needed it because they had to have room for all the kids, it had great mileage, it was a safer car, and many more concepts. But let's be honest, people buy a specific car because the ad appealed to their emotion enough that they went out to look at it and then the new car smell took over. The Institute of Practitioners in Advertising in the UK found that ads with mixed emotional and rational content performed significantly better than those that had only rational content.

When trying to describe the benefit of a feature, define the property as if talking to a friend or relative. They must feel the experience of living there themselves and there must be an emotion attached to it so that the buyer is able to see themselves enjoying what that product can do for them. For example, a "large backyard" can become "Imagine yourself playing catch with the kids in your large, safe backyard." Here's some features of a home.

Spend some time free-flowing some ideas to find two or three benefits for each feature.

Large backyard	Granite Countertops	Stainless steel appliances
Bungalow w/ 3 + 1 bedrooms and 3 bathrooms	4 piece ensuite bath	
Oversized 2 car garage	Unfinished basement	Small deck off family room
Treed backyard	Near school & park	Galley style kitchen

Once you've determined that, you need to write a separate ad for each group. It makes no sense to write an ad targeted at both the first-time buyer and the investor, since these two groups have very different needs and wants and a single ad can't cover the goals of both.

Creativity

Consistency in the ads is extremely important, as every ad for the same property should have the same appearance, layout, content and message. When designing the ad, one technique that greatly increases the writer's ability to be creative is to use a free flow of ideas, avoiding thinking logically. Use flow diagrams to help you develop your ideas.

Don't think about why not to use a description (no self-editing). In other words, when thinking about a feature such as a backyard, the following words may come to mind; play, safe, trees, hockey rink, grass, children, BBQ, catch, dog. By using this free flow of ideas, you can then develop concepts to produce tangible benefits which can be featured in the ad and can be used for headlines or content.

Use the benefits you discovered in the examples above and add an emotion to the benefit. Think of how that benefit might create an emotion in a potential buyer and inspire them to act.

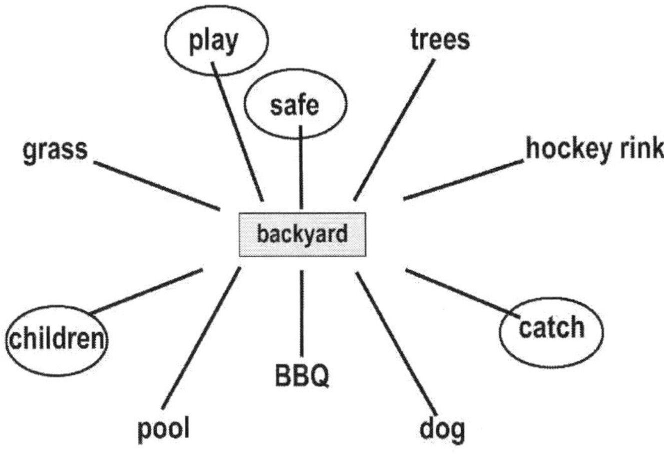

Free Flow Diagram

Target the Right People

Who's your target market? People approach a home purchase from many different angles. An investor will look at the benefits of owning a home in a far different way than a first-time buyer. And yet we see many ads that are written claiming that a home is perfect for an investor or a first-time home buyer. When writing ads, it makes no sense to write an ad that tries to appeal to different potential buyers. You need to take some time and decide to whom your ad should appeal.

When defining your target market, try to describe them with as much detail as you can. To do this you must have an understanding of who they are. You have to put yourself in their place; what are they looking for? What's important to them? What are their needs and wants? And how do they think?

And then create ads that are consistent. Every ad for the same target for the same property should have the same:

- Appearance and Layout
- Content and Message
- Location in the media being used

Knowledge of the Property

When writing an ad, you must become familiar with the property and the community in order to put yourself in the buyers' shoes. Since the people most familiar with these are the sellers, it only makes sense to ask the sellers questions about the property such as: What was it that made them buy? What did they love about the home when they bought it? What do they love about it now? What would they change given the opportunity? What will they miss the most?

Since part of the Pre-listing Package is the Seller's Questionnaire which includes these questions, the answers can be used to create the ads for the home. However, this alone is not enough. You'll also need to research the area to find out about the amenities such as shopping, recreation, schools, transit as well as the service people in the area like doctors, dentists, vets and others. When writing ads, it's important to have as much knowledge as you possibly can.

Structure of the Ad

Any ad you write should have a consistent structure, composed of the following three components.

Headline

The headline must attract the attention of the buyer. It must contain one or more benefit or implied benefit, something new or a curiosity element - a "Huh?" factor. It must also relate to the body of the ad. Studies show that as few as one in five people read past the headline and that you have about seven words and three seconds to get their attention or the ballgame's over! The headline MUST capture the readers' imagination and interest.

As well as tying into the body of the ad, the headline should also tie into the first line of the ad and be reinforced at the end of the ad, as shown below.

"A backyard made for games"

You'll love being able to play catch with the kids in your safe, fenced backyard. This great home, in a quiet cul de sac, offers 3 bedrooms on the main floor, perfect for everyone, especially Mom and Dad, to enjoy some privacy in their own room. Family dinners will be a real pleasure in the generous dining room, with pass-through to the amazing kitchen. ... So, if you can see your family enjoying the luxury of a large, safe backyard, I'd love to show you this home..."

Picture

All too often we see ads with the same boring picture of the front of the house. Only one in five people read past the headline. You have about seven words and three seconds to get their attention or the ballgame's over!

Much like the headline of an ad, the picture must also grab the readers' interest. The headline and the picture must tie in with each other with the picture being visually interesting. If the headline is interesting, why use a boring picture? Include people and pets in your ads. The use of a visually interesting picture that ties into the headline and the body of the ad enables the reader to get a more personal concept of the home, provides warmth, character and allows potential buyers to "see" themselves in the home.

For example, this photo is a sample of the typical picture of a home shown on the MLS®. This home was perfect for investors, close to transit and the downtown core and had never had a vacancy over the 5 years the sellers had owned it. This photo conveys nothing specific or interesting about the home that would indicate its value to investors.

However, with a little creativity and an appropriate headline, the photo of the home was made to stand out from the others and create some interest in the investment community.

Put Some Money in Your Jeans

The headline must also tie into the first line of the ad and must also be reinforced at the end of the ad in the call to action.

Message with a Definite Call to Action

The message of the ad must focus on the benefits of living in the home, not simply the features. The ad should be written as a one-to-one communication with the reader and should evoke an emotion in the reader. It should also flow in a logical sequence; as though you were guiding a tour of the home from the front door to the back yard.

Use active words, not fluff or descriptive adjectives like beautiful, cozy, and wonderful to describe the home. Avoid the use of jargon, words that only someone in the real estate industry would understand. Use plain layman's terms to avoid confusing the readers. It's also advisable to avoid using abbreviations, which may interrupt the flow of the communication.

When I first started in real estate, I was taught never to include the price in an ad, so that I could get more people calling. What I found was that the vast majority of people who called tended to be tire kickers and people who couldn't qualify for a home. Subsequent research has shown that 58% of buyers will not call if the price is not shown in the ad.

In order to get buyers to call, it's necessary to include a clear and directed call to action. This means that, instead of having a statement like *"For more information, call…"*, the call to action must use "Me" statements, i.e. *"If you want to put more money in your jeans and would like a private showing of this perfect investment property, Call me Now!"*

Business Building Exercise

Find two or three properties in your local real estate magazine, look them up on MLS and re-write the ads using the information you learned here.

And Now, The End is Near…

Now that we've reached the end of the series your real journey begins. You've read about how important it is to develop your business plan.

In **"On the Right Foot",** we discussed Business Planning, Time Management, Financial Management, Client Management and Real Estate Etiquette.

Your Business Plan is the road map that will help guide you along the route to success. You've read how to use the business plan to map out the paths you'll need to strategically follow to achieve each of the goals you've set for yourself. It outlines the tools you already have that you can use to build your business as well as the training you'll need to polish your existing skills and develop new ones. The business plan contains your guiding principles, your Life Purpose, and the message you want to bring to your community about how you plan on doing business, your Mission Statement.

You know how many transactions you'll need to have to achieve the income goal you set for yourself, where those transactions will come from and how many of each you'll want to make in order to reach your target. But, don't forget that a plan is only as good as the execution. It's a road map and you can choose to follow it or not.

You've read how to build your business by defining who should be on your sphere of influence, the group of people you're going to rely on to refer other people to you. And you've spent some time developing that list, contacted them and have pared it down to your final referral team.

The next step is to find the businesses with whom you already do business and develop a cross-promotion strategy with them.

Organization is the foundation of any system. In real estate, organization begins with managing your time. As independent contractors it's far too easy to believe that, since we work for ourselves, we can work when we choose. We can fall into the trap of not keeping ourselves on track and on time and suffer both financially and personally.

But, by understanding the potential time vampires and how to avoid them and by setting up and following a schedule that ensures you do what needs to be done, when it needs to be done, you can greatly improve your chances of reaching the goals you set for yourself. As part of that schedule, you'll need to make sure you've prioritized the most important aspects of your business and got them scheduled first thing in the day. Remember, Eat That Frog!

Another often overlooked aspect of the business is having a system to organize and manage your finances. In Volume 1, you read about how to set up a basic accounting system. I would, however, strongly suggest that a consultation with an accountant would be something you may want to consider.

Now that you've defined your sphere of influence and built some strategic alliances, it's time to make sure you stay in regular contact with them and get them working to help you build your business. You've read about, and should have set up, your Referral Management System.

Without a doubt, the most effective and the most important method of prospecting is to mobilize your sphere of influence. Remember, it's not about getting them to buy or sell, it's about getting them to consistently think of, and refer to, you when they know of, or meet, anyone else who's thinking of buying or selling real estate or who may have a question about real estate.

Everything you do in maintaining contact with your sphere of influence must be targeted at maintaining top of mind presence with them.

Which brings me to prospecting. You can ride the real estate roller coaster or you can have a steady, predictable and reproducible income. You can make as much as you want, or you can struggle and make as little as you choose. It's all about choice. And that choice is to either prospect or not.

In **"Good Hunting"**, you read about the various types of prospecting techniques, the mindset required to be successful at it and how to overcome the three main causes of resistance to prospecting; fear, inertia and projection. You've read how to be both a hunter gatherer and a farmer. One of the most important long-term prospecting activities is determining and maintaining a farm. This is an activity which will, in the first few years, result in minimal, if any, actionable leads, but you must go into this activity with a long-term plan to become the best known and most knowledgeable REALTOR® in the area. Remember, you're building long-term relationships.

We reviewed the many different active forms that prospecting may take, including making warm calls around just listed or just sold properties, door-knocking, Open Houses, converting For Sale By Owners, networking, trade shows, and participating in client and community events. You've had a chance to review and modify the scripts so that they sound like you. We discussed the concept of providing value to the prospect before asking them to take some action.

Lead generation is just the beginning of the process in growing a business. Follow up is a critical component of a complete prospecting system. Without a complete and organized lead follow up system, the leads you generate will amount to nothing. A complete lead follow up system includes being able to efficiently complete a tracking form that provides you with information that will allow you to determine who you want to work with and how motivated they are. It should enable you to follow up with leads rapidly, effectively and to set them up on a program that keeps you in touch with them until they're ready to act.

"Listings, Listings, Listings" described how the ability to obtain listing appointments is one of the ultimate goals of your prospecting system. Your listing system should include a pre-listing package that you can send to people who are thinking of selling, so that they're introduced to you and that differentiates you from other REALTORS® before they actually meet with you. Your listing presentation must be able to demonstrate, to the potential client, that you're able to provide them with the value they're seeking and what they feel is important, not what you believe your value is. Provide that value and you'll win more appointments. It's also designed to provide enough information to the client to overcome most of their concerns and reduce the objections you'll need to manage.

You've seen how important it is to have a highly organized listing system in place that ensures you follow a consistent process for every listing. Your system thereby reduces or eliminates the possibility of missing any steps throughout the entire sales cycle.

Offer management is a key component of a well-constructed listing system. The management of offers, both single and multiple, can easily become disorganized and chaotic without a standardized method of handling the many aspects of what can be a complex procedure.

Your listing system should help you continue to provide outstanding service to your sellers once conditions have been removed. It should also include a system to ensure that the transition period between the final sale and the move goes smoothly and that the sellers have the information they need so that each step leading up to the move is clearly defined. It must also include a strategy to prospect for more listings using the existing one.

In **"Buyers, Buyers, Buyers"** you read about the different buyer demographics and what the average buyer in each is looking for when purchasing a home. Your buyer system should include questions that will help you determine what your client is looking for, what type of buyer they are and should help you narrow down their needs and wants. It should also allow you to review the properties for which they're looking and help you find them the right property in the least amount of time.

As with managing listings, your offer management system for your buyer should enable you to protect your client's interests while obtaining the property with the least amount of difficulty. Your post-sale system must be designed to maintain communication with your clients, not only until the property closes, but beyond that in order to ensure they become part of your referral network.

And in this Volume, you read that handling objections will be a critical skill you'll need to develop. Using the BASIQ technique will enable you to quickly and easily determine what the true objection is and by asking the right questions and listening carefully to the answers you'll have the opportunity to understand what the client's concern is and, even more, how to handle it.

The major source of complaints against REALTORS® can, in most cases, be traced back to a lack of communication or a miscommunication that was never resolved. Communication goes far beyond the simple exchange of words or the transfer of information from one person to another. In order to successfully and effectively communicate with your clients, your ongoing task will be to grasp the combination of information, the intention behind the transfer and the non-verbal part of communication being transmitted to you. You'll also have to ensure the client is able to clearly hear and understand the information you're providing. You'll need to ask open ended questions to find out the deeper meaning and clarify that what you've heard is actually what the speaker intended to say. Remember the iceberg; you only hear a very small part of what the client is actually trying to transmit.

Negotiation can be a very disconcerting experience if you're not prepared for it. You'll encounter many instances where you'll need to work hard for a win-win resolution. But by keeping that concept in the forefront, you'll find that you'll ultimately be far more successful than those with a win-lose mentality. Preparation is the key to any negotiation. A well-prepared negotiator has a good understanding of the context and desired outcome of the negotiations. They have and can execute an effective game plan, complete with specific strategies to achieve the desired outcomes.

The main keys to successful negotiation are to focus on interests not positions, to separate people from problems and use objective criteria not emotion. Providing options for mutual gain, making the other side look good and allowing them to participate will encourage more cooperation from the other side during the negotiations and help work towards that win-win result. However, in the event that negotiations don't move smoothly to a resolution acceptable to your client, it's imperative that you've established your bottom line so that you have the ultimate power in negotiation, the ability to walk away from it.

Marketing and advertising are two important components of your marketing strategy. They are, however, distinct from each other. Your marketing strategy must be a long term, consistently applied approach, designed to put your name or brand in front of a selected group of potential clients in order to create awareness, face and name recognition. However, advertising is designed to promote a specific property or service and to encourage or persuade an audience to take some action, such as buying that property or service.

As with any other system, you must have your marketing strategy planned out for the year so that you don't miss any component or spend money where you needn't. A well planned marketing strategy will ensure that your clients and target audience think of you whenever they, or anyone they know, may be thinking about buying or selling a property.

When advertising a property, try to place yourself in the mind of the potential buyer. Be creative and avoid the trap of doing the same thing everyone else is. Your ads must appeal to the buyer. Your headline must create an interest or surprise the reader. It must tie in to the picture you're using. Your picture must have something different in it rather than just the front of the property. Remember, you have about seven words or three seconds to get their attention or they've moved on to the next ad.

When writing your ad, you need to decide who you're trying to reach; you have to define a specific target market. And then you have to write an ad directed specifically at them. Define the benefits of living in the home and let the buyers know what they are. People buy on emotion and you need to be able to appeal to that emotion to get them to act. You also need to tell them to act, so your ads must have a clear and sharp call to action.

And so, this brings everything to a close. If you haven't worked your way through the business building exercises in **Volume 6 - Workbook** as you've gone along, now is the time to complete them. It may seem like a lot of stuff to do, but, by completing them now, at the beginning of your career, it will ensure that you have the systems and procedures in place, as well as the start of the skills and knowledge you'll need, to succeed faster, with less errors and less money wasted. I wish you nothing but success!

FOUNDATIONS FOR SUCCESS

WORKBOOK

Business Building Exercises, Scripts, Checklists and Systems

BUSINESS BUILDING EXERCISES

"One of life's most painful moments comes when we must admit that we didn't do our homework, that we are not prepared."

Merlin Olsen

BUSINESS BUILDING EXERCISES

The steps you'll find in this workbook are designed to help you move forward in developing your systems, skills and confidence. They are divided according to specific time frames and highlighted to help you achieve those goals as efficiently as possible.

While still allowing you time to put the information into practise, they have been carefully structured to ensure you are able to develop the basic systems you'll need to have to ensure predictable, reproducible and consistent results. The foundations for success are all included here and, if you follow them, will provide you with an easy to follow road map to get you through what is generally the most difficult time for new salespeople.

On top of everything included here, try to attend as much training as you can fit into your schedule. Don't just attend sales related sessions. It's important to be a sponge and absorb as much information as you can about as many other topics as you can. You never know when something may come in handy.

One of the best ways to find out how to be successful is to hang around other successful agents. Just hang around and listen. Buy them a coffee and ask them how they got there. And listen. I remember when I was just starting in the business. I was almost broke and was getting to the point that I was seriously questioning whether this was really what I wanted to do or not. One of the more successful agents in our office and I happened to go out for a coffee. I'll never forget the story he told me of when he was at the same point in his career and how just doing what needed to be done consistently paid off for him. It made a huge impact and was something I tried to focus on from that point on.

Take the opportunity to sit in on conferences and seminars, like Richard Robbins' Secrets of the Masters, Brian Buffini's Success Tour and Mike Ferry's Action Workshops. Think about getting a coach, like Bruce Keith. The knowledge and skill development and accountability that having a great coach brings to the table will be career changing.

However, don't let the training distract you from completing the assignments you'll find here on time. This is the foundations for your long-term success that you're building.

WEEK 1

1. Create your Life Purpose Statement

Remember, this is going to be the ultimate goal for your life; what you want your legacy to be and how you want to be remembered.

Expect that this particular exercise may take you more than the first two weeks, so don't wait until you've completed this to move on to the next exercise.

My Life Purpose Statement

2. Develop your Mission Statement

This will be what you want the outside world, including your sphere of influence and potential clients to think of when they think of your services. I generally suggest that you think of four to six key words that describe what you believe to be your greatest customer service strengths. Then create a paragraph that uses these words as key components, for example:

"To consistently provide professional, ethical and dependable real estate services to my clients and to ensure the integration of my core values of service, flexibility, dedication, enthusiasm, and integrity into that service."

My Key Words

____

____

____

____

____

____

____

____

____

____

____

____

____

____

My Mission Statement

3. Complete your Personal SWOT Analysis

Complete your SWOT Analysis by filling in the sections below.

Strengths

***Weakness*es**

Opportunities

Threats

WEEK 1

WEEK 2

1. Business Planning

Step 1 - Set your Goal

Download the Business Planning Worksheets from www.foundationsforsuccess.ca or use the following pages in the workbook. Enter your Income goal for the year. Most new Sales Representatives only achieve 60 – 75% of their target. Set the bar high but make sure it's attainable.

Enter the Average Commission for transactions in your area. If you're a new Sales Representative and don't have any previous commissions to base your goals on, ask your broker/manager for assistance with the average commissions for the brokerage.

Divide the Income by the Commission to determine the number of transactions required.

INCOME GOAL	AVERAGE COMMISSION	TRANSACTIONS NEEDED
$ ___________	$ ___________	___________

Step 2 - Listings or Buyers

Enter the percentage of your business you want to come from Listings and from Buyers.

WEEK 2

LISTINGS	BUYERS
%	%

Using the percentages you entered above and the number of transactions needed, **calculate the number of total listings and buyers needed to reach your goal.**

TRANSACTIONS NEEDED	PERCENTAGE FROM LISTINGS	PERCENTAGE FROM BUYERS
	%	%
	TOTAL SOLD LISTINGS NEEDED	TOTAL SOLD BUYERS NEEDED

Step 3 – How Many Appointments Needed

Listings

Enter the number of sold listings needed from above.

Total Sold Listings needed ____________

Enter your Listings taken to Listings Sold ratio.

It's been my experience that for new Sales Representatives, the following averages are generally appropriate:

Listings Taken to Listings Sold Ratio 50 – 60%

Your Listings Taken to Listings Sold Ratio ____________ %

Total Listings Required	____________

It's been my experience that for new Sales Representatives, the following averages are generally appropriate:

# of Listing Appointments needed for each Listing Taken	5 - 7
# of Listing Appointments needed for each Listing Taken	____________
Number of Listing Appointments needed (Total Listings needed x # of appointments/listing)	____________

Purchases

Enter the number of Sold Buyers required from the chart above.

Total Buyers Needed	____________

It's been my experience that for new Sales Representatives, the following averages are generally appropriate:

Written to Close Percentage	75 - 80%
Your Written to Close Percentage	__________ %
Number of Written Contracts needed (Total Buyers needed x Written to Close ratio)	____________

Enter the number of contacts required for each appointment.

Averages	120 – 130

Contacts needed for each Appointment (1st year)	________
2nd - 5th year	50 - 60
6th year +	30 - 40

Contacts Required per Appointment	________
Total Appointments Needed (Listing + Buyer Appointments)	________
Total Yearly Contacts Required	________
Total Daily Contacts Required, Working 225 Days per Year	________

Step 4 - Create Your Task List

Now that you've calculated the number of contacts you're going to need to make, you'll need to create your task list to define from what sources you'll develop business.

Your 3 Point Stool

As discussed in *Volume 1 – On the Right Foot*, this is where you'll choose your 3 point stool; the three sources which you believe will produce the best opportunities for developing your business. The first of these should always be through the use of referrals from past clients, your Sphere of Influence and repeat clients.

Using the Business Planning Worksheets or the following page, complete the chart, indicating how many transactions you intend to complete for each of the sources you've chosen to pursue and how many you plan on for each quarter.

Goal: Generate ______ Transactions

Source of Business	Number of Transactions	Quarterly Target
Referrals from Past Clients / Sphere of Influence & Repeat Clients		Q1 Q2 Q3 Q4
Open Houses		Q1 Q2 Q3 Q4
Website / Social Media		Q1 Q2 Q3 Q4
Prospecting		Q1 Q2 Q3 Q4
Ad / Sign Calls		Q1 Q2 Q3 Q4
Other Networking		Q1 Q2 Q3 Q4
FSBO / Expireds		Q1 Q2 Q3 Q4
Just Listed / Just Sold Marketing		Q1 Q2 Q3 Q4
Commercial		Q1 Q2 Q3 Q4
Other (Specify)		Q1 Q2 Q3 Q4

Total Quarterly Targets

Q1 - **Q2 -** **Q3 -** **Q4 -**

Define your Tactical Plan

a. Using the Business Planning Worksheet, list the objectives for each source of business you plan on utilizing.

b. **Enter the number of transactions and the source of business you'll be using in the "Task" field**, i.e. Task – 3 Transactions – Referrals.

c. Using the SWOT Analysis you completed earlier, **list each of the assignments you'll need to complete and when your deadline for completion will be.** Remember, each objective takes into account your strengths and opportunities and how you'll use them to achieve each task as well as your weaknesses and the education, skills, tools and people you'll need to help you overcome them.

Task – 3 Referrals from SOI			
		Deadline	Achieved
Objective - Complete Database		Jan. 31	
1	Create Database of friends, family and past clients	Jan. 10	
2	Implement Contact Management System	Jan. 15	
3	Upload Database to CRM System	Jan. 18	
4	Contact SOI and Qualify / Eliminate	Jan. 25	
5	Set up Monthly Newsletter and Initiate Referral Management System	Jan. 31	

2. Complete Your Referral Database

a. **Download the Excel spreadsheet named "Database" from www.foundationsforsuccess.ca.**

b. **Enter as many people you know and who know you by first name as possible.** Do NOT edit anyone out; include everyone. Use the following chart to include people about whom you may not have thought, but who should be included.

c. **Save the file as a CSV file** for export to your Client Retention Management System at a later date.

Who do you know?

Who do you know that is a(n)...

Aerobics Instructor	Airline Employee	Attorney
Barber	Beautician	Business Owner
Cashier	Caterer	Chiropractor
Dentist	Dietitian	Doctor
Educator	Engineer	Executive Assistant
Financial Planner	Florist	Fundraiser
Insurance salesperson	Interior decorator	Limo driver
Massage therapist	Nurse	Office worker
Orthodontist	Physical therapist	PR agent
Project manager	Retired executive	Sales Rep
Telemarketer	Veteran	Waitress

Who sold you or services your...

Alarm system	Bicycle	Bed
Boat	Books	Bridal gown
Camera	Camper	Car
Carpeting	Clothing	Computer
Condominium	Construction	Copier

WEEK 2

Cosmetics	Dry cleaning	Exercise equipment
Fence	Formal wear	Fruit
Furniture	Gas	Horse
Manicure	Mobile phone	Mortgage
Motorcycle	Music	Mutual funds
Office supplies	Payroll	Pet supplies
Photography	Piano	Pool
Printing	Quilting materials	Refrigerator
Rental Equipment	Roofing	Secretarial
Stereo system	Shoe repair	Sporting goods
Tax return	Tires	Tools
Travel		

Other people...

Parents/grandparents	Brother/sister/in law
Aunts/Uncles/Cousins	Past jobs
Coworkers	High school friends

People you grew up with

College friends	Neighbors	Play sports with

Who do you know at ...

Bingo	Book club	Bowling
Camp	Child care	Chamber of commerce
Clubs	Government	Place of worship
Golf course	Garden center	Health club
Hospital	Hotel	Nightclub
Pharmacy	Restaurant	School
Supermarket	Tennis	Volunteer group
Parents of kids friends	Kid's teachers	Military friends
Fraternity/sorority	Bridesmaids	Bridge players
Mailman\UPS\FedEx driver		Other networkers

WEEK 3

1. Learn and Practice Your Scripts (See Appendix)

a. **Use the Just Listed or Just Sold scripts** in the Appendix (or any other one you prefer to work with) and personalize it.

b. **Role play for half an hour daily** with someone at your office.

c. Use different role play partners on a rotating basis, if possible. This ensures that you get different critiques and don't get the same answers. Remember, the role play sessions should be as realistic as possible but should also be kept positive and the critiques constructive.

2. Put the Scripts to Use

a. **Make 100 prospecting calls daily from Monday to Friday.**

   This is, of course, to help you develop your skills and confidence but even more importantly to help you get into a consistent prospecting habit as well as find leads and prospects.

b. **Track the number of contacts you make each day** using the Contact Tracking Form you can find in the Appendix and on www.foundationsforsuccess.ca.

3. Set Up Your Schedule

Set up a schedule that ensures you take care of the most important business when you need to take care of it, as often as you need to take care of it. Time blocking and following your schedule is a major component of successful time management.

Step 1 – Get a Calendar

You're going to need two calendars; one wall calendar and a copy of the weekly schedule you'll find in the Appendix and on www.foundationsforsuccess.ca.

Go to your nearest office supply store and get a wall calendar for the year. A dry erase board may be the best option. **Download the Weekly Schedule.**

Put the calendar up on your wall at the office. An electronic calendar on your mobile and computer are very handy, but there's nothing like seeing your entire schedule every day to keep you on track.

Step 2 – Yearly Holidays

Decide when you'll be taking your holidays and mark the time on your wall calendar and then enter them on your mobile device and sync to your computer (or vice versa). If you don't get away at that time, you can rejig your schedule to correct the dates at a later time.

Step 3 – R&R Time

Set aside, at minimum, one day per week to rest and recuperate and spend time with your family, friends or significant other. **Rule out the day on your yearly calendar and your Weekly Schedule.**

As well, set aside some time to exercise, meditate, or whatever you need to do on a daily basis to look after your own health needs.

Step 4 – Heigh Ho, Heigh Ho, It's off to Work I Go

Decide what time you're going to start work and when your last appointment will finish and mark this off on your weekly schedule, mobile device and computer.

Step 5 – Munchy Time

Schedule time for lunch and dinner. You need to eat and you don't want to end up eating a rushed lunch at some fast food restaurant on a regular basis, or having dinner late at night and then falling into bed. Not healthy prospects! Look after yourself first.

Step 6 – Lead Generation

Schedule your Lead Generation / Prospecting time on your weekly schedule, mobile device and computer. Traditionally, lead generation is done in the mornings, when your energy levels are at their greatest. I would recommend that you **schedule this for at least 3 hours each morning during the week, i.e. 9:00 am – 12:00 pm.**

Mark your quarterly Listing Appointment and Purchase Contract targets on your wall calendar at the end of each quarter.

Step 7 – Follow-Up Time

Lead follow up is generally managed in the early afternoon, at which time your energy is still high.

Schedule 90 minute slots after lunch for your lead follow up.

Step 8 – Preview New Listings

One of the most important things you can do when starting out is to make sure you're as knowledgeable as possible on the available inventory and the best way to accomplish that is to preview them.

Schedule at least one 90 minute appointment slot every week to preview the new listings in your office and its surrounding area.

Step 9 – Open Houses

One of the most effective methods of prospecting is to run effective Open Houses.

Schedule at least one five hour time slot to run an Open Houses per weekend.

Step 10 – R&D Time

Schedule two 60 - 90 minute slots for researching the market weekly.

Take a top producer out for lunch and ask them how they got where they did. And then listen. It's amazing what you'll learn.

Step 11 – Training & Courses

Schedule at least one 90 minute slot every week for training, courses and/or webinars.

Step 12 – All the Rest

Schedule 90 minute appointment slots within the remaining time, giving yourself at least half an hour to get from one appointment to the next.

The Final Step

Post a copy of your schedule in your office, in different places at home and set it up on your mobile device and computer with reminders for each of the time blocks.

Follow the schedule consistently. If you don't have appointments booked, use the time constructively to work on building your business, such as prospecting, training or role playing. Do NOT use it to sit around and socialize with the other salespeople in your office. Remember, if they're sitting around and socializing, they're probably not busy and they're not the people from whom you'll learn good habits.

Sample Weekly Schedule (See Appendix for Blank Schedule)

<table>
<tr><th></th><th>MONDAY</th><th>TUESDAY</th><th>WEDNESDAY</th><th>THURSDAY</th><th>FRIDAY</th><th>SATURDAY</th><th>SUNDAY</th></tr>
<tr><td>8:00 - 8:30 am</td><td>Role Play</td><td>Role Play</td><td>Role Play</td><td>Role Play</td><td>Role Play</td><td>Role Play</td><td rowspan="26">OFF
(Sorry
I'm competely
Booked)</td></tr>
<tr><td>8:30 - 9:00 am</td><td rowspan="4">Prospecting
Calls
&
SOI</td><td rowspan="4">Prospecting
Calls
&
SOI</td><td rowspan="4">Prospecting
Calls
&
SOI</td><td rowspan="4">Prospecting
Calls
&
SOI</td><td rowspan="4">Prospecting
Calls
&
SOI</td><td rowspan="4">Prospecting
Calls
&
SOI</td></tr>
<tr><td>9:00 - 9:30 am</td></tr>
<tr><td>9:30 - 10:00 am</td></tr>
<tr><td>10:00 - 10:30 am</td></tr>
<tr><td>10:30 - 11:00 am</td><td></td><td></td><td></td><td></td><td></td><td></td></tr>
<tr><td>11:00 - 11:30 am</td><td rowspan="3">Appointment
Available</td><td rowspan="3">Appointment
Available</td><td rowspan="3">Appointment
Available</td><td rowspan="3">Appointment
Available</td><td rowspan="3">Appointment
Available</td><td></td></tr>
<tr><td>11:30 - 12:00 pm</td><td></td></tr>
<tr><td>12:00 - 12:30 pm</td><td rowspan="11">Open
House</td></tr>
<tr><td>12:30 - 1:00 pm</td><td></td><td></td><td></td><td></td><td></td></tr>
<tr><td>1:00 - 1:30 pm</td><td rowspan="3">Lead
Follow Up</td><td rowspan="3">Lead
Follow Up</td><td rowspan="3">Lead
Follow Up</td><td rowspan="3">Lead
Follow Up</td><td rowspan="3">Lead
Follow Up</td></tr>
<tr><td>1:30 - 2:00 pm</td></tr>
<tr><td>2:00 - 2:30 pm</td></tr>
<tr><td>2:30 - 3:00 pm</td><td rowspan="3">Appointment
Available</td><td rowspan="3">Appointment
Available</td><td rowspan="3">Appointment
Available</td><td rowspan="3">Appointment
Available</td><td rowspan="4">Preview
New
Listings</td></tr>
<tr><td>3:00 - 3:30 pm</td></tr>
<tr><td>3:30 - 4:00 pm</td></tr>
<tr><td>4:00 - 4:30 pm</td><td></td><td></td><td></td><td></td></tr>
<tr><td>4:30 - 5:00 pm</td><td rowspan="4">Doorknocking
(Farm)</td><td rowspan="3">Appointment
Available</td><td rowspan="4">Doorknocking
(Farm)</td><td rowspan="3">Appointment
Available</td><td rowspan="4">Doorknocking
(Farm)</td></tr>
<tr><td>5:00 - 5:30 pm</td></tr>
<tr><td>5:30 - 6:00 pm</td><td></td></tr>
<tr><td>6:00 - 6:30 pm</td><td></td><td></td><td></td></tr>
<tr><td>6:30 - 7:00 pm</td><td></td><td></td><td></td><td></td><td></td><td></td></tr>
<tr><td>7:00 - 7:30 pm</td><td rowspan="3">Appointment
Available</td><td rowspan="3">Appointment
Available</td><td rowspan="3">Appointment
Available</td><td rowspan="3">Appointment
Available</td><td rowspan="3">Appointment
Available</td><td></td></tr>
<tr><td>7:30 - 8:00 pm</td><td></td></tr>
<tr><td>8:00 - 8:30 pm</td><td></td></tr>
<tr><td>8:30 - 9:00 pm</td><td></td><td></td><td></td><td></td><td></td><td></td></tr>
</table>

4. Eliminate the Time Vampires

a. List as many of your Time Vampires (your time-wasting activities and distractions) as you can.

b. Describe how you can avoid or eliminate them (Your Garlic Bouquets).

a. <u>My Time Vampires</u>

b. <u>My Garlic Bouquets</u>

____

____

____

____

____

____

____

____

____

____

____

____

____

____

____

____

____

5. Referral Management System Part 1

Decide on a Client Retention Management System. Choose one that will allow you to easily and automatically maintain contact with your Sphere of Influence as well as provide a drip marketing campaign to your prospects. Do **NOT** wait until you've completed your database.

WEEK 4

1. Continue Role Playing & Prospecting Calls

a. **Continue your daily role playing sessions.**

b. **Continue making 100 prospecting calls daily and tracking the number of contacts you make each day.** Are you making the number of contacts you need to daily? If not, you'll need to increase the number of calls you make each day.

c. **Using the Daily Activity Tracking Form** in the Appendix or on www.foundationsforsuccess.ca, track your appointments, leads and prospects.

2. Referral Management System Part 2

a. **Transfer the CSV file** you created last week to your CRM system. If you haven't completed your database, transfer the people you have already entered.

b. **Review and modify the Referral Database Qualifying Script.**

c. **Begin calling and Qualify or Eliminate people from your Database using your script.**

d. **Format your Monthly Newsletter**.

e. **Implement it** for distribution to your database beginning next month.

f. **Set up your CRM system to send you birthday and home purchase anniversary reminders** for your database and past clients at least 5 days before the event.

g. **Set up several drip marketing campaigns.** These should include campaigns for the following:

   i. 30 – 60 day Seller prospects

   ii. 60 – 90 day Seller prospects

   iii. > 90 day Seller prospects

   iv. FSBO prospects

   v. 30 – 60 day Buyer prospects

   vi. 60 – 90 day Buyer prospects

   vii. > 90 day Buyer prospects

   viii. Renter to Buyer prospects

h. **Download the Referral Management System Schedule** from www.foundationsforsucces.com

i. **Complete your yearly Referral Management System Schedule** (See next page) to include:

   i. Quarterly calls to your database - schedule these on your calendar

      - Calculate the number of people on your database divided by the number of prospecting days in the quarter, i.e. 120 people / 60 days = 2 people per day

   ii. Birthday cards for the homeowners

      - Go to your nearest dollar store and purchase a series of generic birthday cards or sign up for a service that sends out cards for you

      - Sign as many as possible to have on hand for mailing

   iii. Holiday cards

      - Purchase a series of major holiday cards that are appropriate to your database as well as Mother's Day,

Father's Day and Canada Day or Independence Day cards

- Sign as many as possible to have on hand for mailing

iv. Pop-bys

- Go to www.popbyideas.com for ideas
- On a seasonal basis drop off pop-bys for your database

3. Practice makes Perfect

a. **Find a number of available listings of all different kinds** (single family, condo, multifamily, properties with tenants, rural properties, etc.).

b. **Write offers for each of them.**

c. **Use different conditions and terms** to make them as real as possible.

d. **Have your broker/ manager check them to make sure they're accurate and realistic.**

4. Lead Follow Up System

a. **Download the Lead Tracking Form** from www.foundationsforsuccess.ca

b. **Copy your Lead Tracking Forms** onto bright coloured paper for hot leads and white for other leads.

c. **Place them in a lead follow up binder**.

d. **Create your 8 week prospect follow-up system** based on the drip marketing campaign you established in your CRM system.

e. **Prepare your phone, text and email templates**. Remember, they need to sound like you.

f. **Create your list of qualifying questions** to use to determine a lead's motivation when you receive an ad or sign call and

g. **Role play them with a colleague** until you're comfortable with them.

WEEK 5

1. Continue Role Playing & Prospecting Calls

a. **Continue your daily role playing sessions. Include Objection Handling as part of the role play.**

b. **Continue making at least 100 prospecting calls daily.**

c. **Continue tracking the number of contacts and appointments you make each day.**

2. Become a Farmer

a. **Decide on your farm area** based on the criteria discussed in Volume 2.

b. **Find out about the schools in the area**. How do they rank on the Fraser Institute Report Cards (Canada)? Speak to the vice-principals about the resources they have.

c. **Start walking the area and meeting the business owners.** Become the neighbourhood expert. What services are in the area? What amenities are there? What's the Walkscore for the community?

d. **Create a monthly Area Update** (See Appendix and www.foundationsforsuccess.ca for a sample template) and use it for doorknocking.

e. **Develop your doorknocking dialogue** (See Appendix and www.foundationsforsuccess.ca).

f. **Begin doorknocking in your farm at least 2-3 times per week using your dialogue.**

g. **Talk to 5 businesses in the area** and find out if there's a way to co-market. Begin building your Strategic Alliances.

3. File Management

a. **Set up 5 Listing files** with all the paperwork required by your brokerage, the New Listing Task List, Seller Questionnaire, Feedback Form, Marketing Checklist and Deal Tracking Form.

b. **Set up your Red File** and begin previewing new listings.

c. **Set up 5 Buyer files** with all the paperwork required by your brokerage, your Buyer's Task List, Buyer's Questionnaire and Deal Tracking Form.

4. Practice makes Perfect

Continue practicing writing offers for different types of properties, using different conditions and terms. Have your broker/ manager check them to make sure they're correct and realistic.

WEEK 6

1. Continue Role Playing & Prospecting Calls

a. **Continue your daily role playing sessions.**

b. **Continue making at least 100 prospecting calls daily.**

c. **Continue tracking the number of contacts and appointments you make each day.**

2. Buyers' Presentation

a. **Develop your Buyers' Presentation.**

b. **Rehearse it at least 5 times this week.**

c. Role play it consistently with another REALTOR®.

3. On the Road Again

a. **Download the following items from www.foundationsforsuccess.ca:**

   - Buyers' Questionnaire
   - Home Buyer's Scorecard
   - "Rules of the Road"

b. **Organize your Buyer Showing System.**

   - Modify the downloaded files as needed and include them in your system.

c. Check with your broker or manager for the specifics of booking showings in your area.

d. **Set up your post-sale Buyer's Service System.**

4. Run an Open House this weekend

a. **Download the Open House Checklist from www.foundationsforsuccess.ca.**

b. **Choose the day you want to run it.**

c. **Try to schedule it on Monday or Tuesday.**

d. **Follow the checklist for the Open House.**

5. Doorknock in Your Farm Area

a. **Doorknock in your farm area at least 3 times this week and track your contacts.**

WEEK 7

1. Continue Role Playing & Prospecting Calls

a. **Continue your daily role playing sessions.**

b. **Continue making 100 prospecting calls daily.**

c. **Track the number of contacts and appointments you make each day**.

d. **Track the number of Appointments you make** each day. What's your conversion rate?

2. Listing Presentation

a. **Develop your Listing Presentation**.

b. **Rehearse it at least 5 times this week.**

c. **Role play it consistently with another REALTOR®.**

d. **Develop your Pre-Listing Package**

e. **Have 10 printed and ready to use**.

3. Objection Handling

a. Role play your Objection Handling with a colleague for half an hour every day for the following:
   i. Prospecting Calls
   ii. Listing Presentations
   iii. Buyer's Presentations
   iv. Closing for offers with Buyers

4. Run an Open House this weekend

Track your Contacts and Appointments using the Contact Tracking Form.

5. Doorknock Your Farm Area

Doorknock in your farm area at least 3 times this week and track your contacts.

WEEK 8

1. Continue Role Playing & Prospecting Calls

a. **Continue your daily role playing sessions.**

b. **Make 100 prospecting calls daily.**

c. **Track the number of contacts and appointments you make each day**. Review your conversion rate with your broker/manager to help polish your skills.

2. Get the Word Out

a. Pick 5 properties from your local real estate magazine.

b. Pull up the listings on your local MLS® System.

c. Using the MLS information and the description in the magazine, rewrite the ads.

d. Use the methods described in Volume 5 to develop ads that focus on creating an emotional draw for potential buyers and have a call to action at the end.

   i. Define the benefits to the buyer of the particular features of the house

   ii. Add an emotional component to the benefits

   iii. What's your Target Market?

   iv. Which of the benefits will attract your target market?

   v. Remember to tie the headline, fist line and last line together.

   vi. What's your call to action?

3. Objection Handling

a. Role play your Objection Handling and Closing skills with a colleague for half an hour every day for the following:

   v. Prospecting Calls

   vi. Listing Presentations

   vii. Buyer's Presentations

   viii. Closing for offers with Buyers

4. Run an Open House this weekend

Track your Contacts and Appointments using the Contact Tracking Form and the Weekly Tracker.

5. Doorknock Your Farm Area

Doorknock in your farm area at least 3 times this week and track your contacts.

APPENDIX

All forms, charts and checklists contained in this Appendix are also available for download on www.foundationsforsuccess.ca.

APPENDIX

BUSINESS PLANNING WORKSHEETS

INCOME GOAL	AVERAGE COMMISSION	TRANSACTIONS NEEDED
$ ____________	$ ____________	____________

Enter the percentage of your business you want to come from Listings and from Buyers.

LISTINGS	BUYERS
%	%

Calculate the number of total listings and buyers needed to reach your goal.

TRANSACTIONS NEEDED	PERCENTAGE FROM LISTINGS	PERCENTAGE FROM BUYERS
	%	%
	TOTAL SOLD LISTINGS NEEDED	TOTAL SOLD BUYERS NEEDED

Listings

Enter the number of sold listings needed from above.

Total Sold Listings needed ____________

Average Listings Taken to Listings Sold Ratio 50 – 60%

Your Listings Taken to Listings Sold Ratio ____________ %

Total Listings Required	________
Average # of Listing Appointments needed for each Listing Taken	5 - 7
Your # of Listing Appointments needed for each Listing Taken	________
Number of Listing Appointments needed (Total Listings needed x # of appointments/listing)	________

Purchases

Enter the number of Sold Buyers required from the chart above.

Total Buyers Needed	________
Average Written to Close Percentage	75 - 80%
Your Written to Close Percentage	________ %
Number of Written Contracts needed (Total Buyers needed x Written to Close ratio)	________

Enter the number of contacts required for each appointment.

Averages	
Contacts needed for each Appointment (1st year)	120 – 130
2nd - 5th year	50 - 60
6th year +	30 - 40
Contacts Required per Appointment	________

Total Appointments Needed (Listing + Buyer Appointments)	____________
Total Yearly Contacts Required	____________
Total Daily Contacts Required, Working 225 Days per Year	____________

APPENDIX

Goal: Generate ______ Transactions

Source of Business	Number of Transactions	Quarterly Target
Referrals from Past Clients / Sphere of Influence & Repeat Clients		Q1 Q2 Q3 Q4
Open Houses		Q1 Q2 Q3 Q4
Website / Social Media		Q1 Q2 Q3 Q4
Prospecting		Q1 Q2 Q3 Q4
Ad / Sign Calls		Q1 Q2 Q3 Q4
Other Networking		Q1 Q2 Q3 Q4
FSBO / Expireds		Q1 Q2 Q3 Q4
Just Listed / Just Sold Marketing		Q1 Q2 Q3 Q4
Commercial		Q1 Q2 Q3 Q4
Other (Specify)		Q1 Q2 Q3 Q4

Quarterly Targets Total

Q1 - _______ Q2 - _______ Q3 - _______ Q4 - _______

TACTICAL PLAN

Task –			
		Deadline	Achieved
Objective			
1			
2			
3			
4			
5			

Task –			
		Deadline	Achieved
Objective			
1			
2			
3			
4			
5			

TACTICAL PLAN CONT'D…

Task –			
		Deadline	Achieved
Objective			
1			
2			
3			
4			
5			

Task –			
		Deadline	Achieved
Objective			
1			
2			
3			
4			
5			

WEEKLY SCHEDULE

	MONDAY	TUESDAY	WEDNESDAY	THURSDAY	FRIDAY	SATURDAY	SUNDAY
8:00 - 8:30							
8:30 - 9:00							
9:00 - 9:30							
9:30 - 10:00							
10:00 - 10:30							
10:30 - 11:00							
11:00 - 11:30							
11:30 - 12:00							
12:00 - 12:30							
12:30 - 1:00							
1:00 - 1:30							
1:30 - 2:00							
2:00 - 2:30							
2:30 - 3:00							
3:00 - 3:30							
3:30 - 4:00							
4:00 - 4:30							
4:30 - 5:00							
5:00 - 5:30							
5:30 - 6:00							
6:00 - 6:30							
6:30 - 7:00							
7:00 - 7:30							
7:30 - 8:00							
8:00 - 8:30							
8:30 - 9:00							

CONTACT TRACKING SHEET

Daily Target_____ Weekly Target _____

1	2	3	4	5	6	7	8	9	10
11	12	13	14	15	16	17	18	19	20
21	22	23	24	25	26	27	28	29	30
31	32	33	34	35	36	37	38	39	40
41	42	43	44	45	46	47	48	49	50
51	52	53	54	55	56	57	58	59	60
61	62	63	64	65	66	67	68	69	70
71	72	73	74	75	76	77	78	79	80
81	82	83	84	85	86	87	88	89	90
91	92	93	94	95	96	97	98	99	100
101	102	103	104	105	106	107	108	109	110
111	112	113	114	115	116	117	118	119	120
121	122	123	124	125	126	127	128	129	130
131	132	133	134	135	136	137	138	139	140
141	142	143	144	145	146	147	148	149	150

Place an "X" in box for each contact that doesn't lead to an appointment.

Place an "L" in the box for a Listing Appointment or a "B" for a Buyer's Appointment.

WEEKLY ACTIVITY TRACKER

Activity	Mon	Tues	Wed	Thurs	Fri	Sat	Sun	Totals
Prospecting								
Warm Calls								
Doorknocking								
Pop-bys								
FSBOs								
Open Houses								
Contacts								
Listing Appointments								
Buyer Appointments								
Additions to Database								

Activity	Mon	Tues	Wed	Thurs	Fri	Sat	Sun	Totals
Prospecting								
Warm Calls								
Doorknocking								
Pop-bys								
FSBOs								
Open Houses								
Contacts								
Listing Appointments								
Buyer Appointments								
Additions to Database								

Monthly Referral Team Marketing Schedule						
Event	**Newsletter**	**Calls**	**Mini-CMA**	**Pop-Bys**	**Cards**	**Other**
Jan						
Feb						
Mar						
Apr						
May						
Jun						
Jul						
Aug						
Sep						
Oct						
Nov						
Dec						

REFERRAL DATABASE QUALIFYING SCRIPT

Hi ____________________, it's ________________________.

I was thinking about you the other day and I just thought I'd give you a call and see how everything is going.

I also wanted to let you know that I'm taking a more serious approach to my real estate business and my ultimate goal is to become the person that people think of when they have a real estate question or are thinking about making a move.

I'm calling because when I was reviewing my database I noticed that I'm missing some information. It looks like I'm missing your email addresses / phone numbers / etc. So that we can stay in touch with you, I need to get my records updated, is that okay?"

Great! So let's see, it looks like I need your email address… (Obtain address and ask for any other information needed).

Perfect, thank you! Can I ask you a quick question? If you were thinking about buying or selling a property, or knew anyone who was, would you be comfortable referring them to me?

Yes: Great. I send out a free monthly newsletter with information for homeowners and current market statistics. Does this sound like something you might be interested in?

Yes: Excellent, I'll get you started on my monthly newsletter right away.

No / They know someone they have to refer to: OK. Thanks for your time. If you find that you do need any information, please remember that I'm always available to help. (Eliminate them from your database)

One last thing, would you mind if I stayed in touch with you every few months or so to keep you informed of any market changes and of course answer any real estate questions you may have at that time?

That's great.

I look forward to keeping in touch with you. In the meantime, remember, I'm never too busy for any of your referrals and if you have any questions or know of someone thinking of making a move, please feel free to contact me anytime.

REFERRAL DATABASE QUALIFYING SCRIPT WITH APOLOGY

Hi ____________________, it's ________________________.

I was thinking about you the other day and I realized we haven't spoken in (quite) a while. I want to apologize for that.

I also wanted to let you know that I'm taking a more serious approach to my real estate business and my ultimate goal is to become the person that people think of when they have a real estate question or are thinking about making a move.

I'm calling because when I was reviewing my database I noticed that I'm missing some information. It looks like I'm missing your email addresses / phone numbers / etc. So that we can stay in touch with you, I need to get my records updated, is that okay?"

Great! So let's see, it looks like I need your email address... (Obtain address and ask for any other information needed).

Perfect, thank you! Can I ask you a quick question? If you were thinking about buying or selling a property, or knew anyone who was, would you be comfortable referring them to me?

Yes: Great. I send out a free monthly newsletter with information for homeowners and current market statistics. Does this sound like something you might be interested in?

Yes: Excellent, I'll get you started on my monthly newsletter right away.

No / They know someone they have to refer to: OK. Thanks for your time. If you find that you do need any information, please remember that I'm always available to help. (Eliminate them from your database)

One last thing, would you mind if I stayed in touch with you every few months or so to keep you informed of any market changes and of course answer any real estate questions you may have at that time?

That's great.

I look forward to keeping in touch with you. In the meantime, remember, I'm never too busy for any of your referrals and if you have any questions or know of someone thinking of making a move, please feel free to contact me anytime.

LEAD FOLLOW UP TOOLS

LEAD TRACKING FORM

TACTICAL LEAD FOLLOW-UP

<table>
<tr><td colspan="2">LEAD NAME</td><td colspan="2">DATE OF FIRST CONTACT</td></tr>
<tr><td>RES. PHONE</td><td>CELL PHONE</td><td colspan="2">DATE OF FIRST CONTACT</td></tr>
<tr><td>BUS. PHONE</td><td>EMAIL</td><td>FOLLOW-UP DATE</td><td>FOLLOW UP DONE</td></tr>
<tr><td colspan="2">BUYER</td><td colspan="2">SELLER</td></tr>
<tr><td colspan="2">WANTS:
SINGLE FAMILY ☐ CONDO ☐
PRICE RANGE: AREA:
TYPE: STYLE:
DETACHED ☐ 2 STOREY ☐
SEMI DETACHED ☐ BUNGALOW ☐
TOWNHOME ☐ SPLIT ☐
GARAGE: BEDROOMS:
BATHROOMS:
BASEMENT: OTHER:</td><td colspan="2">NOW:
SINGLE FAMILY ☐ CONDO ☐
STYLE: BASEMENT:
SQ. FT.: BEDROOMS:
BATHS: GARAGE:
COMMUNITY:</td></tr>
<tr><td colspan="2">LEAD SOURCE:
REFERRAL ☐ AD ☐ SIGN ☐ CALL ☐ DK ☐</td><td>THANK YOU NOTE SENT</td><td>GIFT SENT</td></tr>
<tr><td colspan="4">ADDITIONAL INFO:</td></tr>
</table>

SAMPLE SELLER EMAIL TEMPLATE

Dear Mr. and Mrs. Smith,

Thanks for speaking with me yesterday at our Open House at 123 Cherry Tree Lane.

You expressed an interest in selling your home and I wanted to make sure I followed up and answered any questions you had about that process.

Selling your home can sometimes be a daunting procedure, but it's my job to eliminate the stress and worry from the process. The most important difference in the way I do things is to tailor the services I offer to the specific ways you want them provided, rather than providing the same services to everyone.

Sound intriguing? Then let's connect by Tuesday, so I can demonstrate more about how I can help you get your home sold, in the time frame that best suits you, for more money, with truly personalized, worry-free service. Call me at 123-456-7890 and we can schedule a time.

SAMPLE BUYER EMAIL TEMPLATE

Dear Mr. and Mrs. Smith,

Thanks for speaking with me yesterday at our Open House at 123 Cherry Tree Lane.

You expressed an interest in buying a new home and I wanted to make sure I followed up and answered any questions you had about that process.

Buying a home can sometimes be a daunting procedure, but it's my job to eliminate the stress and worry from the process. The most important difference in the way I do things is to tailor the services I offer to the specific ways you want them provided, rather than providing the same services to everyone.

Sound intriguing? Then let's connect by Tuesday, so I can demonstrate more about how I can help you find your next home, in the time frame that best suits you, for the best price, with truly personalized, worry-free service. Call me at 123-456-7890 and we can schedule a time.

SAMPLE SELLER TEXT MESSAGE TEMPLATE

Hi Mr. and Mrs. Smith,

Thanks for speaking with me yesterday at our Open House at 123 Cherry Tree Lane.

I wanted to make sure I followed up and answered any questions you had about selling your home.

It's my job to eliminate the stress and worry from the process by tailoring the services I offer to you, rather than providing the same services to everyone.

Sound intriguing? Then let's connect by Tuesday, so I can demonstrate more about how I can help you get your home sold, in the time frame that best suits you, for more money, with truly personalized, worry-free service. Call me at 123-456-7890 and we can schedule a time.

SAMPLE BUYER TEXT MESSAGE TEMPLATE

Hi Mr. and Mrs. Smith,

Thanks for speaking with me yesterday at our Open House at 123 Cherry Tree Lane.

I wanted to make sure I followed up and answered any questions you had about buying a new home.

It's my job to eliminate the stress and worry from the process by tailoring the services I offer to you, rather than providing the same services to everyone.

Sound intriguing? Then let's connect by Tuesday, so I can demonstrate more about how I can help you find your next home, in the time frame that best suits you, for the best price, with truly personalized, worry-free service. Call me at 123-456-7890 and we can schedule a time.

APPENDIX

SAMPLE SELLER PHONE CALL MESSAGE SCRIPT

Hi Mr. / Mrs. Smith,

It's ____________ with ______________ calling. We met yesterday at our Open House at 123 Cherry Tree Lane.

You expressed an interest in selling your home and I wanted to make sure I followed up and answered any questions you had about that process.

I know that selling your home can sometimes be a daunting procedure, but it's my job to eliminate the stress and worry from the process. The most important difference in the way I do things is to tailor the services I offer to the specific ways you want them provided, rather than providing the same services to everyone.

Does that sound intriguing?

Then let's schedule a time when I can demonstrate how I can help you get your home sold, in the time frame that best suits you, for more money, with truly personalized, worry-free service. Call me at 123-456-7890 and we can schedule a time.

SAMPLE BUYER PHONE CALL MESSAGE SCRIPT

Hi Mr. / Mrs. Smith,

It's ____________ with ____________ calling. We met yesterday at our Open House at 123 Cherry Tree Lane.

You expressed an interest in buying a new home and I wanted to make sure I followed up and answered any questions you had about that process.

I know that buying a home can sometimes be a daunting procedure, but it's my job to eliminate the stress and worry from the process. The most important difference in the way I do things is to tailor the services I offer to the specific ways you want them provided, rather than providing the same services to everyone.

Does that sound intriguing?

Then let's schedule a time when I can demonstrate how I can help you find your next home, in the time frame that best suits you, for the best price, with truly personalized, worry-free service. Call me at 123-456-7890 and we can schedule a time.

APPENDIX

SCRIPTS

APPENDIX

Building Rapport

The ability to build rapport, to connect with someone, is vital in successful prospecting. Communication is much more than the ability to talk or listen to someone; it's a combination of verbal and non-verbal components within the conversation. About 55% of communication is non-verbal, which means that when you're speaking to someone on the other end of a phone you've lost 55% of your ability to influence them. So your words, tone, inflection, timing and ability to actively listen are even more important.

Some key points to remember, when speaking on the phone, at someone's door or in a meeting are:

1) Mirror – match the other person's speech patterns and body language. If they're speaking quickly or loudly, you must speak quickly or loudly. If they're standing with their arms crossed, match them. This technique increases the other person's sense that you're "in tune" with them.

2) Actively Listen – There's an old saying that God gave us two ears and one mouth so that we can listen twice as much as we talk. Active listening is the skill of being able to listen to what the other person means, rather than what they're saying.

    a. Start by asking a Question and then Listen
    Most of us try to decide what the other person is saying and come up with a response before the other person is finished speaking. This creates a barrier to our ability to truly hear the meaning behind what the person is saying and creates a more confrontational approach to the conversation. "They're saying this, so I'll need to say that."

    b. Repeat the Answer back to them

A large part of active listening is to confirm with the other person that what you're hearing is actually what they're saying. "So, what I'm hearing you say is… Is that right?"

c. Express Your Understanding

Confirming that you understand their point of view, even if you disagree with it, eliminates the possibility of the conversation becoming confrontational.

3) Find Common Ground – People want to deal with like-minded people. Try to find something that will allow you to establish a connection to the other person, like kids, a dog, a similar hobby, etc. This will help the other person become more comfortable with you and establish a mutual connection.

4) Be Honest And Authentic – Don't try to be someone you're not. Always be yourself and answer any questions honestly. People can sense when someone is trying to be someone they're not or is lying and this will eliminate any trust or connection that may have been built to this point. If you don't know an answer, tell them and then find out later.

5) Provide Value – Jim Rohn said that "Giving is better than receiving because giving starts the receiving process." Providing the other person with something of value to them demonstrates that you're focussing on their interests, rather than yours and begins the process of building trust and respect. When answering an ad or sign call, give the other person the answer they're looking for, but remember to ask them for something in return.

6) Always Follow a Script or a Guide - Having a specific dialogue / script prepared and rehearsed reduces the opportunity of getting drawn off track or "stepping on your tongue". Any

script should be thoroughly rehearsed. It should become part of your natural cadence and conversational style.

7) Practice – The only way for a script to truly become your own is to rehearse it over and over. And the only way to make it perfect is to make sure you get it right each time you rehearse. Vince Lombardi said "Practice does not make perfect. Only perfect practice makes perfect."

RESPONSES TO ANTICIPATED OBJECTIONS

1. No Interest in You or Your Offer

2. No Authority to Act

3. No Need

4. No Time

5. Previous Bad Experience

____
____
____
____
____
____

6. Likes the Competition

____
____
____
____
____
____

7. Wants Lower Commission

____
____
____
____
____
____

8. Family Member / Friend in the Business

____
____
____
____
____
____

APPENDIX

PHONE PROSPECTING SCRIPTS

General Approach

You: "Hello Mr./Miss/Ms./Mrs.________________. My name is ________________ with XYZ Realty.

"I just want to let you know that I'll be really brief. The reason I'm calling today is that I wanted to get a chance to speak to people about the real estate market in the area. I'm sure you've heard that it's a hot market right now. I was wondering if you had any questions about the market?

Prospect: No.

You: OK. Can I ask how long you've lived there?

Prospect: 10 years

You: (engage them – ask questions)

OK. I was wondering if you know what your home is worth in this market.

Prospect: We think it's worth $______________. / No.

You: OK. Would it be helpful if I came out and took a look at it and gave you a better idea of what homes are selling for in the area and what your home is worth?

Yes: OK. How would ______am/pm tomorrow would work for you, or would ___________am/pm on ___________ work better?

No: OK. I'd like to ask whether you are thinking about moving in the near future." (Y/N)

Yes: OK. (Qualify them – open ended questions. Close for appointment)

No: Do you know of anyone who may be? (Y/N)

Yes: Would you be able to give me their name and perhaps their number and I'll give them a call to follow up.

No: And you're definitely not thinking about it?

No: Can I ask you one last question? If you were thinking about buying or selling, or knew anyone who was, do you have a REALTOR® that you'd work with?

Yes: OK. Thanks for your time.

No: Well, you know, I'd love to be that REALTOR®. Would it be alright if I sent you some information about who I am and what I do and then follow up in a few days to see if you have any questions?

Yes: OK. May I have your email address and I'll get that out to you right away. Thanks again.

No: OK. Thanks again.

Just Listed Approach

You: "Hello Mr./Miss/Ms./Mrs.________________. My name is ________________ with XYZ Realty.

"I just want to let you know that I'll be really brief. The reason I'm calling today is that we just listed a home (a home was just listed) in your neighbourhood. It's listed at $____________ and there's a real demand for homes in your area right now. I was wondering if you had any questions about the market in your area / neighbourhood. (Answer their questions if they have any.)

Prospect: No.

You: OK. Can I ask how long you've lived there?

Prospect: We've been here __________

You: OK. I was wondering if you know what your home is worth in this market.

Prospect: We think it's worth $______________.

You: OK. Would it be helpful if I came out and took a look at it and gave you a better idea of what homes are selling for in the area and what your home is worth?

Yes: Great. How would ______am/pm tomorrow work for you, or would ___________am/pm on ___________ work better?

No: OK. Thanks. Can I ask you one last question? If you were thinking about buying or selling, or knew anyone who was, do you have a REALTOR® that you'd work with?

Yes: OK. Thanks for your time.

No: Well, you know, I'd love to be that REALTOR®. Would it be alright if I sent you some information about who I am and what I do and then follow up in a few days to see if you have any questions?

Yes: Great. Would you prefer it by mail or email?

OK. Thanks again.

Just Sold Approach

You: "Hello Mr./Miss/Ms./Mrs.________________. My name is _________________ with XYZ Realty.

"I just want to let you know that I'll be really brief. The reason I'm calling today is that we just sold a home (a home was just sold) in your neighbourhood. It sold at _____% of asking in ________ days. There's a real demand for homes in your area right now and I was wondering if you had any questions about the market in your area / neighbourhood. Answer their questions if they have any.

Prospect: No.

You: OK. Can I ask how long you've lived there?

Prospect: We've been here __________

You: OK. I was wondering if you know what your home is worth in this market.

Prospect: We think it's worth $______________. / No.

You: OK. Would it be helpful if I came out and took a look at it and gave you a better idea of what homes are selling for in the area and what your home is worth?

Yes: Great. How would ______am/pm tomorrow work for you, or would ___________am/pm on ___________ work better?

No: OK. Thanks. Can I ask you one last question? If you were thinking about buying or selling, or knew anyone who was, do you have a REALTOR® that you'd work with?

Yes: OK. Thanks for your time.

No: Well, you know, I'd love to be that REALTOR®. Would it be alright if I sent you some information about who I am and what I do and then follow up in a few days to see if you have any questions?

Yes: Great. Would you prefer it by mail or email?

No: OK. Thanks again.

Buyer Specific Approach

You: "Hello Mr./Miss/Ms./Mrs.________________. My name is ________________ with XYZ Realty.

"I just want to let you know that I'll be really brief. The reason I'm calling today is that I'm working with a family who's really interested in buying a home in your neighbourhood. I'd like to ask whether you are thinking about moving in the near future." (Y/N)

Yes: OK. (Qualify them – open ended questions. Close for appointment)

No: If I could get you a price that you'd be happy with, would you consider selling to them?

Yes: Great. (Qualify them – open ended questions. Close for appointment)

No: Thanks for considering it. Do you know of anyone who may be? (Y/N)

Yes: Would you be able to give me their name and perhaps their number and I'll give them a call to follow up.

No: And you're definitely not thinking about it?

No: OK. Thanks. Can I ask you one last question? If you were thinking about buying or selling, or knew anyone who was, do you have a REALTOR® that you'd work with?

Yes: OK. Thanks for your time.

No: Well, you know, I'd love to be that REALTOR®. Would it be alright if I sent you some information about who I am and what I do and then follow up in a few days to see if you have any questions?

Yes: Great. Would you prefer it by mail or email?

No: OK. Thanks again.

Yes: OK. May I have your email address and I'll get that out to you right away. Thanks again.

No: OK. Thanks again.

DOORKNOCKING SCRIPTS

General Approach

You: Good morning / afternoon. My name is _________________ with XYZ Realty.

I'm working in your neighbourhood and wanted to make sure I introduced myself. As the neighbourhood professional I like to make sure I keep up to speed on everything that's going on. Here are the latest stats for this community (Hand them the Area Market Update).

I was wondering if you have any questions about the real estate market?

Them: Yes. (Answer their questions as completely as possible. You want to demonstrate that you're the person they want to deal with.)

No: OK. Can I ask how long you've lived there?

Prospect: We've been here __________

You: OK. *(Engage them in a conversation about the community – Build Rapport)*

I was wondering if you know what your home is worth in this market.

Prospect: We think it's worth $______________. / No.

You: OK. Would it be helpful if I came out and took a look at it and gave you a better idea of what homes are selling for in the area and what your home is worth?

Yes: Great. How would ______am/pm tomorrow work for you, or would ___________am/pm on ___________ work better?

No: OK. Thanks. Can I ask you one last question? If you were thinking about buying or selling, or knew anyone who was, do you have a REALTOR® that you'd work with?

Yes: OK. Thanks for your time.

No: Well, you know, I'd love to be that REALTOR®. Would it be alright if I sent you some information about who I am and what I do and then follow up in a few days to see if you have any questions?

Yes: Great. Would you prefer it by mail or email?

No: OK. Thanks. Just before I go, I send a monthly Area Market Update to quite a few people in the area and was wondering if you'd be interested in receiving it, with no obligation? (Y/N)

Yes: OK. May I have your email address and I'll get that out to you right away. By the way, do you know of anyone who may be thinking about moving in the near future? (Y/N)

Yes: Would you be able to give me their name and perhaps their number and I'll give them a call to follow up?

No: And you're definitely not thinking about it? *No*. OK. Thanks again.

Just Listed Approach

You: Hi, my name is ________________ with XYZ Realty.

I just want to let you know that I'll be really brief. The reason I'm here today is to let you know that 123 Anywhere Street just listed at $____________ and there's a real demand for homes in your area right now. I was wondering if you have any questions about the real estate market?

Them: Yes. (Answer their questions as completely as possible. You want to demonstrate that you're the person they want to deal with.)

No: OK. Can I ask how long you've lived there?

Prospect: We've been here __________

You: OK. *(Engage them in a conversation about the community – Build Rapport)*

I was wondering if you know what your home is worth in this market.

Prospect: We think it's worth $_____________.

You: OK. Would it be helpful if I took a look at it and gave you a better idea of what homes are selling for in the area and what your home is worth?

Yes: OK. How would ______am/pm tomorrow would work for you, or would ___________am/pm on ___________ work better?

No: OK. Thanks. Can I ask you one last question? If you were thinking about buying or selling, or knew anyone who was, do you have a REALTOR® that you'd work with?

Yes: OK. Thanks for your time.

No: Well, you know, I'd love to be that REALTOR®. Would it be alright if I sent you some information about who I am and what I do and then follow up in a few days to see if you have any questions?

Yes: Great. Would you prefer it by mail or email?

No: OK. Thanks. Just before I go, I send a monthly Area Market Update to quite a few people in the area and was wondering if you'd be interested in receiving it, with no obligation? (Y/N)

Yes: OK. May I have your email address and I'll get that out to you right away. By the way, do you know of anyone who may be thinking about moving in the near future? (Y/N)

Yes: Would you be able to give me their name and perhaps their number and I'll give them a call to follow up?

No: And you're definitely not thinking about it? *No.* OK. Thanks again.

Just Sold Approach

You: Hi, my name is ________________ with XYZ REALTY.

I just want to let you know that I'll be really brief. The reason I'm here today is to let you know that 123 Anywhere Street just sold at ________% of asking, in _____ days. There's a real demand for homes in your area right now and I was wondering if you have any questions about the real estate market?

Them: Yes. (Answer their questions as completely as possible. You want to demonstrate that you're the person they want to deal with.)

No: OK. Can I ask how long you've lived there?

Prospect: We've been here __________

You: OK. *(Engage them in a conversation about the community – Build Rapport)*

I was wondering if you know what your home is worth in this market.

Prospect: We think it's worth $______________.

You: OK. Would it be helpful if I took a look at it and gave you a better idea of what homes are selling for in the area and what your home is worth?

Yes: OK. How would ______am/pm tomorrow would work for you, or would ___________am/pm on ___________ work better?

No: OK. Thanks. Can I ask you one last question? If you were thinking about buying or selling, or knew anyone who was, do you have a REALTOR® that you'd work with?

Yes: OK. Thanks for your time.

No: Well, you know, I'd love to be that REALTOR®. Would it be alright if I sent you some information about who I am and what I do and then follow up in a few days to see if you have any questions?

Yes: Great. Would you prefer it by mail or email?

No: OK. Thanks. Just before I go, I send a monthly Area Market Update to quite a few people in the area and was wondering if you'd be interested in receiving it, with no obligation? (Y/N)

Yes: OK. May I have your email address and I'll get that out to you right away. By the way, do you know of anyone who may be thinking about moving in the near future? (Y/N)

Yes: Would you be able to give me their name and perhaps their number and I'll give them a call to follow up?

No: And you're definitely not thinking about it? *No.* OK. Thanks again.

Buyer Specific Approach

You: Hi, my name is ________________ with XYZ Realty.

I just want to let you know that I'll be really brief. The reason I'm here today is that I'm working with a family who's really interested in buying a home in your neighbourhood. I'd like to ask whether you are thinking about moving in the near future." (Y/N)

Yes: OK. (Qualify them – open ended questions. Close for appointment)

No: If I could get you a price that you'd be happy with, would you consider selling to them?

Yes: Great. (Qualify them – open ended questions. Close for appointment)

No: Thanks for considering it. Do you know of anyone who may be? (Y/N)

Yes: Would you be able to give me their name and perhaps their number and I'll give them a call to follow up.

No: And you're definitely not thinking about it?

No: OK. Thanks. Can I ask you one last question? If you were thinking about buying or selling, or knew anyone who was, do you have a REALTOR® that you'd work with?

Yes: OK. Thanks for your time.

No: Well, you know, I'd love to be that REALTOR®. Would it be alright if I sent you some information about who I am and what I do and then follow up in a few days to see if you have any questions?

Yes: Great. Would you prefer it by mail or email?

No: OK. Thanks again.

Yes: OK. May I have your email address and I'll get that out to you right away. Thanks again.

No: OK. Thanks again.

SAMPLE QUALIFYING QUESTIONS FOR AD / SIGN CALL

How long have you been looking?

When do you want to move / How soon do you want to be in your new property?

Why are you thinking of buying?

If you could design the ideal moving situation for your family, what would it look like?

Have you seen anything you really like?

Do you need to sell your current home before you can buy? Is your home currently on the market?

Have you bought a property in the past?

Have you met with a lender yet? What Price Range are you looking in?

When can we meet to discuss your property search?

Are you working with another agent?

What can I do to make it easier for you to get the kind of real estate information you are looking for?

Tell me the process you typically use to make decisions like this?

What is the most important service you want from a real estate agent like myself?

Besides that, what's next? (Go 3 deep)

AD/SIGN CALL SCRIPTS

The secret to success when dealing with ad or sign calls is to engage the caller, build rapport and avoid giving them all the information they want all at once. The whole purpose is to **close the caller for a face to face appointment** rather than just meeting them and showing them the property they're calling about.

Inbound Calls

You: Hello, ______________ speaking. May I help you?

Them: I'm calling about your ad in the paper…

You: Great, thanks for calling. Can you tell me a little bit about which property you're calling about? Oh, by the way, just in case we get cut off, can I get your name and number so I can call you back?

They give you their name and number.

You: Thanks. Now, which home were you calling about?

Them: The two storey with four bedrooms and three baths.

You: Oh yes, that's a great house. What would you like to know about it?

Them: I'd like to know where it is and the price.

You: It's in the ______________ area of ______________. Is that an area you're interested in? (Where)

Them: It's one of the areas we're thinking about… Yes…Not really…

You: OK. What other areas were you thinking about? (Where)

Them: *lists several*

You: How soon where you thinking of moving? (When)

Them: When we find the right place... When we sell our other house... Very shortly.....

You: And what kind of price range are you looking in? (How much)

Them: *provides a price range*

You: Unfortunately, that house isn't in that price range. But I have several homes in those areas that are. Would you like to hear about some of them? (Use Red File)

(or)

OK, well that house is listed at $______________. Would that work for you?

Them: Yes it would.

You: Great. Let me tell you a little about the home. *(Describe the home for them)* Does that sound like what you're looking for?

1)

Them: Yes.

You: OK. Why don't we get together and I can show it to you? Would __________ at ________ work for you or is ________ at _________ better?

2)

Them: No.

You: OK. So that's not what you're looking for. Would you like to hear about some of the other properties that are available in the same area and price range?

Them: Sure.

You: *Read the remarks from 2 listings.* Do any of those sound interesting?

Them: Yes…I like the one…

You: Great. Why don't we get together and I can show it/them to you? Would ____________ at ________ work for you or is ________ at _______ better?

Outbound Calls

You: Hi _______________, this is _____________ from ______________ calling. You called me looking for some information on a home that I have advertised. How can I help you?

Them: I'm calling about the two storey with four bedrooms and three baths.

You: Oh yes, that's a great house. What would you like to know about it?

Them: I'd like to know where it is and the price.

You: It's in the _____________ area of ______________. Is that an area you're interested in? (Where)

Them: It's one of the areas we're thinking about… Yes…Not really…

You: OK. What other areas were you thinking about? (Where)

Them: *lists several*

You: How soon where you thinking of moving? (When)

Them: When we find the right place... When we sell our other house... Very shortly…..

You: And what kind of price range are you looking in? (How much)

Them: *provides a price range*

You: Unfortunately, that house isn't in that price range. But I have several homes in those areas that are. Would you like to hear about some of them? (Use Red File)

(or)

OK, well that house is listed at $______________. Would that work for you?

Them: Yes it would.

You: Great. Let me tell you a little about the home. *(Describe the home for them)* Does that sound like what you're looking for?

1)

Them: Yes.

You: OK. Why don't we get together and I can show it to you? Would ____________ at ___________ work for you or is ______________ at _____________ better?

2)

Them: No.

You: OK. So that's not what you're looking for. Would you like to hear about some of the other properties that are available in the same area and price range?

Them: Sure.

You: *Read the remarks from 2 listings.* Do any of those sound interesting?

Them: Yes…I like the one…

You: Great. Why don't we get together and I can show it/them to you? Would ____________ at ________ work for you or is __________ at __________ better?

APPENDIX

OBJECTION HANDLING

AD / SIGN CALL OBJECTIONS

CAN YOU GIVE ME THE ADDRESS

Them: I just want the address. We want to drive by and take a look and then we'll get back to you.

You: OK. I understand how you feel. A lot of people feel the same. But what I've found is that just driving by doesn't give you the real feel of the house. Let me ask you, when you bought your current place, did you buy it because of how it looked outside, or how you felt when you were in it?

Most people will reply that it was how they felt when they were inside. Except investors.

You: OK, so wouldn`t it make sense to take a look at the interior of this house to see if it`s the right feel?

1)

Them: Yeah, I guess so.

You: OK. I'm free at _______ today, or would _________ work better for you? And while we're out, I'll set up a couple of other places for you to see. How does that sound? *(Make sure both buyers will be available)*

Them: Sure.

You: *Confirm time, address and contact info.*

2)

Them: Maybe, but I'd just like the address.

You: OK. It's ______________. *(It's OK to give them the address of your listing)* Would you like to hear about some of the other properties that are available in the same area and price range?

Them: Sure. (Read the remarks from 2 listings)

You: Do any of those sound interesting?

Them: Yes. Could I get the addresses of those as well?

You: Can I ask you a quick question? Is this the neighbourhood you want to be in?

Them: Yes

You: Great. So can you tell a bit more about why you feel driving by the home will help you make a decision? *(They just want to see what it looks like).*

I understand. But I only give out those addresses to my clients. I'd be happy to arrange a time for us to meet to discuss how I can help you find a home, if you're interested and then I can show you the homes that meet your needs. Would today at ________ or tomorrow at _______ work best for you?

I JUST WANT TO SEE THE HOUSE

You: I can understand that, a lot of people I've spoken to feel that way and I'd be happy to show you the home. But what I've found is that when we show someone a home, it's rarely the home they're looking for.

Would you agree that we don't want to waste time looking at homes that aren't what you want?

Them: That makes sense.

In order to do that, I'd suggest we get together and I can find out exactly what it is you're looking for in your new home. I also want to make sure that you're completely up to date on what's happening in the real estate market. That way you can make the best decision when you decide to purchase. Would that be helpful?

Them: That sounds OK.

You: Great. It usually takes about 20 or 30 minutes. Why don't we meet and go over it? How does _______ today sound, or would ________ tomorrow work better for you?

If the Buyer is still insisting on only seeing that home

You: OK. I understand. Unfortunately, my sellers have asked me not to bring anybody through the home without making sure they're qualified to buy it. I'm sure you can understand their concern for safety and that they don't want waste their time with anyone who's not able to buy it.

Buyer: Yes, I can understand that.

You: Great. I can still show you the home, but in order to do that, we'll need to meet for about 20 minutes first. How does _______ today sound, or would ________ tomorrow work better for you?

CAN YOU JUST EMAIL ME THE INFORMATION ON THE HOME?

You: I can certainly do that, but let me ask you; are you already getting listings emailed from other agents?

Buyer: I'm working with a couple of other agents and they're sending me listings.

You: OK. And are you looking in the same areas with all of them?

Buyer: Yes

You: Let me ask you, have you noticed that the homes they're sending are the same ones?

Them: Yes.

You: Here's why. All agents have access to the same information through the MLS system. So the agents you've spoken with have taken what you've told them and plugged that into their system. As a result, they're sending you the same information.

Now, here's how I work. In order to make sure we're not wasting your time or sending you repeats of the same listings, I'd suggest we get together and I can find out exactly what it is you're looking for in your new home. I also want to make sure that you're completely up to date on what's happening in the real estate market. That way you can make the best decision when you decide to purchase. Would that be helpful?

Buyer: That makes sense.

You: Great. It usually takes about 20 or 30 minutes. Why don't we meet and go over it? How does _______ today sound, or would ________ tomorrow work better for you?

WE'RE JUST STARTING THE PROCESS AND NOT SURE WHAT WE'RE LOOKING FOR.

You: That's great. You know, I can help with that. Why don't I send you my Informed Buyer Guide? It's got great information on what steps are most important when buying a home. Would you like me to send it to you?

Them: Yes

You: Great! What address should I send it to? I'll also follow up on _____ at _____ to make sure you received it.

Do you mind me asking if you've been preapproved for a mortgage yet?

I strongly recommend this as your first step before you begin looking for a home. That way you'll know how much you can spend and won't waste your time or get frustrated looking at homes you can't afford.

Knowing everything is in order will also make it easier when it comes to negotiating. Best of all, if interest rates rise, you'll get the benefit of having locked in at a lower rate.

So, why don't we set up a time to get together so that we can discuss what you're looking for in your next home? That usually takes about 20 or 30 minutes. How does _______ today sound, or would ________ tomorrow work better for you?

WE ONLY WANT TO WORK WITH THE LISTING AGENT

You: Do you mind me asking why?

Buyer: We can get a better deal by buying through the listing agent because they can reduce their commission.

You: You know ___________, I've heard that a lot, and you're right, some agents may offer to reduce their commission to get the home sold. However, may I explain why that strategy can actually work as a disadvantage?

Buyer: Sure

You: When an agent lists a home, they have a legal obligation to work in the seller's best interest at all times. This means that the listing agent isn't allowed to disclose any market information that would be harmful to the seller.

That means that if you decide to buy through them, their first obligation is to the seller and not you.

Would you agree that it's impossible to try to get the highest price for one party while at the same time trying to get the lowest price for the other person?

Buyer: That makes sense.

You: That means that even if they have you under contract as a buyer, they can't negotiate for your best price, while trying to get the top dollar for the seller. Do you see what I mean?

Buyer: Yes

You: So it only makes sense to have someone working for you, who's committed to acting in your best interests, doesn't it?

Buyer: Yes

You: So, when I work with buyers, my job is to find them the right house at the right price and to work only for you, and your best interests.

Why don't we get together and I can show you how I work. Would that be of interest to you?

Great. I'm available ________ and ________, do one of those work for you?

ANOTHER AGENT IS WILLING TO GIVE US PART OF THEIR COMMISSION

You: I understand that every dollar counts for you. But, can I tell you why that concerns me?

If the other agent isn't able to stand up for themselves when it comes to negotiating their own salary, how strong do you feel they can possibly be when it comes to negotiating the price of your home against an experienced agent?

I have that strength and the strong negotiating skills so you can rest easy knowing I'll get you the best purchase price possible.

Why don't we get together and go over the value I can bring to your home purchase?

Excellent, I have an opening in my schedule _______ or _______, which would you prefer?

Develop your own objection handling using the examples above.

I just want to drive by it. Can you give me the address?

____

____

____

____

____

____

Are you the listing agent? I only look at homes with the listing agent.

____

____

____

____

____

____

Can you just email the information on the home / on what's available?

____

____

____

____

____

____

We're just starting the process and not sure what we're looking for.

____

____

____

I want to wait because I think the market will go down.

BUYER OBJECTIONS

In order to make objection handling less complicated, I've broken down the steps in managing the most common buyer objections into two categories; basic and advanced. The basic skill level utilizes tried and true stock answers that are easily learned. These can be used while practicing and improving your skills using the advanced techniques.

WE THINK IT'S OVERPRICED / WE WANT TO GO IN LOWER

You: OK. I can appreciate that. If you were going to write an offer, what price would you like to pay for the home? ….

Once they give you a price, you have to decide if it's reasonable or unreasonable as a starting point.

You: OK. But I need to explain that at that price we should expect a counteroffer, so my question is, do you absolutely want to buy this home?

Buyer: Yes we do.

You: OK. So in order to make sure you get the home you want at a price you're comfortable with, what I've found is that if we take a closer look at the comparable properties that have sold, it may help you to understand why they're at that asking price. Would that help you?

Buyer: Yes.

Review the comparables to help them better understand why the home is priced where it is.

You: So, now that we've taken a closer look at the properties that have sold in the area, does that help you better understand their pricing?

Buyer: Yes.

Close for the purchase.

SHARP ANGLE CLOSING QUESTION - Financing concern

"If I could show you how you could still get this home, and pay a very minimal amount more for it, would that help you make a decision?"

FEEL, FELT, FOUND - Financing concern

"What I've found is that by helping you understand how you can still get this home by paying a very minimal amount more for it, it might help you make a more informed decision. Would that help?"

Demonstrate how; "Let's say you pay the additional $20,000 for this house. How long do you expect to live here? (5 years)

At 3% interest that's $4,300 per year, right? That works out to $82 per week or $12 a day. You really like this home, am I right? You want to move, right? Can you afford an extra $12 a day to get the home you want, now?"

WE WANT TO WAIT. WE THINK THAT PRICES ARE GOING TO DROP

SHARP ANGLE CLOSING QUESTION

You: "If I could show you that by waiting for the market to drop, you could actually end up in a position where it costs you more, would that make it easier for you to make a decision about buying this house?"

FEEL, FELT, FOUND

You: "I understand how you feel. A lot of my clients have felt that way. But what I've found is that by waiting for the market to drop, you could actually end up in a position where it costs you more. If I could show you how, would that make it easier for you to make a decision about buying this house?"

Buyer: Yes.

Use the latest market trends, stats and demonstrate to them that that, overall, housing prices tend to increase over time.

WE WANT TO THINK ABOUT IT

Them: "We need to talk to our parents about it."…"We like to take our time to think things over."

You: "Buying a house is a big deal and I understand that you would want to think about it. Let me ask you this, you like the house, right? It has what you're looking for, doesn't it?

OK. So, what is it about the purchase that concerns you?"

"So you're not sure about (concern) is that right?"

SHARP ANGLE CLOSING QUESTION

"If we take some time to discuss what you like and don't like about this house, would that help clear things up for you?"

FEEL, FELT, FOUND

"What I've found is that if we take some time to discuss what you like and don't like about the house, it'll help clear things up for you. Would that help?"

Review their Pain / Fear. Why are they making the move? What's their concern? Is the pain of staying greater than their concern about the move?

THE HOME IS RUN DOWN

SHARP ANGLE CLOSING QUESTION

"I understand. But, this home offers you a chance to add your own personal touches. If we took a look at what it might cost to bring it up to your standards, compared with the cost of buying a renovated home, would that help you make a decision?"

FEEL, FELT, FOUND

"What I've found is that if we look at what the cost would be to renovate, compared with the price of a renovated home, it might help you make a decision. Would that help?"

Review their Motivation. Compare their needs and wants to the available homes and their budget.

WHAT'S YOUR COMMISSION? (OVER THE PHONE / AT THE DOOR)

Reply #1.

You: "Mr. / Mrs. Seller, that's a great question. That's one of the first things we'll talk about when I see you. While I understand that you need to know the answer to that, at the same time let me ask you, if you're like most people I talk to, isn't the most important question how much you're going to net on the sale of your property? I'll cover my marketing plan, the timing of your move, my fees, everything you need to know to make the right decision. How does that sound? Why don't we get together to discuss it _______ at ________?"

Reply #2.

You: "That's a great question Mr. / Mrs. Seller. I don't charge a commission unless I sell your home. Why don't we get together so I can see your home and then let's decide on the commission amount after we've talked about what marketing's required to get your home sold for the most amount of money."

Them: But can't you just tell me what percent you charge?

You: "Not really – not until I see your home and we decide what marketing I'm going to do. I can tell you one thing though, before I ask you to sign a contract, I assure you that you will be very satisfied. Fair enough? (Alright) Great, how's __________ at ________?"

HOW MUCH DO YOU THINK MY HOME'S WORTH? (OVER THE PHONE / AT THE DOOR)

You: "Mr. / Mrs. Seller, that's a great question and one I'm sure you'd want a really accurate answer to. Without having a chance to take a look at your home, it would be unprofessional of me to give you an opinion of its market value. Why don't we set up a time for us to get together so I can take a look through your home and then we can compare it to the other homes that are for sale and have sold in the area? That way I can give you a realistic, accurate figure. How would ____________ at ____________ work for you?"

Them: But you're supposed to be the neighbourhood expert, right. So can't you just give me an idea of what I could get?)

You: "Well, I could let you know what the average house is selling for in the area, but your house isn't average is it? Would you say your home has different features than the other homes in the area? What about the things you've done to make it home? I'd have to make some adjustments to the average price and I can't do that without seeing your home. Let's set up a time for me to take a look and then discuss what it's worth. Would ______________ at __________ work for you?"

LISTING APPOINTMENT OBJECTIONS

I WANT TO FIND A HOUSE BEFORE I PUT MINE ON THE MARKET

Reply #1

"I understand, finding your new home is important. The concern that I have is that it may take a while to sell your home and then another month to close. Any home you find may be sold before you get yours sold.

What I'd recommend is that we get your home listed and then, when we have an offer on it, we can find your next one. Does that make sense? Why don't we get the paperwork going so I can help you make your move?"

Reply #2

"I understand your concern. I've brought you a list of current listings that fit your needs. Check these out and we will start looking. Once we have this house listed, we can find you the home you're looking for. That way we can close both homes on the same day and you only have to make one move. How does that sound?"

Reply #3

"I understand. We have some options that might help. Once we've got your home on the market, we'll start looking at homes. When we get an offer on yours we can do a couple of things. The first is to set a longer closing date so we have time to continue looking or we can include a condition that ensures that you find a suitable home within a specific time period. How does that sound?"

WE WANT A HIGHER LIST PRICE....

Reply #1

"I understand. Let me ask you this, do you have any questions about the Comparative Analysis I've shown you? You understand that the price range I've recommended is based on the prices that people are paying for homes like yours in this area, right? You've seen the prices of the homes that didn't sell, and remember, houses sell because of price. So, if I can show you how pricing your home higher than the price range I've recommended could actually cost you money as well as valuable time, would you be willing to set a price for your home that reflects what the market is paying?"

Reply #2

"I understand that you want to leave room for negotiation. What I've found is that when people try that, it can create some problems. Can I explain?

First, people decide which homes they want to look at based on price. So if your home is priced above the market, many people will not even consider it for two reasons; it may be above the price range they want, but, even more importantly, buyers nowadays are very savvy. They know the prices in the area where they're looking and won't even consider a home that they feel is overpriced.

So, what does this mean to you? If we price your home out of the market range, we reduce the number of buyers just looking at your home, meaning that there's less of a chance of getting an offer and a higher chance of not getting one for an extended period. That could result, if we do get an offer, in it likely being somewhere at the lower end of the price range.

That means you'd have the potential for ending up with less and taking longer to sell than if we price it properly right out of the gate.

So, doesn't it make more sense to price it properly, get it sold in a better time frame and for more money by listing it within the range we've discussed?"

ANOTHER AGENT SAID THEY COULD SELL IT FOR MORE MONEY

Reply #1

"I understand your concern. It's kind of confusing isn't it? I mean, you interview four agents and you get four different prices ... right?

Well, here's why. There's a big difference in the way that I operate and the way that a lot of agents operate. Most agents manipulate the stats to show figures that they think you want to hear, because they're desperate to get your listing. Getting your listing makes them feel like they are accomplishing something. That's why they'll tell you whatever price they think you want to hear.

However, I believe that I'm doing both you and me a disservice by listing a home above market price. First, I believe that when I list your home, we've started building a relationship and I don't want to start that relationship off with a lie. Secondly, as your agent, my main goal is to help you achieve your goals, one of which is getting your home sold so you can move onward. So why don't we review the numbers and let's get your home listed at a price that's going to achieve your goals."

Reply #2

"I understand your concern. Did you know that only ___% (currently 56%) of the homes that are listed for sale actually sell?

That's because the other ______% are overpriced. And that happens because some agents are so concerned about just getting a listing that they'll take any listing and they don't care about the seller.

There are three real comparables to understand in the real estate market. The first is the currently listed homes. The second is the homes that have sold in the area. And the third are the homes that haven't sold because they were overpriced, the expireds. The first can also be called the "Wish list" because that what people hope to get. The second is the reality; that's what buyers are prepared to pay for similar homes. And the third is what I call no-man's land. That's where overpriced listings go after they've sat on the market until the contract expires.

So you can list your home to sell, or list it to sit. Why don't we list it at the right price and get you moving?"

Reply #3

"I understand your concern. Of course you want to sell it for the best amount you possibly can and that makes perfect sense.

Let me ask you this. If the other agents told you that once you'd listed your home with them, that you'd have blue skies every day until it sold, would you believe them?

Of course not. That's impossible. Well, it's the same as promising that your house will sell above what the market says it will. It's impossible to predict. So, why don't we review the numbers and let's get your home listed at a price that's going to get it sold."

THEY CAN ALWAYS MAKE AN OFFER / WE WANT TO TRY IT HIGH FOR A COUPLE OF WEEKS

"I understand that you want to leave room for negotiation. What I've found is that when people try that, it can create some problems. Can I explain?

First, people decide which homes they want to look at based on price. So if your home is priced above the market, many people will not even consider it for two reasons; it may be above the price range they want, but, even more importantly, buyers nowadays are very savvy. They know the prices in the area where they're looking and won't even consider a home that they feel is overpriced.

So, what does this mean to you? If we price your home out of the market range, we reduce the number of buyers just looking at your home, meaning that there's less of a chance of getting an offer and a higher chance of not getting one for an extended period. That could result, if we do get an offer, in it likely being somewhere at the lower end of the price range.

That means you'd have the potential for ending up with less and taking longer to sell than if we price it properly right out of the gate.

So, doesn't it make more sense to price it properly, get it sold in a better time frame and for more money by listing it within the range we've discussed?"

WILL YOU REDUCE YOUR COMMISSION?

Reply #1

"You obviously need to feel comfortable that the fee being charged is justified by the services being provided, am I right? Let me begin by asking you, how do you feel about everything I've presented to you? (We like it)

May I ask if you're looking for the best bottom line or the lowest commission rate?

As a real estate sales professional, I'm confident that my abilities as a marketer and negotiator will ensure you achieve the highest possible sales price, in the least amount of time adding potentially thousands of dollars to your bottom line. May I show you exactly how working with me will actually net you more? (Demonstrate value and an increase in bottom line) Sound fair?"

Reply #2

"One of the most important reasons to hire a REALTOR® is to negotiate on your behalf to achieve the highest possible price for your property, right?"

If I can't negotiate my own salary, wouldn't you be concerned that I may not be the best negotiator for the sale of your home?"

Reply #3

"I don't charge a commission. Just like your lawyer or dentist, I provide a service and charge a fee for it. I can cut my fees, but I need to know which of the services I provide, which are specifically designed to get your home sold for the most money in the best possible time, would you prefer I not use?"

Reply #4

"Mr. / Mrs. Seller, Let me ask you this. If your boss asked you to do your normal work, but came to you one day and wanted you to do it for a lower salary, how would you feel? Would that be fair? Would you agree?"

WILL YOU REDUCE YOUR COMMISSION IF MY HOME SELLS QUICKLY?

"Mr. and Mrs. Seller, let me ask you this. Would you pay someone more for doing a good job or a poor job?"

This is a performance based business, which means that the better we perform and the more background work we've done, the shorter time it takes to sell your home.

So what you're saying is that if I do a poor job and take a longer time to sell your home you're willing to pay me more than if I do a good job and sell it faster. Does that make sense to you?"

FOUNDATIONS FOR SUCCESS

SYSTEMS CHECKLISTS

LISTING MANAGEMENT CHECKLIST

MLS #:
Initial Price:
Contract Date:
Expires:
Lockbox:
Added to Market Watch:

Prior to Appointment

- ☐ Pre-Listing Package Delivered 24 - 48 Hrs before appointment
- ☐ Appointment Confirmed - all decision makers to be present
- ☐ Seller's Advertising Questionnaire Completed by Seller for Appointment
- ☐ CMA Completed
- ☐ Listing Presentation Completed
- ☐ Current Competitors previewed

Paperwork to Complete

- ☐ Working with a Realtor
- ☐ Listing Agreement
- ☐ MLS Data Information Sheet
- ☐ SPIS
- ☐ Service Guarantee
- ☐ FINTRAC Individual Identification Information Record (One per Seller)
- ☐ Sellers Directions for Offer Presentations & Appointment Info
- ☐ Seller's Consent & Acknowledgement Form
- ☐ Taxes Confirmed
- ☐ Mortgage Verification Form signed
- ☐ Mortgage Verification Form sent to bank
- ☐ Mortgage Verification Form returned
- ☐ Survey, if available

- ☐ GeoWarehouse (Ontario) / Title Printout
- ☐ Property History

Discuss with Seller

- ☐ Seller's Advertising Questionnaire
- ☐ Ideal Closing Date
- ☐ If Winter, do they have summer yard photos?
- ☐ Bridge Financing Discussion
- ☐ Plan for Existing Mortgage
- ☐ Showing Instructions / Times
- ☐ How Office handles Appointments
- ☐ Buyer Showings - What To Do/Not To do
- ☐ Set Agent Open House Date
- ☐ Set First Public Open House Date
- ☐ Offer Management (Date - if holding offers, Handling Bully Offers)
- ☐ Realtor.ca Delay
- ☐ Lawyer Info
- ☐ If Feature Sheets are running low
- ☐ Feedback from Realtors
- ☐ Share Listing with Friends

Listing Procedures

Day of Listing Appointment

- ☐ All Paperwork Signed and dated for 2-3 days later
- ☐ Key from the Seller and copy made
- ☐ Book Photographer / Videographer
- ☐ Order Sign
- ☐ Lockbox Installed w/ key
- ☐ Files Uploaded to Evernote
- ☐ Files Sent to Office Administrator
- ☐ Enter Client into CRM
- ☐ Enter Files into CRM
- ☐ Enter Listing into Evernote

Day after Listing

- ☐ Send Letter to Referral
- ☐ Write Ad Copy for Feature Sheets
- ☐ Write Ad Copy for MLS
- ☐ Write Ad Copy for other advertising media
- ☐ Prepare Feature Sheets
- ☐ Design and Print Just Listed Flyer for Home Office
- ☐ Design and Print Just Listed Flyer for RE Offices
- ☐ Design & Print Open House Invitation for Neighbourhood
- ☐ Prepare Thank You Letter
- ☐ Deliver Feature Sheets to Home

Activation Day

- ☐ Upload on MLS
- ☐ Upload Photos
- ☐ Check MLS for Correct Information
- ☐ E-mail Listing to Clients
- ☐ Upload Virtual Tour
- ☐ Video sent out across social media platforms (Facebook Business Page, YouTube, Instagram, Blog)
- ☐ Video embedded on website
- ☐ Doorknock & Distribute Open House Invitations to neighbours
- ☐ Upload Listing to Kijiji
- ☐ Upload Listing to Housingblock.com
- ☐ Upload Listing to Backpage.ca
- ☐ Upload Listing to Craigslist.ca
- ☐ Email Blast to agents in area

Weekly Activities

- ☐ Open House scheduled
- ☐ Warm calls to neighbours for Open House
- ☐ Preview Listings in area
- ☐ Open House held ☐ ☐ ☐ ☐ ☐
- ☐ Weekly Activity Report completed and sent to Seller ☐ ☐ ☐ ☐ ☐

APPENDIX

Price Reductions

- ☐ Amendment to Listing Contract signed
- ☐ Amendment Sent to Office
- ☐ Price Changed on MLS
- ☐ Update Blog Post
- ☐ E-mail Clients
- ☐ Email sent to all agents who have shown property
- ☐ Upload Amendment to Evernote
- ☐ Upload Amendment to CRM

Multiple Offers

- ☐ Time set for Offer Presentation
- ☐ Deadline for Offer Registration set
- ☐ Every agent notified of new offers
- ☐ Upload Copy of Each Offer to Evernote
- ☐ Thank All Agents for their offers

Conditional Procedures

- ☐ APS & Confirmation of Co-Operation signed by all parties
- ☐ Copy of APS & Confirmation of Co-Operation Sent to Client
- ☐ Deposit Cheque delivered by Purchaser
- ☐ Deposit Cheque & Paperwork to Deals Secretary (APS, Conf. of Coop., Trade Record)
- ☐ Upload Copy of Files to Evernote (Cheque, Trade Record, APS)
- ☐ Inspection date set & Clients notified
- ☐ Mortgage Condition waived
- ☐ Inspection completed
- ☐ Inspection Condition waived
- ☐ Status Certificate ordered
- ☐ Status Certificate delivered to Purchaser's Agent
- ☐ Status Certificate Condition waived
- ☐ Additional conditions waived
- ☐ Copies of waivers sent to Office
- ☐ Copies of waivers sent to client

- ☐ Upload Copies of waivers to Evernote

Firm Procedures

- ☐ Update CRM
- ☐ Update Evernote
- ☐ Send Client Survey
- ☐ Update Website
- ☐ Sold Sign up
- ☐ Remove Lockbox
- ☐ Call for Sign Removal
- ☐ Thank You Gift to Seller
- ☐ Update Closing Date on CRM
- ☐ Move File to Pending Closings
- ☐ Update Trade Record Sheet
- ☐ Update Address for Client in CRM
- ☐ Send Survey to Referral Contact
- ☐ Provide referral to movers if required

Closing Procedures

2 weeks prior to closing

- ☐ Call Seller's Lawyer to confirm receipt of all paperwork
- ☐ Confirm any repairs required completed
- ☐ All receipts left for new owners
- ☐ Buyers' visit scheduled

1 week prior to closing

- ☐ Call client to confirm visit with lawyer
- ☐ Confirm movers
- ☐ Thank You Letter
- ☐ File Cheque
- ☐ Send Copy of Feedback to Referral
- ☐ Update CRM
- ☐ Buyers' visit held

Closing Day

- ☐ Confirm closing with lawyer
- ☐ Move File to Closed Clients Notebook

OPEN HOUSE CHECKLIST

Monday / Tuesday

- ☐ Open House Scheduled
- ☐ Call the neighbours and invite them to the VIP Open House

Wednesday

- ☐ Prepare your Open House Gift Bags
- ☐ Inspector Brochure
- ☐ Lawyer Brochure
- ☐ Contractor Brochure
- ☐ Area Information (schools, maps, trails, etc.)
- ☐ Cookie / Bar
- ☐ Prepare Feature Sheets, including Walkscore
- ☐ Prepare Open House Invitations for neighbours

Thursday

- ☐ Doorknock and distribute Invitations
- ☐ Preview all available listings in area
- ☐ Familiarize yourself with area (schools, transit, shopping, etc.)
- ☐ Organize files needed
- ☐ Feature Sheets
- ☐ Info from Mortgage Broker
- ☐ BRA / Customer Status
- ☐ Sign In Sheets
- ☐ APS
- ☐ Print Labels for Water Bottles

Friday

- ☐ Buy food and water bottles for VIP Open House

Day of Open House

- ☐ Place signs at intersections and leading to home
- ☐ Sign / flag in front of house
- ☐ Set up food and water

- [ ] Set up laptop with map search
- [ ] Gift Bags out
- [ ] Windows open
- [ ] Doors unlocked
- [ ] Lights On

After Open House

- [ ] Pick up all flyers, sheets, food
- [ ] Windows closed and locked
- [ ] Doors closed and locked
- [ ] Final walkthrough
- [ ] Note for client
- [ ] Front door locked
- [ ] Collect all signs

BUYER MANAGEMENT CHECKLIST

Client Name:
Phone: Home: Cell: Work:
Email:
Lawyer's Name:
Phone:
Fax:
Email:
Mortgage Broker:
Phone:
Fax:
Email:

Prior to Appointment

- ☐ Informed Buyer's Guide Delivered 24 - 48 Hrs before appointment
- ☐ Appointment Confirmed - all decision makers to be present
- ☐ Buyer's Presentation Completed

Paperwork to Complete

- ☐ Working with a Realtor
- ☐ Buyer Representation Agreement
- ☐ FINTRAC Individual Identification Information Record (One per Buyer)

Discuss with Buyer

- ☐ Pre-Approved? Price Range:
- ☐ Buyer Questionnaire / Home Buying Wishlist Completed
- ☐ Ideal Closing Date
- ☐ Bridge Financing Discussion
- ☐ Plan for Existing Mortgage
- ☐ What Times are they available for Showings

- ☐ How Offices handle Appointments
- ☐ 6 Step Buying Process
- ☐ "Rules of the Road"
- ☐ Showing Procedures - What to Do / Not to do
- ☐ Set First Showing Date
- ☐ Open House Procedures
- ☐ Offer Management - sellers holding offers, Bully Offers, negotiating, multiple offers
- ☐ Managing Conditions
- ☐ Lawyer Info
- ☐ Feedback for REALTORS®

Weekly Activities

- ☐ Preview Listings in area
- ☐ Open Houses viewed ☐☐☐ ☐
- ☐ Weekly Activity Report completed and sent to Buyer

Multiple Offers

- ☐ Client notified of Multiple Offers
- ☐ Client given chance to improve offer
- ☐ Time set for Offer Presentation
- ☐ Offer Registered prior to Deadline for Offer Registration
- ☐ Meet clients at location for Offer Presentation
- ☐ Upload Copy of Offer to Evernote

Property Info

MLS#:

Address:

Offer Date:

Closing:

Condition Date:

Inspection Date:

Conditional Procedures

- ☐ APS & Confirmation of Co-Operation signed by all parties
- ☐ Copy of APS & Confirmation of Co-Operation Sent to Client
- ☐ Deposit Cheque delivered to Listing Office
- ☐ Copy of Deposit Cheque, Receipt & Paperwork to Deals Secretary (APS, Conf. of Coop., Trade Record)
- ☐ Upload Copy of Files to Evernote (Cheque, Trade Record, APS)
- ☐ Inspection date set, Listing agent notified
- ☐ APS sent to Financial Institution / Mortgage Broker
- ☐ Mortgage Condition waived
- ☐ Inspection date confirmed 1 day prior
- ☐ Inspection completed
- ☐ Inspection Condition waived & Sent to Listing Agent / Transmission record filed
- ☐ Status Certificate ordered
- ☐ Status Certificate delivered by Listing Agent
- ☐ Status Certificate delivered to Client / Lawyer
- ☐ Status Certificate Condition waived & Sent to Listing Agent / Transmission record filed
- ☐ Additional conditions waived & Sent to Listing Agent / Transmission record filed
- ☐ Copies of waivers sent to Office
- ☐ Copies of waivers sent to client
- ☐ Upload Copies of waivers to Evernote

Firm Procedures

- ☐ Update CRM
- ☐ Update Evernote
- ☐ Send Client Survey

- ☐ Update Website
- ☐ Sold Sign up
- ☐ Update Closing Date on CRM
- ☐ Move File to Pending Closings
- ☐ Update Trade Record Sheet
- ☐ Update Address for Client in CRM
- ☐ Send Survey to Referral Contact
- ☐ Provide referral to movers if required

Closing Procedures

2 weeks prior to closing

- ☐ Call Lawyer to confirm receipt of all paperwork
- ☐ Confirm any repairs required completed
- ☐ All receipts left for new owners
- ☐ Buyers' visit scheduled

1 week prior to closing

- ☐ Call client to confirm visit with lawyer
- ☐ Confirm movers
- ☐ Thank You Letter
- ☐ File Cheque
- ☐ Send Copy of Feedback to Referral
- ☐ Update CRM
- ☐ Buyers' visit held

Closing Day

- ☐ Confirm closing with lawyer
- ☐ Meet client at new home
- ☐ Provide lunch for client on moving day
- ☐ Move File to Closed Clients Notebook
- ☐ Implement 1, 1, 1 System

FOUNDATIONS FOR SUCCESS SERIES

Volume 1 - "On the Right Foot"
Business Planning, Organization and Real Estate Etiquette

Volume 2 - "Good Hunting"
Prospecting and Lead Follow Up,

Volume 3 - "Listings, Listings, Listings"
Listings and Listing Systems,

Volume 4 - "Buyers, Buyers, Buyers"
Buyers and Buyers Systems

Volume 5 - "I'm Just Sayin"
Objection Handling, Communication and Negotiation and Advertising

Volume 6 - Workbook
Specific Business Building Exercises

Volume 7 – The Complete Series
All the volumes in one book, including the Workbook.

ABOUT THE AUTHOR

Steve began his real estate career in Edmonton, Alberta in 2001. He worked as an Associate Broker with Realty Executives North Star until 2008 when he opened his own brokerage. He moved back to Toronto in 2010, has been the Director of Agent Development for HomeLife/Cimerman Real Estate Ltd., Director of Training and Development for RE/MAX West Realty Inc., and Manager and Coach for The Daryl King Team at Royal LePage Your Community Realty and has designed and overseen the training, development and coaching of the sales personnel at each. He is the author of ''List to Last - The Definitive Guide to Finding, Closing and Managing Residential Listings''.

NOTES

Made in the USA
Columbia, SC
11 July 2018